ROYALWISE

QuickBooks® Online Bootcamp:

From Setup to Tax Time

Alicia Katz Pollock, MAT
Royalwise Solutions, Inc.

Top 50 Women in Accounting
Top 10 ProAdvisor
Intuit Subject Matter Expert
Advanced Certified ProAdvisor

info@royalwise.com
www.RoyalWise.com

Published 2025 in the United States of America
ISBN: 978-0-9893992-6-5

Dedication

This book is dedicated to Zip, Grace, and my husband and business partner, Jamie Pollock. Our house of love is an inspiration, and I'm grateful that with you I get to live my best life.

I would also like to dedicate this book to our Royalwise OWLS Community members. Your passion shines through in every course you take and every meeting you attend. I'm inspired to answer your questions because I can see the impact on your clients and customers. Together we are making the world a better place. Hoot hoot!

Acknowledgements

A sincere thank you to the members of Intuit®'s ProAdvisor® community.

Over the years you have become not just my colleagues, but my friends. I spend more time with you over Zooms and conferences than I do with people IRL.

You're smart, funny, and collaborative. You inspire me to learn and expand. Whoever thinks accounting is boring is doing it wrong!

You're also literally what keeps me going as I tirelessly update my content to keep up with QuickBooks. Thank you for your kind words, handmade gifts, and endless encouragement.

About This Book

This book was originally written as the "handouts" for Alicia's QuickBooks Online Bootcamp video course for the Royalwise OWLS ("On-demand Web-based Learning Solutions") at Royalwise.com.

Ten years later, it stands alone as a handy reference book that everybody can hold in their hands. That way you can dog-ear, bookmark, and look things up quickly, which is a great way to learn.

But sometimes, watching and hearing the explanations is sometimes easier than reading! When you need more information about a particular topic, keep an eye out for graphics that look like this:

The **Companion Course** on the left is the *QBO Bootcamp* video course that matches this book and brings it to life with personality and demos. It also gives you a place where you can ask questions!

The **Deep Dive** course on the right is a full course just about the specific topic discussed in that section. Royalwise.com has published over 50 QuickBooks Online courses that pick up where this book leaves off! Each one goes into detail about the features you need to make your QBO experience easier, and help your business thrive.

To access these supplemental courses:

- Type the orange URL into your browser, or
- Use your phone's camera to tap the black and white square to be taken right to the course page.

All courses come with a Class Discussion Forum where you can ask questions. You get lifetime access, including updates as the interface changes. If the course has a date on it, that's the next webinar to update the content…and you'll be invited!

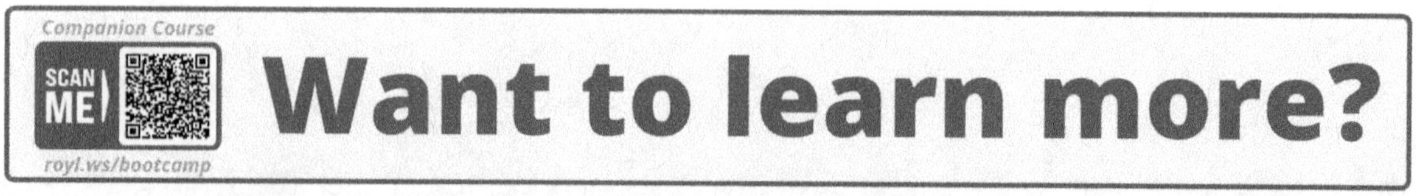

The Quizzes

Yes, I can hear you: **"What! A quiz? I hate quizzes!"**

The quizzes at the end of each chapter in this book have been carefully and strategically designed to make you think about how the features are used in real life. Answering the questions helps you cement the concepts in your mind.

Yes, they are optional. And yes, I even give you the answers on the same page!

For those of you who need to earn NASBA CPE credit (Continuing Professional Education), you can enroll in the online course and take the quizzes there.

Hoot Tips

I have years of experience helping small businesses use QuickBooks to their fullest potential. Along the way I've learned a lot of cool tips and tricks that speed up your work. Owlfred will do his best to get your attention!

Watch out for PEBCAK!

("Problem Exists <u>Between</u> Chair and Keyboard")

"**PEBCAK**" is an expression jokingly used in the tech support industry to describe customer calls where the problem isn't with the software, but with how it's being used.

Look for ***PEBCAK!*** alerts throughout this book to describe common errors that my clients make, so that you don't make them too.

It's crucial that you set up and use QuickBooks Online correctly. Your reports are only as good as the information you enter.

If you're not sure what to do with a transaction...***DON'T GUESS!*** Make a quick phone call to me, to your bookkeeper, or to your accountant. Or make use of an "Ask My Accountant" expense account to put the transaction in a safe holding tank (what we call a "suspense" account) for later, so you don't forget about it.

It's infinitely easier to fix a mistake before it's made than it is to spend hours tracking down an error, or having to undo additional transactions that were incorrect as a result.

My goal in this book is to be proactive, building your QBO skills so that you do everything correctly from the start!

Companion Course

SCAN ME

royl.ws/bootcamp

Want to learn more?

Table of Contents

PART 1:

SETTING UP QUICKBOOKS ONLINE

Chapter 1: Why QuickBooks Online

This book covers the necessary fundamentals for using QuickBooks Online (QBO) as an easy and efficient tool to manage your business and grow your company.

> The screenshots in this book are from the test drive QBO Plus file:
>
> ***https://qbo.intuit.com/redir/testdrive/***
>
> **Use an Incognito Chrome browser.**
>
> **Open the sample file, follow along, and practice using QuickBooks Online!**
>
> As we explore and modify the Craig's Landscaping company, your changes are not saved because the sandbox file resets automatically when you begin a new session so that you can start fresh each time.

Why is Bookkeeping Important?

Bookkeeping is an undervalued and underutilized facet of running your business. Knowing how to keep accurate financial records helps you understand the business behind your business. Learning how to read a Profit and Loss statement and a Balance Sheet helps you monitor the health of your company.

Then at tax time, you'll be ready for your accountant in a few hours…instead of a few weeks.

You'll be able to quickly determine which of your products and services are your best-sellers, and which make you the most money (they may not be the same!). You'll uncover your best type of customers to help you better target your marketing.

And if you are NOT doing well, using QuickBooks Online will help you track your expenses and analyze exactly WHY you're losing money.

Do You Need a Bookkeeper?

Good bookkeeping can improve cash flow and increase profits. Bad bookkeeping can lead to business failure.

A bookkeeper enters daily transactions, keeping you up to date so that you can log in and have instant accuracy. Even more importantly, she understands where to put the transactions, and why.

Many small businesses don't think they need a bookkeeper, rationalizing that it's an extra expense they can't afford...AND that they can do it themselves!

To those owners I ask these four revealing questions:

1. Do you like doing data entry, coding transactions, and balancing check registers?
2. Are you GOOD at it?
3. Do you know what to do in unusual circumstances?
4. Is it the best use of your time?

If the answer is NO to any of these questions, HIRE A BOOKKEEPER!!!

The Pareto Principle: The 80/20 Rule

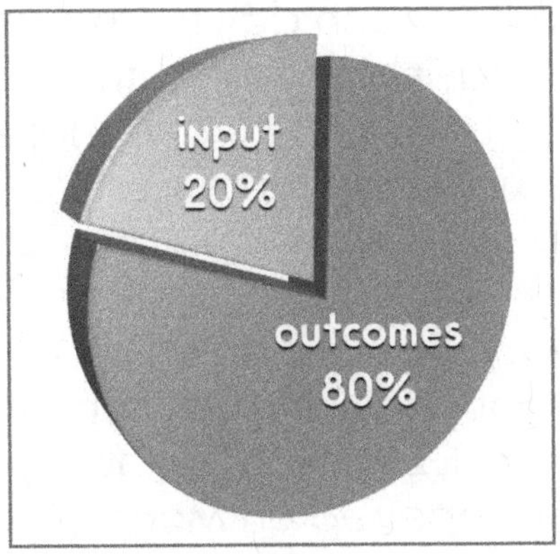

The 80/20 rule, also known as the "Pareto Principle," is a universal truth in business:

- 20% of your customers generate 80% of your net profit
- 20% of your products or services contribute 80% of your revenue
- 20% of your staff create 80% of your customers' experience

Not surprisingly, only 20% of all the hours you work actually add value to your bottom line.

Good bookkeeping helps you find where your 20% is hidden.

You can use QuickBooks minimally like a glorified checkbook, or extensively to track a lot of detail in every transaction. The former is quick and easy. The latter may be more time consuming and require more attention to detail; however, it gives you the valuable ability to slice and dice your data to generate usable analysis.

QuickBooks Online has dozens of reports that uncover your best customers, services, products, and time spent. The higher your subscription level, the more reports you can run. Using the more sophisticated versions of QuickBooks Online helps you analyze which direction to allocate your resources to help you grow.

Putting the "Quick" in QuickBooks

Allocate a few quick minutes each day for the daily maintenance of your QuickBooks Online data. Staying current with your data entry not only keeps the burden from mounting, but it also makes the data entry workflows easier to remember and more accurate as transactions are fresh in your mind.

Think of the benefit this way: If you sit down at 4:45pm each day, it will take 15 minutes to enter your daily transactions. If you wait until Friday, not only will it take a combined 1.25 hours, but now you'll have to spend extra time to go look up what happened on Monday, since your exhausted brain will have forgotten the details by then, adding at least another 15 minutes to the process.

And if you wait until the end of the month, what would have only taken 5 hours may now take an entire stressful day!

Doing your books is like exercising: the more you do it, the better shape you'll be in.

3 essential actions to take at the end of each day:

1. Make that day's **Sales Receipts** or **Invoices,** and record the **Payments.**

2. **Make Deposits.** Group your cash and checks, and batch your credit cards. Your deposits need to exactly match the amount posted in the bank, and your Undeposited Funds account should only contain pending transactions.

3. **Accept your Bank Transactions.** Clean out the list of transactions downloaded from your bank that cleared today. Match the deposits, and categorize the new expenses. Data entry is faster while you still remember what happened, as opposed to waiting until the end of the month and having to look everything up.

By reviewing your regularly updated books, you can monitor the financial health of your company and determine where you need to focus your attention.

5 essential reports to review:

1. **A daily, monthly, and year-to-date Profit and Loss Statement.** By reviewing each day's profits in real time, you will be able to notice what is or isn't working, then adjust accordingly.

   Turn on the column to compare to the past period to see if you did better or worse than last year!

2. **Sales reports by Product and by Customer.** The customers who spend the most with you may not be the ones who drive the most profit. Your most popular products may not have the highest margin.

3. **Accounts Receivable.** Cash flow problems are frequently due to uncollected invoices. Review what your customers owe you and make plans to collect!

4. **Accounts Payable.** If you know what you owe in the next 30 days, you're more likely to pay it on time.

5. **Balance Sheet/Cash on Hand.** Each day you must know exactly how much cash is available in your bank accounts and how much you owe on your liabilities. Ignoring your credit cards won't make the debt go away!

Check Your Understanding: Introduction to QuickBooks Online

1) ________ One of the best features of QBO vs. Desktop is:
   a. You can use it in a browser or on a smartphone
   b. Works on both Mac & PC
   c. Many simultaneous users without running a server
   d. Your accountant can take a look any time
   e. All of the above

2) ________ This QBO book may not exactly match your screen because:
   a. I'm using the Plus version, and you may have QuickBooks Lite or Essentials
   b. QBO receives updates with new features and improvements every month
   c. Everybody sees things differently
   d. A & B

3) ________ Only medium and large-sized companies need a bookkeeper
   a. True
   b. False

4) ________ The Pareto Principle says:
   a. 80% of your customers make 80% of your revenue.
   b. 20% of your customers make 80% of your revenue.
   c. 80% of your customers make 20% of your revenue.
   d. 20% of your customers make 20% of your revenue.

5) ________ You should process your Invoices and expenses:
   a. Every day
   b. Every other day
   c. On Fridays
   d. Once a month
   e. Whenever you can squeeze in the time

6) ________ If you set up your QuickBooks with a lot of detail:
   a. It will take longer to do
   b. It requires more attention to detail
   c. It will give you far more reporting detail
   d. All of the above

7) ________ You should hire a bookkeeper if:
   a. You don't have enough time to do it yourself
   b. You're prone to making errors
   c. You don't think you can afford it
   d. All of the above

Answers: 1) e, 2) d, 3) b, 4) b, 5) a, 6) d, 7) d

Chapter 2: Getting Around in QuickBooks Online

Using a Browser

Instead of software installed on your computer, QBO is web-based and requires an internet connection. One benefit is that you never have to buy upgrades – Intuit just releases new features as they are developed.

Chrome is the preferred browser for QuickBooks Online. You can make use of all its features like bookmarks, tabs, refresh, and back buttons.

If QBO ever isn't behaving properly, try an Incognito window (found under the 3 dots in the upper right corner) to help you figure out if the problem is with your computer or with QBO. Because it doesn't save a cache or cookies, it's a pristine environment. If you don't have the issue while in Incognito, the problem is with your computer. If you still have the problem, something is wrong with QBO – wait a few minutes and try again!

Opening Multiple Windows

It's helpful to have three or four separate tabs open in your browser window for different sections of QBO. This allows you to toggle between all the screens you need and avoid having to constantly open and close pages!

For example, keep the Bank Transactions feed open in one window, while creating the corresponding Deposits in another tab.

I usually keep a third tab open, dedicated to Advanced Searches.

To do this, right-click on the button you need (it's a 2-finger click on a trackpad), and choose **Open in New Tab** (the wording may vary depending on your browser). A new tab opens to the right, allowing you to click back and forth between screens to your heart's content.

Suggestion: Add bookmarks to your browser's shortcut that go directly to the screens you use frequently. To turn on your Bookmarks Bar, click on the 3 dots in the upper right corner, hover over **Bookmarks and Lists**, then click **Show Bookmarks Bar**). When you need to access a new area in QBO, create a new tab and click on your bookmark to navigate right to it.

Advanced: Chrome also has **Profiles**, using the circle with your initials in the upper right. Create a profile specifically for your QuickBooks work, with its own bookmarks and settings.

If you have multiple QBO files you need to see at the same time, open each one in a separate Profile!

A "hoot tip" for bookkeepers: create a Profile for each of your clients with bookmarks directly to their custom reports, banks, eCommerce, and other frequently-used websites.

The Interface

QBO is Always Evolving

One important thing to understand about QBO is that it's a perpetual work-in-progress. Intuit strives to be cutting-edge in technology, adding new features and artificial intelligence.

As users submit suggestions and **Feedback** (see page 186), Intuit continuously updates the interface and features with improvements.

As a result, your interface may vary slightly from the instructions in this book depending on which version of QBO you are using. The instructions contained in this book are based on QBO Plus and feature the new platform introduced in Summer 2025.

Part of being a successful QuickBooks User is getting comfortable with the unknown. When you see something new, take a moment to explore; it may be the perfect solution for one of your problems!

The Left Navigation Pane

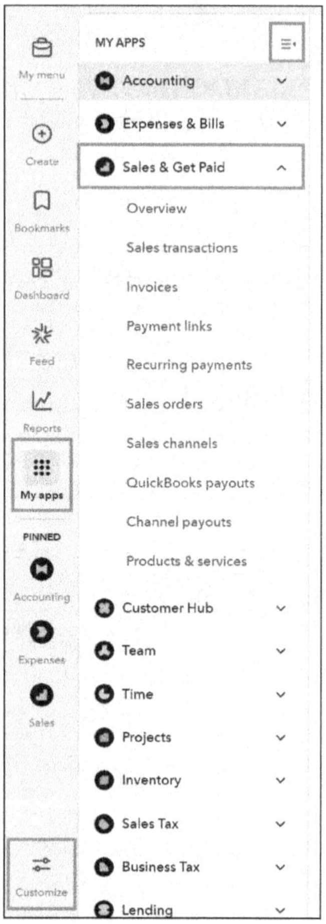

On the left side, the **Left Navigation Pane** takes you to the major centers.

It has two panes, the **Rail** and the **Apps Panel**.

When you want to open a screen, hover your cursor over the icons in the rail, and menus will fly out with additional subsections.

My Apps is the most important button, taking you to all of your most common tasks.

After you click on one of the features, you'll know where you are by the gray shading.

The section headers in the My Apps panel are expandable and collapsible so that you can focus on related tasks.

The "hamburger" (3 lines) at the top right collapses the entire panel to give you more screen real estate.

QBO for Accountants users will also see a **My Menu** button shaped like a briefcase. It's fully customizable and contains the tools bookkeepers use for QuickBooks administration.

HOOT TIP

Instead of flying your mouse around as the options open and close, click on any of the buttons in the rail, and the apps panel will open so you can switch between sections easily.

This also makes it easy to find the Customize buttons so that you can create your own menu system.

Companion Course
SCAN ME
royl.ws/bootcamp
Want to learn more?

While most of the features on the Apps Panel will be explained in detail, the following are optional depending on the needs of your company, and are complex to address. Therefore, they are not included in this book:

Projects. If you manage project-based clients, turn on this center in Accounts and Settings in QBO Plus (see page 34). It includes job costing with a project-specific P&L, and Unbilled Time and Expense reports.

Payroll and *Team*. All levels of QBO allow for an available add-on with built-in Full-Service payroll that also pays Contractors.

Taxes. QBO has built-in Sales Tax management to calculate taxes owed to your state and local authorities. If you are running QuickBooks Payroll, submit your tax payments here as well.

My Accountant. Share bank statements and other documents with your bookkeeper or tax preparer.

Inventory. Manage inventory and e-commerce websites including Amazon, Shopify, eBay, and Square.

For more information about these features, please visit our video courses at learn.royalwise.com.

The +Create Button

The **+Create Button** in the upper left corner is how you add new transactions of all types.

If you need a blank form to fill in, look for it here.

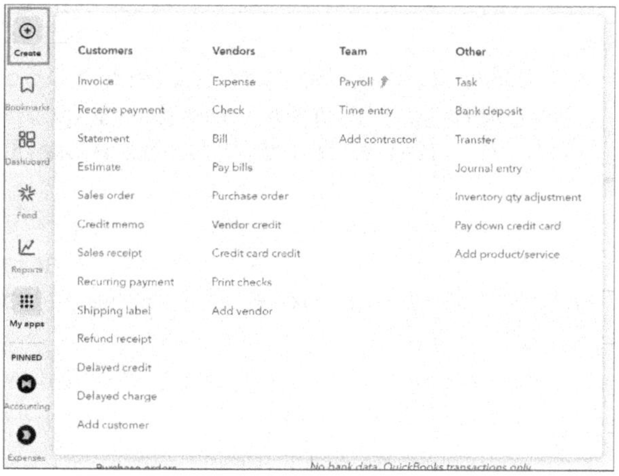

The Settings Gear

The **Settings gear** in the upper right corner takes you behind the scenes to the settings and tools needed to administer your company file.

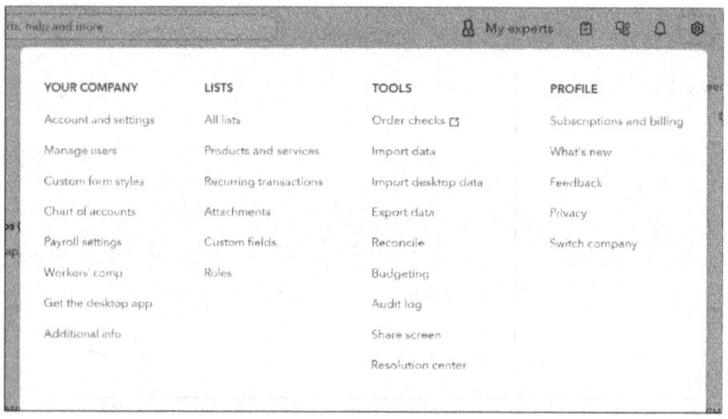

Bookmarks

Click on the **Bookmark** next to each menu item to create a list of your favorite shortcuts.

In the **Bookmarks** list, click the pencil to edit and rearrange the shortcuts.

Use the **Customize** button at the very bottom left of the screen to pin your top 3 favorite centers for quick access.

The Dashboard

The Dashboard provides an overview of your company status at a glance. Click the Customize button to arrange or resize the tiles, and turn them on and off.

Some of the **Dashboard's** handy tools include:

1. ***Shortcut actions*** to your favorite forms.

2. A ***Sales and Get Paid Funnel*** keeps an eye on your cash flow by showing a pipeline of your income.

3. ***Invoices, Expenses, Profit and Loss***, ***Cash Flow Trend***, and ***Sales*** charts offer a quick glimpse of your statistics.

4. The ***Bank Accounts*** click straight through to your Bank Transactions feed to pull in transactions that have cleared your bank.

5. The brand-new ***Customers Hub*** surveys your customers after they pay your invoices, collecting **Work Requests** and **Referrals**!

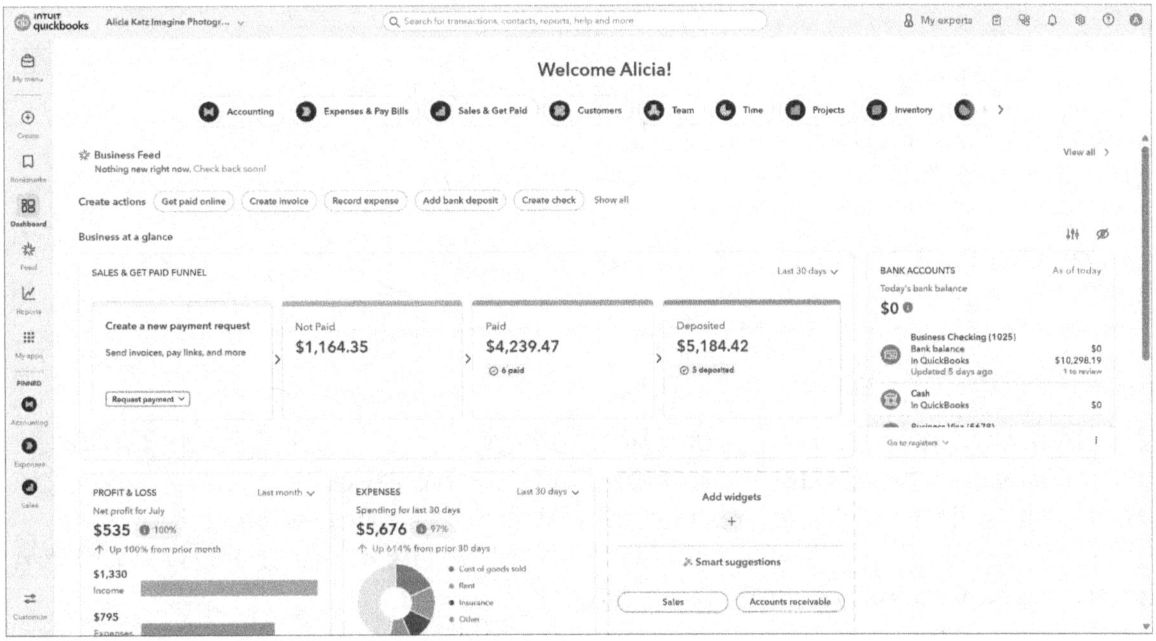

The Search Bar

The **Search** bar in the top middle of the window allows you to instantly jump to any transaction.

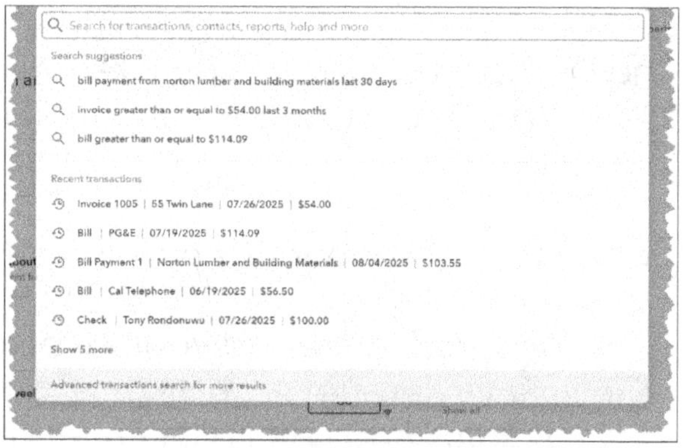

The **Search** bar even brings up a list of your most **Recent Transactions.** Click on a transaction to jump right back into what you were doing.

Enter a customer name, a vendor, an invoice number, a memo, or a dollar amount and you'll pull up a list of all matching items. Type in a report name to run it instantly.

You can even use natural language searches like "open invoices greater than $500 that are more than 90 days old." That's four different filters all in one request!

To refine a search using multiple criteria, click **Advanced Transactions Search** at the bottom to open a dedicated search window. You can use multiple fields to look for your exact transaction. There are additional options under the Filters button.

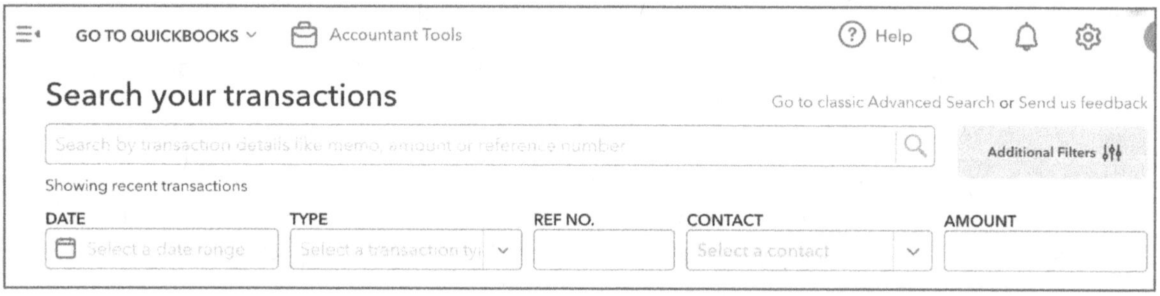

Searching for text on a page

This trick uses a feature of your Chrome browser, not QuickBooks Online. Chrome's Search, **CTRL+F,** scans all the text on the screen you're looking at. Use it to find anything on a page instantly, without wasting time skimming around looking for it. Use the **Find** field's < > arrows to jump from instance to instance of matching text.

Keyboard Shortcuts

Keyboard shortcuts speed up navigation and data entry in QuickBooks Online, even though you're working in a browser.

Zoom in on the Interface

- **Ctrl-.** to hide and show the toolbars
- **Ctrl-+** and **Ctrl- –** to zoom in and out
- **Esc** to cancel a form without saving

Moving Around Forms

- Press the **Tab** key to move from box to box
- Press **Shift+Tab** to go back again
- Press the **Space Bar** to check a check box
- Press **Alt + down arrow** to open a drop-down list, or the pop-up calendar icon to the right of any date field

Drop-down Lists

You don't have to click on every drop-down arrow and scroll through long lists to find what you want. Start typing the entry you are looking for, and your list will instantly reduce itself to matching items. Indented items show that they are sub-accounts.

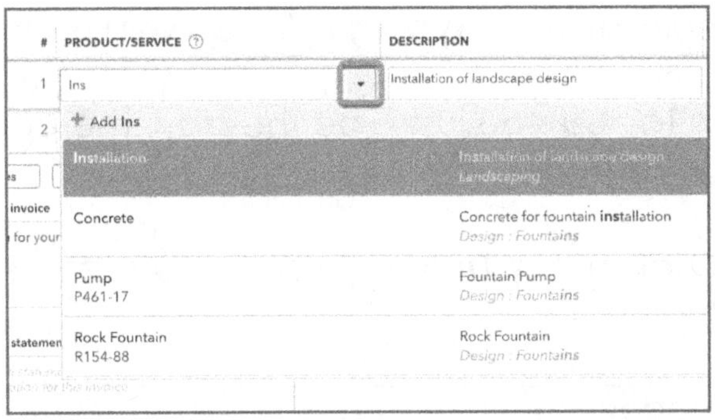

What's extra-cool is that you don't even have to start at the beginning of the word – type the most unique text for the shortest list of matching options!

Press **up arrow** or **down arrow** to move through the items in the list.

Keyboard Commands

Hold down the **Ctrl** and **Alt** (or **Option** on a Mac) and type the **?/** key on your keyboard. A window opens with your **Company ID**, as well as a master list of keyboard shortcuts. Hold down **Ctrl+Alt** and press letters in the list below to open those windows.

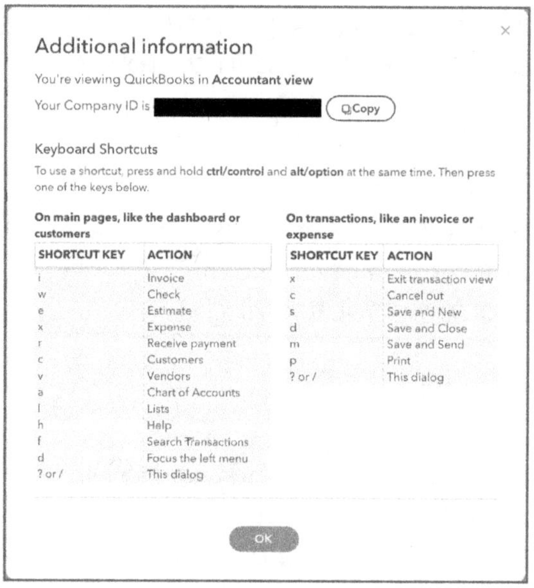

Entering Dates

When entering dates, you don't need leading 0s or the current year. Typing **6/3, Tab** will resolve to 06/03/2026.

In fact, if you just type the *day*, the current month and year will autofill!

Click in any **Date** field and tap these letters to jump to a key date without typing:

Today	**T**
Tomorrow, next day	**+ (plus)**
Yesterday, previous day	**- (minus)**
First day of the Year (1/1)	**Y**
Last day of the Year (12/31)	**R**

First day of the Month (1st)	**M**
Last day of the Month (28th, 30th, 31st)	**H**
First day of the Week (last Sun)	**W**
Last day of the Week (next Sat)	**K**

Built-in Calculators

There is no need to pull out your calculator! In every **Quantity, Rate, and Amount** field, you can use +, -, *, /, and () to do instant math. Press **Tab** to calculate the result.

Dynamic Buttons

The buttons at the bottom right corner of each window are dynamic. When you click on a Save button's drop-down arrow, it gives the option to **Save** this window and stay where you are, Save and Close it, or save this transaction and start a **New** one (so that you can process several similar transactions quickly).

In Sales Receipts and Invoices you can also **Review and send**, emailing them directly to the Customer.

What's nice about these buttons is that they're sticky. Once you change the button, it will stay that way until you change it again.

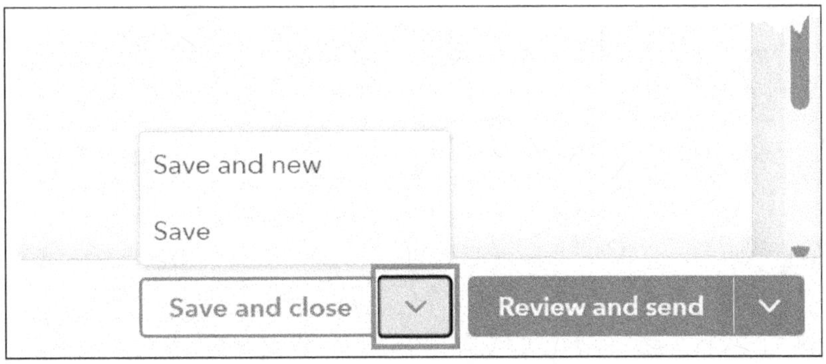

The More Actions Button

Keep an eye out for the **More Actions** button in the bottom center of many transactions. This is where you go to **Delete** or **Void** a transaction, **Audit** its history, view its **Transaction Journal**, **Copy** it to make a new one, and perform other actions related to that form.

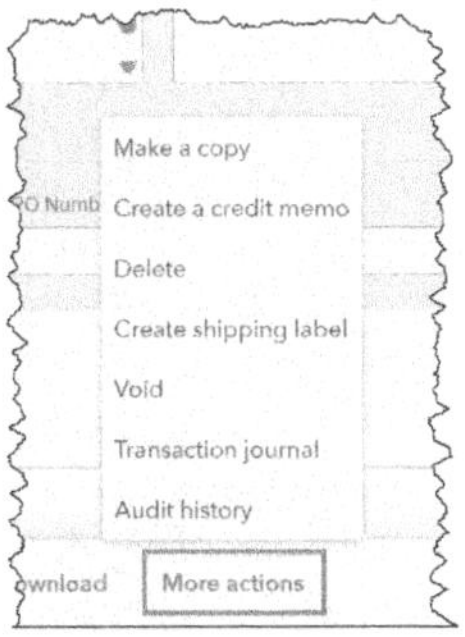

The Business Feed

The Business Feed is the hub for the Intuit Assist artificial intelligence agents. Head here for actions to speed up your cash flow, and alerts to call your attention to overlooked business activity.

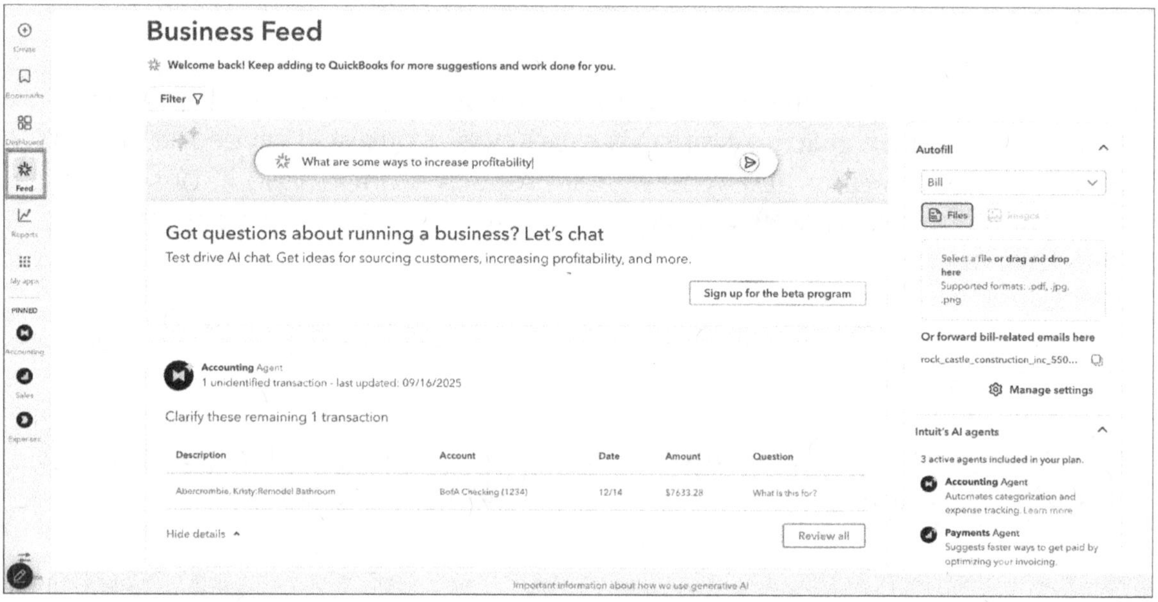

Check Your Understanding: The Interface

1) _______ The Left Navigation Pane contains:
   a. QBO's behind-the-scenes tools
   b. New transactions you create
   c. The main Centers for different functions
   d. Shortcuts to the most commonly used forms

2) _______ The Dashboard:
   a. Shows a workflow so you know what to do next
   b. Is a collection of important information
   c. Help you use QuickBooks Online properly
   d. B & C

3) _______ To quickly find a transaction by dollar amount:
   a. Use the Bank Transactions
   b. Use the Search Bar
   c. Go to the Center where you were when you made it
   d. Run a Report

4) _______ To find a transaction you were just working on:
   a. Use the Back button on your browser
   b. Use the Sales or Expenses Center
   c. Click the Search Bar
   d. Search by the date of the transaction

5) _______ To create a new transaction:
   a. Use the Settings in the upper right corner
   b. Use the Left Navigation Bar
   c. Use the +Create button at the top left of the screen
   d. Use Ctrl-N (PC) or Cmd-N (Mac)

6) _______ The Settings gear contains:
   a. QBO's behind-the-scenes tools
   b. New transactions you create
   c. The main Centers for different functions
   d. Shortcuts to the most commonly used screens

7) _______ Go here to see your Bank Transactions feeds:
   a. Accounting
   b. Sales & Get Paid
   c. Expenses & Bills
   d. Chart of Accounts

8) _______ Go here to see your income transactions:
   a. Accounting
   b. Sales & Get Paid
   c. Expenses & Bills

d. Chart of Accounts

9) _______ Go here to see the money you spend:
   a. Accounting
   b. Sales & Get Paid
   c. Expenses & Bills
   d. Chart of Accounts

10) _______ Dynamic Save buttons:
   a. Are the same on every screen
   b. Allow you to select the mode leading you to your next action
   c. Are customizable to say what you want them to say

11) _______ There are no keyboard shortcuts because QBO works in a browser.
   a. True
   b. False

12) _______ You can find your Company ID under the:
   a. Keyboard Shortcuts window
   b. Settings > Account and Settings
   c. The Dashboard
   d. A and B

13) _______ Your choices for changing dates include:
   a. M & H
   b. + and –
   c. T
   d. All of the above

14) _______ If you need to do a calculation, the most efficient method is to:
   a. Use a calculator and type the result in a field
   b. Use Excel and copy/paste the number
   c. Type the calculation right in the Quantity or Rate fields
   d. All of the above

Answers:
1) c, 2) d, 3) b, 4) c, 5) c, 6) a, 7) a, 8) b, 9) c, 10) b, 11) b, 12) d, 13) d, 14) c

Chapter 3: Setting Up Your Company

Which Version Should You Choose?

There are four main suites of QuickBooks Online: **QuickBooks Lite**, **Essentials**, **Plus**, and **Advanced**. You can start basic and small and easily upgrade to a more complex version any time. If you start with a higher-level subscription and later decide you do not need all the features, you can also downgrade.

There are three lighter versions including **QuickBooks Ledger, QuickBooks Solopreneur**, and **QuickBooks Money**, but they are not sufficient for most businesses.

Last but not least is the mid-market version, **Intuit Enterprise Suite**. This edition has tools for multi-company entity management, more complex Projects reporting, and multiple Dimensions (like having as many Classes as you need.

To compare versions to determine which one you need, visit http://www.quickbooks.com.

In a nutshell, if you're the only user and you use QBO just to track income and expenses, you can choose **QuickBooks Lite**. If you need 3 users, **eCommerce**, and **Accounts Payable**, look to the **Essentials Suite**.

If you want **Class Tracking** (page 67), will pass on your expenses to **customers** for reimbursement (page 120), keep **Inventory** (page 61), or like to run reports, choose the **Plus** version.

If you have over 250 categories in your **Chart of Accounts**, thousands of customers, need to bulk import transactions, would like additional custom fields, need granular user access for up to 25 employees, would love complex reporting tools and charts, and want to sync with Excel, the **Advanced** version is worth every penny.

Creating Your File

Sign up for QBO at http://www.quickbooks.com. If you know a bookkeeper who is a ProAdvisor, sign up through them instead, as they can offer you discounted subscription rates. If you don't have a bookkeeper to ask, visit our self-service subscription page at https://completebusinessgroup.com/royalwise-solutions/ and receive a 30% discount off your subscription for the first year...including QuickBooks Payments and Payroll!

When you create your account, QBO walks you through entering your company information. All forms, checks, invoices, tax forms, etc. will populate with the information you enter during the interview. BE SURE TO USE PROPER CAPITALIZATION AND PUNCTUATION!

Should You Import Your Existing File or Start Fresh?

To help you decide whether you should convert your current file or start over from scratch:

- Do you trust all the numbers in your current QuickBooks file? Are there errors?
- Have you been using the same QuickBooks file for years without cleaning it up or condensing it? If you have old customers, products, services, and vendors, a fresh start can make a big difference.
- Do you need all the historical detail, or would past summaries be sufficient? Can you just use correct opening balances for all accounts, and enter new transactions going forward?

Always keep your old file for reference!

Converting an Existing File

If you are going to import your QuickBooks Desktop file into QBO, start by signing up for QuickBooks Online and creating the QBO file.

The first step make sure your desktop version of QuickBooks is up to date. Go to **Help > Update QuickBooks.** Choose **Update Now**.

The second step is to Verify and Rebuild your QuickBooks Desktop file. This affirms that you have no errors in your data. Go to **File > Utilities > Verify**. If necessary, then choose **Utilities > Rebuild**.

Then go to the **Company Menu > Export Company File to QuickBooks Online**.

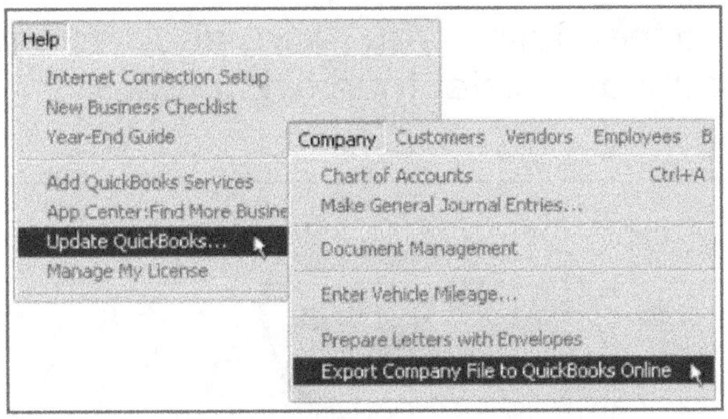

Enter your **username** and **password** for QuickBooks Online.

It takes a few minutes to transfer your data to QuickBooks Online. You'll receive an email when the file is ready.

When you get the email, click the link to log into ***qbo.intuit.com*** to view your new company file!

Your customers, vendors, and transaction history will have imported nicely.

To verify the data, run **Profit and Loss** and **Balance Sheet** reports in both files. Set the **date range** to "All" and the basis to "Accrual." Do all the line totals match? If they don't, there is something wrong with your Desktop file preventing a successful import.

Companion Course SCAN ME *royl.ws/bootcamp*

Want to learn more?

Deep Dive SCAN ME *royl.ws/ConvertingQBDT*

Note that if you are running **Inventory**, QBO natively uses FIFO ("First In, First Out"). You may see the choice to calculate your inventory values using MAC (Moving Average Cost), which is what QB Desktop uses. If you start using FIFO, it's more accurate, but your Inventory Asset and Cost of Goods values will be different when you compare your initial reports. Don't forget to fill in the necessary forms with the IRS to let them know there was a change in your inventory calculation method!

There are a few features available in QuickBooks Desktop versions that are not available in QuickBooks Online. Confirm that QBO has what you need, and develop ways to adapt your workflow if needed.

There are more features in QBO that are not in Desktop for you to discover! Be patient as you learn your new system. It will take time at first until you get used to the routine. You'll love discovering new things QBO can do that are easier and faster than ever before.

PEBCAK! Bad data that was hidden in QB Desktop becomes glaringly obvious in QBO. Take some time to refine your Chart of Accounts, Customer list, Vendor list, and Product list. Look for Unbilled Expenses. Look again at your Accounts Payable and Accounts Receivable reports to confirm that your balances reflect reality.

Don't carry your bad habits forward with you!

Starting from Scratch

If your company is new or you want a fresh start, your mission is to create the structure, enter the open transactions, and plan how to do your daily workflows making best use of the software's features.

Choosing a Start Date

Carefully choose an appropriate **Start Date** to begin using QuickBooks Online. When do you want your reports to start?

Your options are to choose a Start Date that represents either the **first day of your fiscal year**, or **a milestone accounting period** (end of quarter, end of month, etc.).

The start date also signifies how much historical data you'll have to enter. If your business is new, you won't have many transactions. If it's still early in the year, it shouldn't be too difficult to reconstruct the history. Later in the year, the Bank Transactions feed can make short order of entering a lot of data in a little time, and there are apps that can help batch import.

Whatever you choose, you'll enter a **Journal Entry** with period totals before that date, create the actual transactions still pending from before that date, and enter ALL transactions after the date (see page 29).

Setting up the File

The steps in setting up a fresh QBO file include adjusting Settings, creating your Lists, connecting the Bank Transactions, and entering in all open current transactions so that you have what you need for your day-to-day operations moving forward.

Instructions for all these steps appear later in this book.

1. Adjust the Settings:
Visit **Account and Settings** to turn on and off the features you need. See page 30.

2. Create your Chart of Accounts list:
Your **Chart of Accounts** contains all the income, expense, equity, asset, and liability categories for your company. It's the fundamental structure

for your company file, and needs to be refined before you do anything else. See page 42.

3. Create your Products and Services list:
Your Products and Services are the items you charge to customers. They appear on all invoices & sales receipts, and can be used for purchasing and expenses as well. See page 56.

4. Enter open Customer Invoices:
Enter all open unpaid invoices and Credit Memos with the date they were originally created, so that when a customer pays, you know what they're paying for! It's fine if the date is before your start date. See page 86.

5. Enter Vendor bills:
Enter unpaid bills and vendor credits using the dates of the original transactions. Be sure to use Products and Services in the bottom **Item Details** section if you purchased goods or labor. See page 119 and 126.

6. Connect Bank Transactions Feeds:
When you set up your bank accounts and connect them using your bank login, QBO imports your bank history. Every bank is different, so you'll be able to import somewhere between 30 days and two years' worth of transactions. If you need transactions further back, upload a manual export from your bank's website. Your history is then available for easy entry into QBO, following the instructions on page 149.

Entering Historical Transactions

Now that open and current customer and vendor transactions are entered, it's time to create any remaining historical data. As we've discussed in the beginning of this chapter, when you get started with a new QuickBooks Online file, you have a choice to either enter every single transaction after your start date, or to enter monthly summary journal entries until you're caught up.

If you are entering all historical transactions, which is the route most companies take, recreate them one month at a time and reconcile all bank accounts before going to the next month. Use **Bank Transactions** as your guide!

If you decide to enter summarized histories, decide whether you just need one grand total, or it would be helpful to see the previous years, quarters, or months. Refer back to your previous accounting software and run Trial Balance reports for the desired periods.

Create a **Journal Entry** (**+Create > Journal Entry**) for each period, entering the balance for every category in your **Chart of Accounts**. Use Opening Balance Equity (OBE) to offset the grand total. When you're done, transfer the OBE balance to Retained Earnings to zero it out.

Enlist the help of a QuickBooks ProAdvisor, your bookkeeper, or your accountant to ensure that this is done correctly.

> Summarized histories are particularly useful for entering data from the fiscal years before your QuickBooks Online file's start date.
>
> It is optional and potentially time-consuming, but it allows you to compare your company's growth to the years before you got started with this QBO file.

Account and Settings (Preferences)

Your next step is to adjust your **Company Settings** so that QBO behaves the way you want it to.

Select **Account and Settings** from under the **Settings Gear** in the upper right corner.

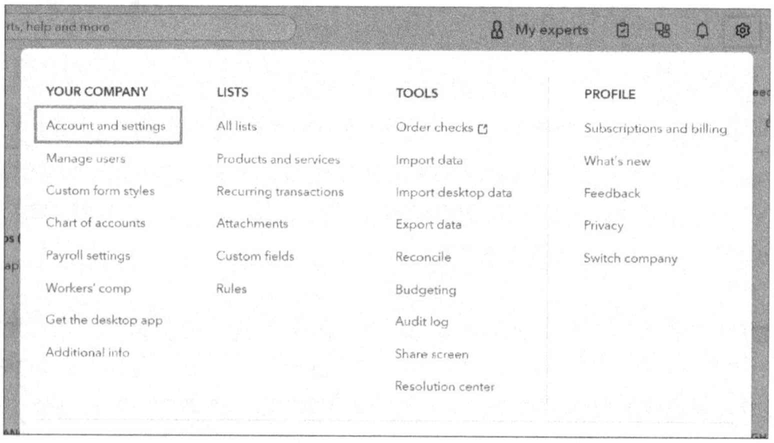

Company info

1. Make sure your Company name is correct.
2. Upload your logo.
3. Add your EIN or SSN.
4. Select your company formation (are you a sole proprietorship, LLC, S-Corp, or something else?).
5. Go through the Contact info and make sure your company name, address, phone numbers, and email addresses are all correct. You have several options for contact info for the back office, corporation, and customer-facing.
6. Choose to receive promotional offers from Intuit...or not.

Sales, Expenses, and Payments Settings

We will later explore these in their respective chapters.

Companion Course
SCAN ME
royl.ws/bootcamp

Want to learn more?

Deep Dive
SCAN ME
royl.ws/Setting-Up-QBO

Advanced Settings

Here are some of the most important settings to turn on or off. Be sure to click **Save** between sections, and **Done** when you're ready to go back.

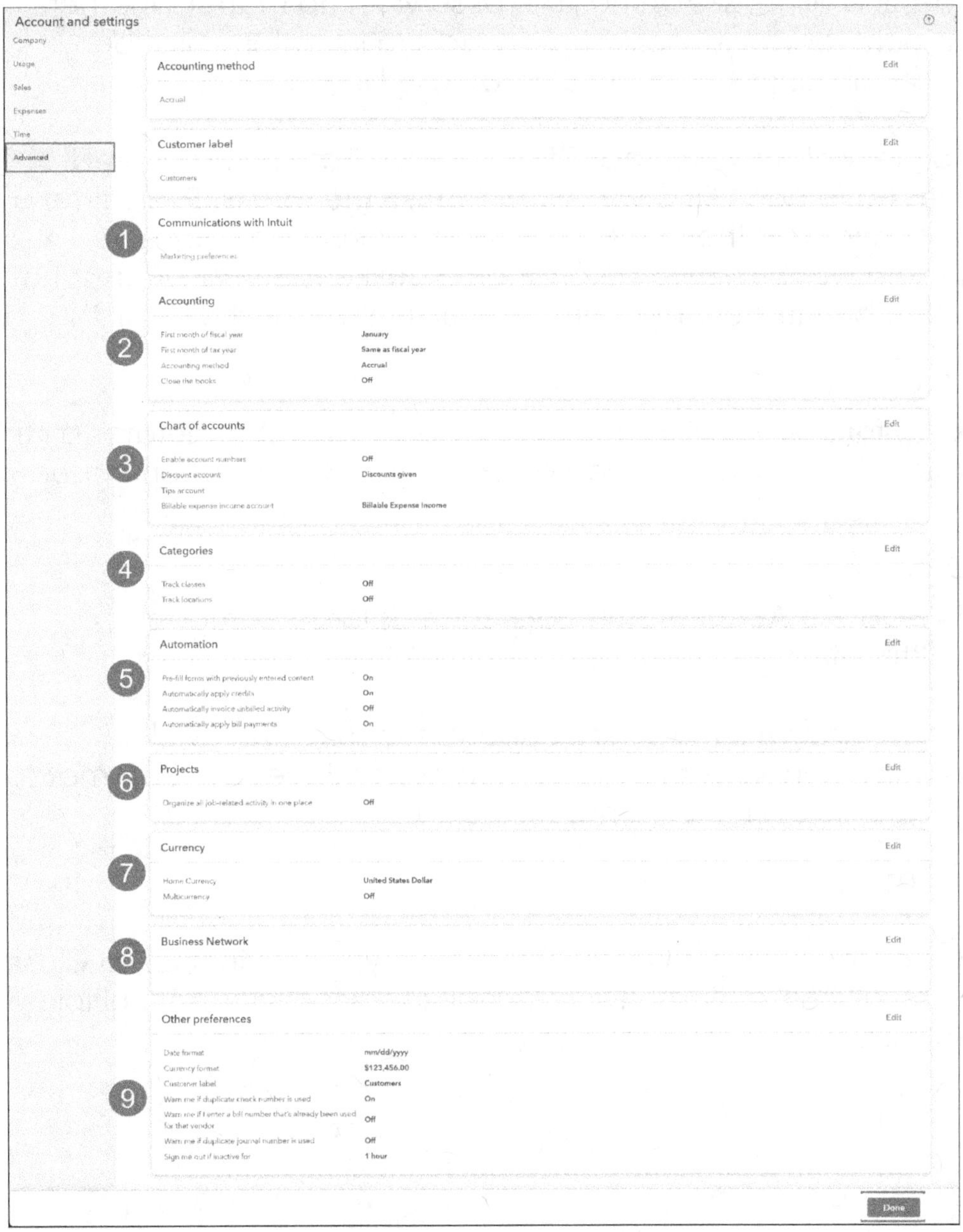

1. Communications with Intuit

Click **Marketing Preferences** to log into your Intuit account to modify your email preferences.

2. Accounting

First, set your **Fiscal Year**.

Next, select whether you are **Cash or Accrual** based. If you're not sure, ask your accountant. A cash-based business reports income and expenses when the money changes hands. An accrual-based company counts income and expenses at the time of service, no matter whether they've been paid for yet. All companies tracking Inventory must be accrual. Most small businesses in the US are cash-based.

If you want to prevent previous years' transactions from being altered, after your taxes have been filed you should **Close the books**. Every time a transaction is changed in the closed period, a warning box appears asking if you really want to save the change. Bookkeepers will often set a password so that business owners can't edit past history without authorization.

A **Closing Exceptions report** (Plus and Advanced versions) generates a list of all transactions that have changed after the books have been closed.

3. Chart of Accounts

If you would like to use **Account Numbers**, such as large companies do, turn that on in this window.

Here you will also map which ledger accounts the forms will use for discounts, tips, and billable expenses. All of these activities are automated as you create your sales and expense transactions.

4. Class and Location Tracking

If you have QuickBooks Online Plus or Advanced, you can include a **Class** and **Location** on all transactions. This feature is ideal for tracking multiple revenue streams.

QuickBooks Online prompts you to enter the Class on each transaction, or even each line, making them extremely useful.

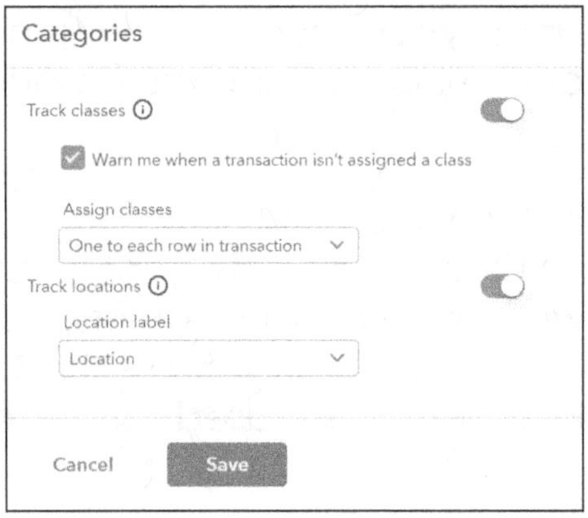

Locations label each transaction with a single physical Location, Department, Division, Store, and more. If you're deciding which one to use, Locations work well on Balance Sheet accounts, and Classes work well on Profit and Loss reports. Sometimes you need both!

See Classes on page 66 for more information.

5. Automation

Automations will either help you or confuse you. When they save you time, they're great! However, if you find that they take important steps out of your hands that you need to control, the automations can actually interfere.

Pre-fill forms with previously entered content. As soon as you enter the Payee on an expense, QBO automatically fills in the rest of the transaction, repeating the most recent categories and amounts. All you have to do is update the description or change the amounts as needed.

However, if this function creates more work for you because you have to constantly delete unneeded rows, then simply turn this option *Off*.

Automatically apply credits. If a customer has a credit on account, and you create a new invoice, this option automatically applies the Credit to the Invoice to pay it down. This is great if it's hard for you to remember when your customers have credits to apply...however, sometimes you need more control about which invoice you want to reduce.

Automatically invoice unbilled activity. If you are marking expenses as billable to a customer, this option invoices them automatically. However, you may not want to charge a client until you are ready, so you can generally leave this function *Off*.

Automatically apply bill payments. If you have a credit with a vendor, and you create a new bill, this option automatically applies the credit to your bill, paying it down. This is great if it's hard for you to remember to apply your account credits to open bills…but it can sometimes be confusing because the amount you owe the vendor instantly changes.

6. Projects

QBO has a Projects Center to track all the revenue and expenses for the work you do for customers. It's a step up from the Customer/Sub-customer relationship that was used in QuickBooks Desktop (see page 75). It includes a job-based P&L report, Labor Costing, Billable Expenses, and a Transaction List.

7. Currency

If your clients pay you with international currencies, this option will allow you to track the exchange rate on a daily basis. But only turn it on if you really need it, like when you have a bank account in another country or do business across borders. Don't use it for international PayPal payments. Once it's on, you can't turn it off!

8. Business Network

This innovation from Intuit connects QuickBooks users together.

Add your address and contact information. When a new Customer (who is also a QuickBooks Online user) adds you to their QBO, your contact info will autofill.

If you add your ACH information, your customers can use it to pay you.

When your vendor is part of the network, you can automatically use Online Bill Pay for direct deposit bill payments.

When you create an invoice to a customer also in the network, a bill will appear in their file automatically…and if you create a bill, your vendor will find a new invoice created in *their* system.

At least, that's the rumor. I haven't seen it happen yet.

The Business Network is turned on by default. Be sure to opt out if you don't want to participate.

9. Other preferences

You can change the **Customer label** to Clients, Tenants, Members, Donors, Patients, and more.

Be sure to change the **Sign me out if inactive for** to *3 hours* so that you don't have to log in repeatedly all day long!

Setting Up Users

Company Users

QuickBooks Online allows for multiple users without needing a server or hosting service. QuickBooks Lite allows for 1 user. **Essentials** allows up to 3 users. With **Plus**, you can have up to 5 users, and **Advanced** opens you up to 25 users.

To add and manage users, go into the **Settings** and choose **Manage Users.**

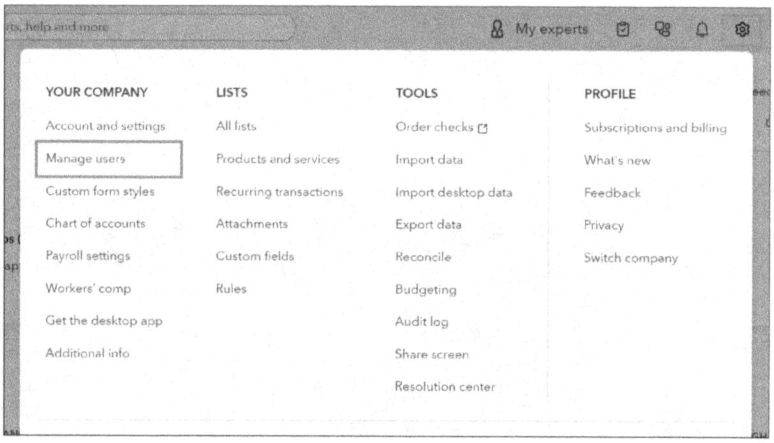

Click the green **Add User** button and choose their user type. Enter their first and last name, and email address. The user will receive an email with a link to sign into the company. They will create their own password when they log in for the first time.

Until the user receives that email and signs in, your Manage Users page will show that they have been "Invited." After they sign in, their status becomes "Active."

The next step is to assign a role. The available roles will change depending on your QBO version level and the features you have turned on.

You can open the **Permissions** sections to see what each role can and can't do. I usually assign the appropriate role with the least permissions for that employee's needs, and then increase it as necessary.

Companion Course — SCAN ME — royl.ws/bootcamp

Want to learn more?

Deep Dive — SCAN ME — royl.ws/Setting-Up-QBO

Assign the **Company administrator** role only to people who need full access to QuickBooks, Payroll, Merchant Services, and third-party apps.

QBO Advanced users have the ability to further define **Roles** with granular detail for what each user can and can't do.

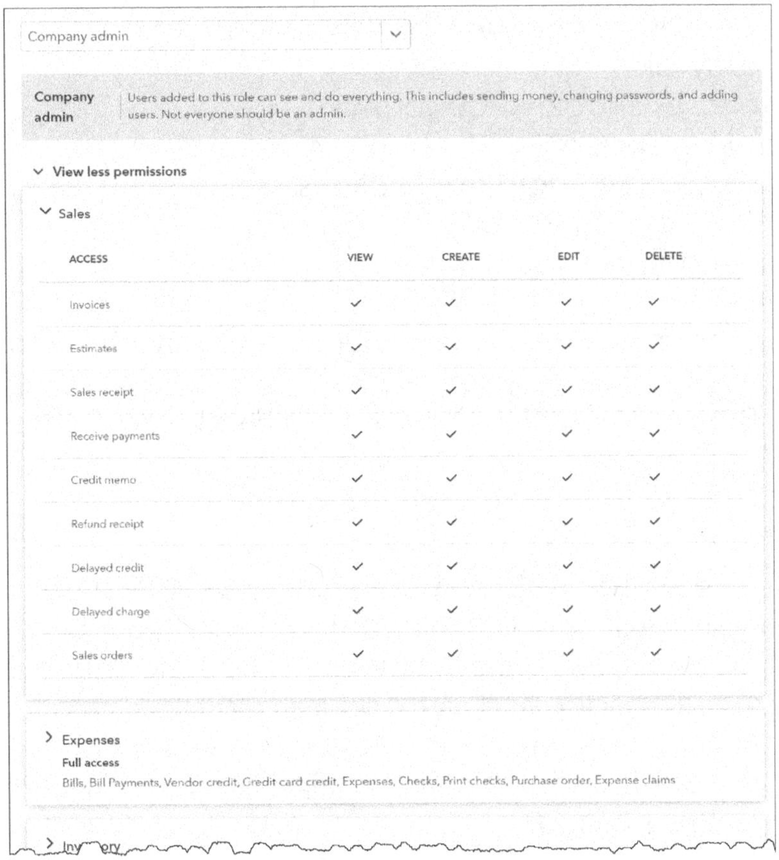

The Plus and Advanced versions have unlimited **View Company Reports** users for those who only pull reports and shouldn't touch the transactions. These are great for CEOs and Board Members.

Track Time Only users allow employees to log into QuickBooks Online to fill in their timesheets. Timesheet-only employees do not count towards your total number of users.

Most employees will be set up using a **Standard user**. The benefit of **Standard** is that they limit access to **Customers & Sales**, **Vendors & Purchases**, and/or **Payroll**.

Users with access as an **Accounts Receivable Manager** can:

- Enter Estimates, Invoices, Sales Receipts, Credit Memos, and Refunds

- Receive payments from clients
- Fill out time sheets for all Employees
- Add, edit, and inactivate Customers
- Add, edit, and inactivate Products and Services
- View Customer and A/R reports

Users with access as an **Accounts Payable Manager** can:
- Enter and pay Bills
- Make purchases Billable to customers
- Write and print Checks
- Enter cash and credit card transactions
- Add, edit, and delete Vendors
- View Vendor and A/P reports

There is an option to restrict any user's **access to Payroll** information. When this box is checked, users only see "Payroll" as the Payee on paychecks and reports. They are also blocked from the Employee Center.

Accounting Firm Users

In addition to these user seats, all businesses are allotted up to two free **Accountant** logins (Advanced has three). This way, your bookkeeper and CPA can log into your file and get to work without having to come into your office, send files back and forth, or use a VPN.

Create their accounts under the **Accounting Firms** section on the right tab of the **Manage Users** window.

Check Your Understanding: Setting Up Your Company

1) _______The QBO version that allows up to 3 users is:
   a. QuickBooks Lite
   b. Essentials
   c. Plus
   d. Advanced

2) _______If you work with 1099 Subcontractors and would like to automate your year-end reporting, choose this version:
   a. QuickBooks Lite
   b. Essentials
   c. Plus
   d. Any of the above

3) _______If you start with the Essentials version but decide you need more users, it's easy to upgrade to Plus.
   a. True
   b. False

4) _______If you start with the Plus or Advanced versions but decide you don't need all the features, it's easy to downgrade.
   a. True
   b. False
   c. Sometimes

5) _______If your current QuickBooks file is full of errors, old customers & vendors, or you don't trust its accuracy, you should:
   a. Fix your existing file before converting
   b. Import it into QBO to fix it
   c. Start over from scratch

6) _______If you start over from scratch, you can do this to maintain access to your old records:
   a. Reactivate the accounts you deleted in QBO
   b. Refer to your previous copy of QB
   c. Print out all your reports and lists from the old file
   d. B & C

7) _______If you import your file from QuickBooks Desktop into QBO, you should:
   a. Deactivate unused customers, vendors, and items before you import
   b. Wait until you're up and running in QBO to clean up your lists

8) _______When you choose a Start Date partway through the year, you can
   a. Run reports from your old and new copies to do your taxes
   b. Enter in all the transactions since the start of the year
   c. Enter in month-end summary totals so you can still run comparison reports

d. Any of the above

9) _______ Capitalization and punctuation don't matter when entering your company's information.
a. True
b. False

10) _______ The Company Settings can be found here:
a. The Left Navigation Pane
b. The +Create button
c. The Dashboard
d. The Settings gear

11) _______ An Accrual-based company counts its income:
a. When an invoice is created
b. When the payment is received
c. When the money is deposited
d. After all expenses have been deducted

12) _______ Companies with inventory must be:
a. Cash-based
b. Accrual-based
c. It doesn't matter
d. Ask your CPA

13) _______ Can you choose any name for your customers?
a. They must be called Customers
b. You can enter the name you call them
c. You can choose from QBO's list

14) _______ If you want your forms to autofill with the most recent transaction, choose this option:
a. Automatically apply credits
b. Automatically Invoice unbilled activity
c. Copy estimates to Invoices
d. Pre-fill forms with previously entered content

15) _______ To limit a user's access to Invoices & Payments, but block them from seeing Accounts Payable, choose this level of access:
a. Accounts Receivable Manager
b. Company administrator
c. View company reports
d. Track Time only

Answers: 1) b, 2) d, 3) a, 4) c, 5) c, 6) d, 7) a, 8) d, 9) b, 10) d, 11) a, 12) b, 13) c, 14) d, 15) a

Companion Course
SCAN ME
royl.ws/bootcamp

Want to learn more?

Deep Dive
SCAN ME
royl.ws/Setting-Up-QBO

Chapter 4: Working with Lists

Lists are the backbone of QuickBooks Online. Most screens in QBO get their content from different "lists" of information. This ensures that the data is entered consistently from day to day.

Lists you work with every day also include **Customers** and **Vendors**, along with the **Chart of Accounts** and **Products and Services**.

To see what's on every drop-down menu in QBO, click on the **Settings** and choose **All Lists**. Lists including **Payment Methods**, **Terms**, and **Classes** can be set up one time and modified as your needs evolve.

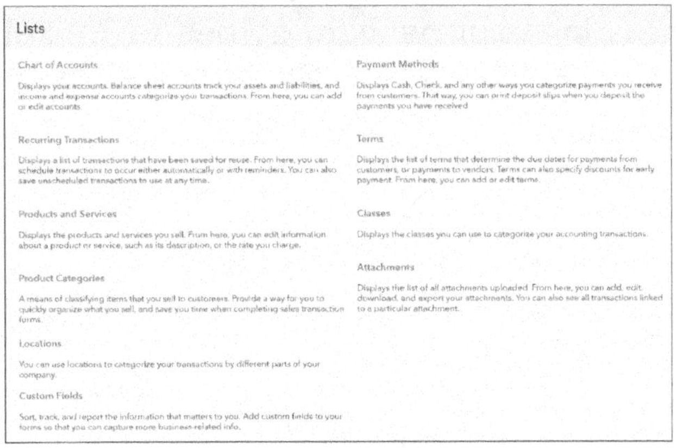

The same name cannot appear on more than one list. For example, you may have a vendor who also buys things from you as a customer. In that case, as long as the names are slightly different, you'll be fine. One method is to add the business designator, like LLC or Inc. to the vendor name. Another is to add on an extension code such as -V and -C to the Display name.

List items can be deleted, inactivated, and merged. For example, if you find you have the same customer twice, once under the company name and again under the contact's name, copying the correct **Display Name** and pasting it into the "bad" one will merge the two, combining all their transactions into one.

The Chart of Accounts

The **Chart of Accounts** is the most important list in your QuickBooks Online file. Just as a house needs a foundation, frame, and roof, your company's reporting won't make any sense without a properly designed **Chart of Accounts (COA).**

This section discusses the fundamentals of a COA; however, tapping the expertise of a QuickBooks ProAdvisor, your accountant, or bookkeeper is ***highly recommended*** to make sure your Chart of Accounts is correct from the very beginning!

During the setup process when you tell QBO which industry you're in, QBO creates a default Chart of Accounts, but you do need to customize it to fit your unique business. In the upper right corner, select **Settings > Chart of Accounts,** or in the left sidebar select **My Apps > Accounting > Chart of Accounts.**

Let's start by analyzing the structure of your COA so that you understand exactly what it all means.

Companion Course

SCAN ME

royl.ws/bootcamp

Want to learn more?

Deep Dive

SCAN ME

royl.ws/COA

The top part of a Chart of Accounts contains the categories found on a **Balance Sheet** (see page 171). The bottom part contains the categories found on a **Profit and Loss** report (page 169).

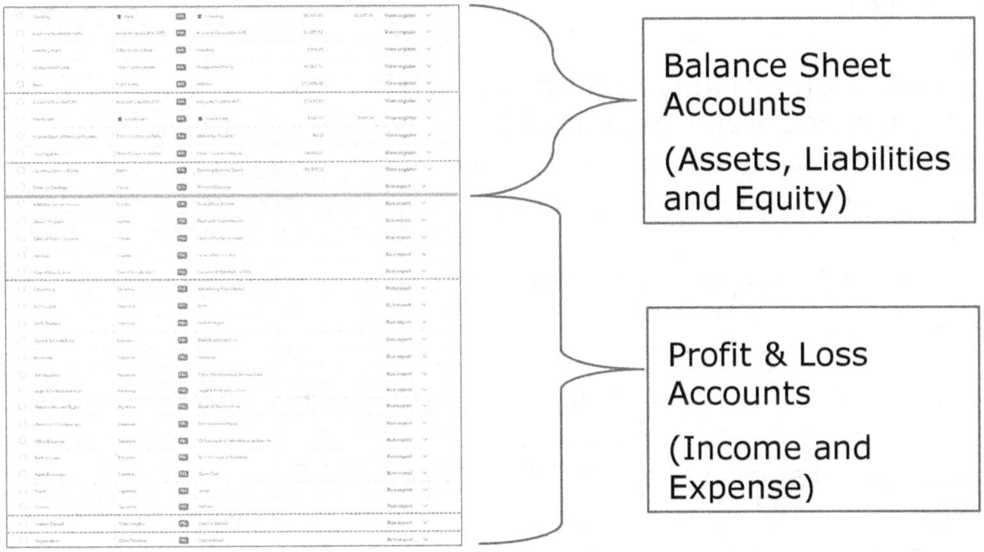

Assets include all the things your company ***has***: bank accounts, fixed assets including equipment and trucks, and inventory. **Assets** also include ***what your customers owe you***. This is called your **Accounts Receivable,** or **A/R.**

Liabilities include ***what your company owes to other people.*** This is called your **Accounts Payable**, or **A/P** for short. Additional liabilities include credit cards, loans, sales tax, and payroll taxes you owe to the state and federal governments.

Equity describes ***the investment in your company***. Equity equals the company's total assets minus its total liabilities. On a Balance Sheet, it looks like this: **Assets = Liabilities + Equity**. This makes sense because everything your company has originally came from getting a loan, putting it on a credit card, turning a profit, or contributing through the owners' capital.

A practical way to think about it is **Assets – Liabilities = Equity**. In other words, what a company *owns* minus what it *owes* equals the equity in the company.

Profit and Loss: Income and Expenses

The **Profit and Loss Statement (P&L)** lays out your income and costs, showing you how much profit (or loss) you made. A sample P&L can be found on page 170.

Income categories refer to the ways the company makes money. Create a separate Income account for each distinct revenue stream. Income accounts are general bucket categories that total up all the specific Services and Products that get listed on customer invoices (see page 56).

Expenses include all the overhead administrative costs of running your business.

Cost of Goods are direct costs associated with delivering your goods or services. They are deducted from Income to calculate Gross Profit. Cost of Goods includes Supplies and Materials, Shipping expenses, Cost of Labor, Equipment Rental, and other miscellaneous costs. If you had to pay for a product or labor in order to earn the income, it's COGS.

Accounts Created Automatically

These Accounts are created by QuickBooks Online automatically as you need them:

Accounts Receivable (A/R) – How much money customers owe you. This account is the default every time you create an Invoice.

Inventory Asset – What is the value of the current inventory in your warehouse? This account is the default every time you enter an Inventory Item.

Uncategorized Asset – ***PEBCAK!*** This is the default for Deposits, Transfers, and Refunds entered into QuickBooks Online through the Bank Transactions feed, but accidentally not assigned to a specific source account. This account should be empty.

Undeposited Funds or Payments to Deposit – This account holds the money you have collected until you physically deposit it in a bank account. Use this in the **Deposit to** field in every Sales Receipt and Invoice Payment. This name varies in different QBO files.

Accounts Payable (A/P) – How much money do you currently owe to vendors? This account is the default every time you create a Bill.

Sales Tax Payable – Created when you turn on the Sales Tax feature. You will see categories for each state.

Uncategorized Income – PEBCAK! Transactions entered into QuickBooks Online through the Bank Transactions feed, but accidentally not matched to a Deposit or assigned to a specific income account. This account should be empty, although it can be used as a holding tank for transactions you need to research.

Uncategorized Expense – PEBCAK! Transactions entered into QuickBooks Online through the Bank Transactions feed, but accidentally not assigned to a specific expense account. This account should be empty, although it can be used as a holding tank for transactions you need to research.

Unapplied Cash Payment Income – PEBCAK (usually)! When you run a cash-based Profit and Loss Statement with an invoice payment dated before the invoice itself, that revenue is Unapplied during that date range.

Unapplied Cash Payment Expense – PEBCAK (maybe)! When you run a cash-based Profit and Loss Statement with bill payments dated before the bill itself, that expense is Unapplied during that date range.

Cost of Goods Sold (COGS or COS) – The COGS account tracks the expenses incurred in order to provide your services. If you would not be able to deliver the product or service without purchasing consumable items, hiring a subcontractor, or renting a piece of equipment, those costs go into this account.

Payroll Liabilities and Expenses – Created when the payroll feature is turned on. All QBO Payroll's transactions are mapped to these accounts by default.

Opening Balance Equity – QuickBooks Online records the beginning balance of each account on the day before you started your QBO file in Opening Balance Equity. After setup is complete, transfer the total in OBE to Retained Earnings, so that its final balance equals $0. If you see a balance here after the initial setup, you made a mistake in that transaction.

Retained Earnings – This tracks your company's cumulative net profit from previous fiscal years. QuickBooks Online automatically transfers your undistributed profit (or loss, as the case may be) from Net Income on the last day of your fiscal year to the Retained Earnings equity account on the first day of each new fiscal year.

REMEMBER TO KEEP THE CHART OF ACCOUNTS LIST <u>GENERAL</u>.

Its main function is to classify your business income and expenses for <u>tax purposes</u> and <u>business advisory</u>.

Add your specific offerings to your Products and Services Items List instead.

It is an extremely good idea to work with a professional to dial in your Chart of Accounts! Errors here trickle down, and make all your yearlong efforts useless come tax time!

Modifying the Chart of Accounts

You can create up to 250 custom categories on your Chart of Accounts. If you need more than that, you'll need to upgrade to QuickBooks Online Advanced.

Add a New Account

Click on the **Settings** or **My Apps > Accounting** and choose **Chart of Accounts**. Select **New Account.**

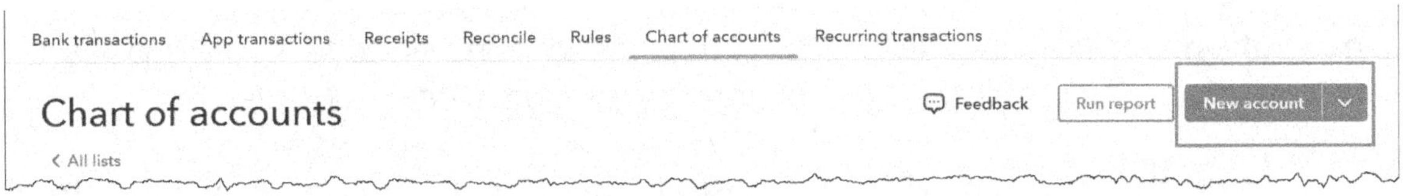

As a demonstration, we'll add an Equity account for when the owner takes cash out of the business's bank account for their own personal use (as opposed to running payroll).

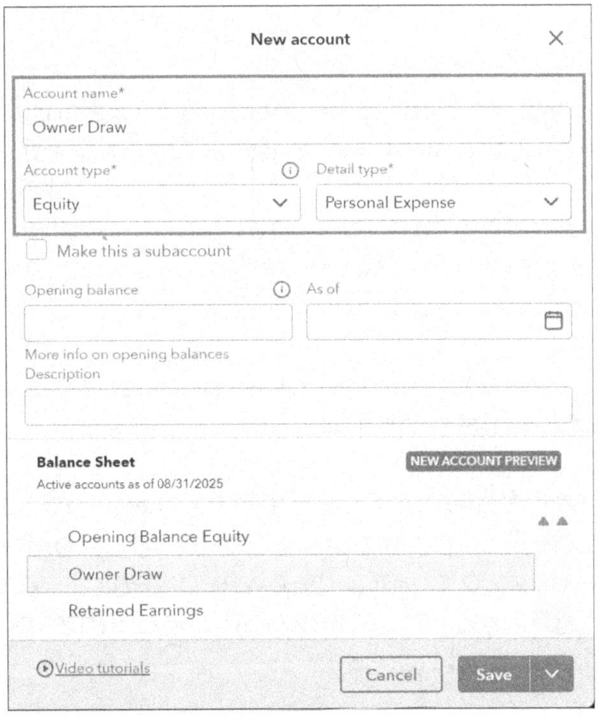

Account Name: call it **Owner Draw**, which is the terminology a sole proprietor uses. Alternatively, LLCs name it a "Partner Distribution" and corporations use a "Shareholder Distribution."

Select the **Account Type*** you want to set up. There are 15 preset Account Types in QuickBooks Online. Your trusted advisor will need to assist you in selecting the correct one, since mistakes here can affect your reports…and your taxes!

Choose **Equity.**

Detail Type*: choose the Tax line associated with this Equity account. This makes it easier to integrate with tax software. Select **Personal Expense.**

In most cases, you will skip the **Opening Balance** and **As Of** fields.

Description: (optional). Use this as a training reminder as to the purpose of the category. It doesn't show up anywhere but here.

Drop down the arrow next to the **Save** button and choose **Save and New.**

Now, **add another account.** Also create an **Owner Contribution** account with the **Detail Type** set to **Owner's Equity** for any personal out-of-pocket money you use to pay business expenses.

Creating Subaccounts

Subaccounts allow you to further analyze your expenses. The idea is to use a main header account to sum the smaller categories.

If you implement Subaccounts, you'll get greater detail, but it also adds to the complexity of your system...and opens the door to ***PEBCAK!***

It's important NEVER to post into the main header account, or you won't get accurate subtotals.

It's also important to create subaccounts to cover all contingencies, or at least create an "Other" category as a catch-all for one-off transactions. For example, if you have a company-owned vehicle, create a main account for Auto Expenses, you'll need subaccounts for Fuel, Repairs and Maintenance, Parking, and Licenses.

Another common use is to break down Utilities into Electricity, Water, Gas, Garbage, Internet, and Telephone.

To create a **Utilities** subaccount, click the **New Account** button, then set up the new category with the identical **Account Type** and **Detail Type** as the main account, **Expenses** and **Utilities**. Check off **Make This a Subaccount**. In **Parent Account**, choose the main root level category, **Utilities**. Give it the account name **Water**. Select **Save and New.**

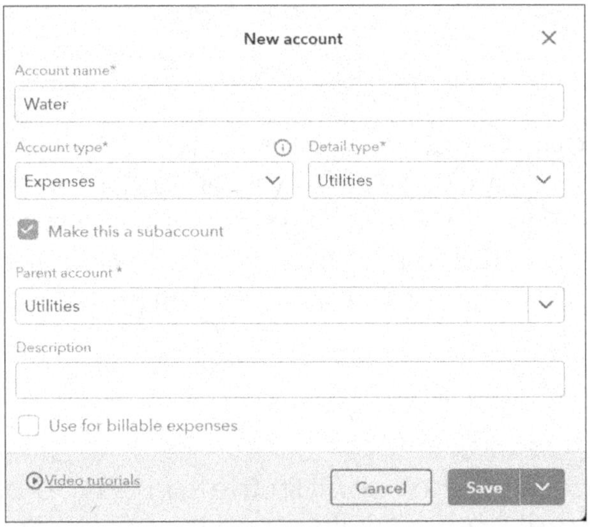

Repeat these same steps to create all of your utility categories.

The new subaccounts are added to the Chart of Accounts list, and are indented in the hierarchy.

Editing an Account

If you need to change anything about how an account is set up, select the drop-down arrow on the far right in the **Action** column, and choose **Edit.**

Deleting and Inactivating an Account

There's really no such thing as deleting an account in QBO. Rather than being deleted, categories are inactivated. They can still be viewed, calculated in reports, and reactivated with no loss of data.

To Delete/Inactivate an account on the Chart of Accounts list, click on the drop-down arrow on the far right of the account to be deleted. Select **Make inactive.**

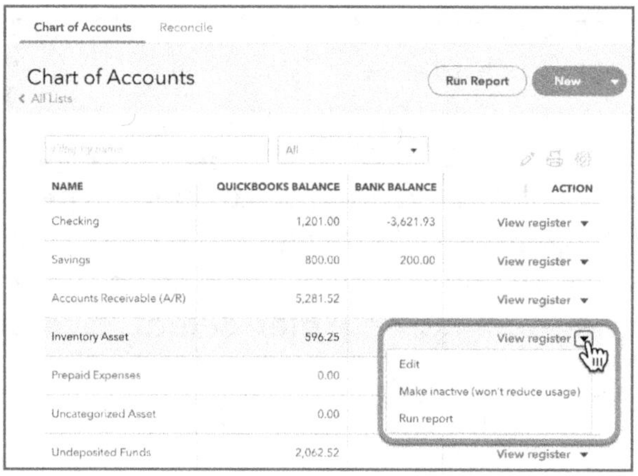

Balance Sheet accounts can only be Inactivated if they have a $0 balance. If it has a balance, decide where the balance goes and move it appropriately (for example, if you close a bank account, where did you transfer the balance?). If you Inactivate a Balance Sheet account that still has a balance, it will be offset to Opening Balance Equity, creating bad data.

Merging Two Accounts

If you have two accounts that contain the same type of transactions, but you used two different names, or if you no longer want the same itemized level of detail, you can **Merge** them.

If you do use Subaccounts,
create a Subaccount for every need, or call one "Other ____".
DO NOT POST into the header account.
The header account is only used to total the Subaccounts.

First, **Edit** the account you want to *keep*. Highlight the name of the account and copy it. Make note of the **Account Type** and **Detail Type** sections so that you can replicate them. **Cancel** the window.

Then **Edit** the account you want to *delete*. Erase the **Account Name*** of the account, and paste the preferred name into the field so that it replaces the old one.

Update the **Account Type** and **Detail Type** if necessary so that they match.

When you scroll down to the bottom of the pane, the two accounts will turn red, indicating that they are identical.

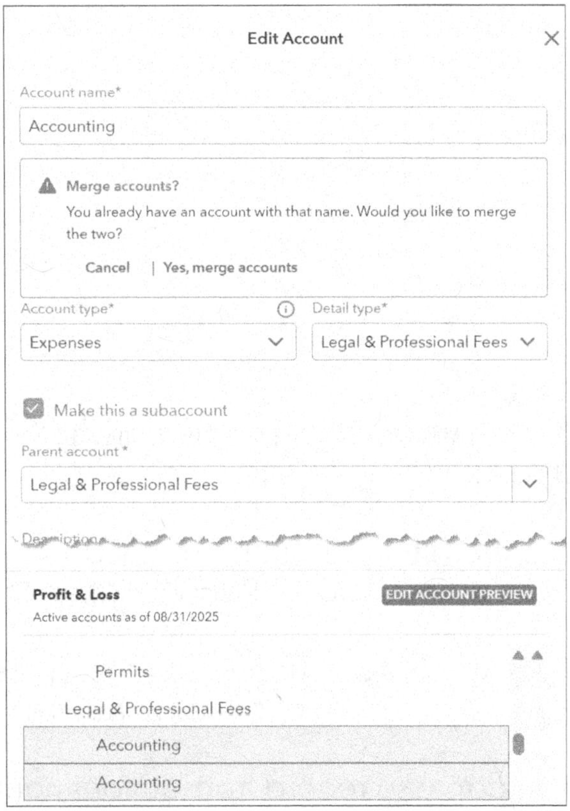

When you **Save** the change, it will recognize that the names are the same, and ask if you want to **Merge** them. Click **Yes, Merge Accounts**.

All the transactions in the second account are moved into the first account. The second is inactivated, disappearing off all Lists.

This technique also works to merge any two Customers, Vendors, or Products & Services. This is great for typos, names entered incorrectly, and correcting redundant payees created by the Bank Transaction feeds.

Always keep a record of when two accounts were merged in case of an audit.

Using the Register

To see the transactions in a Balance Sheet account, double-click on it from the Chart of Accounts, or click the **View Register** action link on the right.

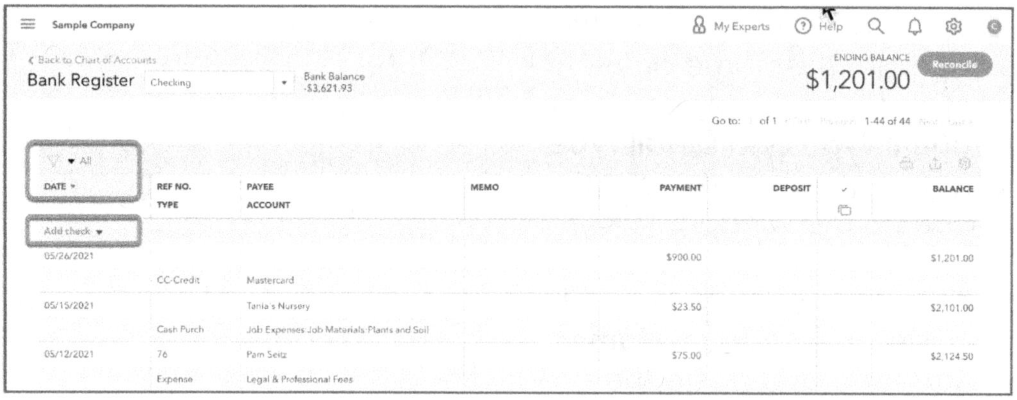

This allows you to view the transactions in a familiar checkbook-register style list.

Use the **Filter** button to narrow down the transaction list by date, Payee, Transaction Type, or Reconciliation Status.

Click the **Date** button to sort the entire register, or your filtered results, from newest to oldest, or oldest to newest.

You can also record transactions right in the register by clicking the **Add Check** dropdown arrow, then selecting the type of transaction. Enter the **Payee, the amount of the Payment or Deposit**, and the **Account.** There's also a place for a **Memo** explaining the transaction, as well as a place to specify **Classes** and **Locations** if you have them turned on.

You can view, edit, and delete transactions by clicking on them. To change a transaction via the register, **click on the transaction**, then the **Edit button** to open the transaction in its own window. Make the changes and **Save** the transaction.

While many people instinctively want to enter transactions here in the register, you're usually better off using the **+Create button** and creating the actual transaction using its form. This will both make additional fields available, and reduce data entry errors.

On Your Own!

Go through your Chart of Accounts and set up general "bucket" categories for:

1) Bank Accounts: Checking & Savings Accounts, Petty Cash, Till
2) Credit Cards
3) Income accounts for the distinct categories of goods and services you offer
4) Cost of Goods or Cost of Sales accounts for labor, materials, and direct costs incurred to deliver your products and services
5) Fixed Assets for Equipment, Furniture, and Vehicles
6) Liability accounts for Loans
7) Expense accounts for costs that are not already listed
8) Equity accounts for Owner Contributions and Distributions

You may also inactivate accounts created by QBO that don't apply to your company. You can always reactivate them or replace them as needed.

Take time to study your COA so that you're familiar with the accounts. This will make it faster when you're deciding what to do with various transactions!

Check Your Understanding: The Chart of Accounts

Match the Account with the function:

_____ Bank
_____ Fixed Assets
_____ Other Current Assets
_____ Accounts Receivable
_____ Accounts Payable
_____ Other Current Liabilities
_____ Long Term Liabilities
_____ Equity
_____ Cost of Goods Sold
_____ Income
_____ Expense
_____ Other Income
_____ Other Expense

a) Money the owners have invested and withdrawn from the business
b) The money customers owe you for services you already provided
c) The money you spend for business overhead
d) Where you keep your money
e) Money you earned, but in a way different than your main revenue streams
f) Money you borrowed and are paying back over time
g) Money spent specifically to deliver your services
h) Money you receive for your services or products
i) Money you spent, not because of operations
j) Large amounts of money spent for equipment and vehicles
k) Money you owe to vendors
l) Money you owe that will be paid in less than a year
m) Value in your company that fluctuates, like inventory

1) _______ The accounts that show up on a Balance Sheet Include:
   a. Income, Cost of Goods, and Expenses
   b. Bank Accounts, Liabilities, and Assets
   c. Products and Services
   d. All of the above.

2) _______ You can edit an existing account by
   a. Double-clicking on it
   b. Choosing Edit from the drop-down menu
   c. Right-clicking on it and choosing Edit.

3) _______Undeposited Funds and Payments to Deposit
   a. Holds the money between receiving it and depositing it in the bank
   b. Is only used for cash & checks
   c. Should be zero when your books are up to date
   d. A & C

4) _______Opening Balance Equity
   a. Holds the starting balances on your bank accounts
   b. Is moved to Retained Earnings
   c. Should be $0 when you're done with your setup
   d. All of the above

5) _______Contributions and Distributions are used for personal money the owner puts in and takes out of the company
   a. True
   b. False

6) _______Income accounts should include:
   a. The starting balances on your bank accounts
   b. The ones the system creates automatically
   c. Your distinct revenue streams
   d. One for every service you offer

7) _______Uncategorized Income should be used for:
   a. Income that doesn't fit into other categories
   b. Income pulled out of the Bank Transactions feeds
   c. Nothing. If you see something here, move it.
   d. Items you need to talk to your accountant about.

8) _______Cost of Goods Sold refers to:
   a. The expenses incurred in order to deliver your products and service
   b. The cost of your products
   c. The money you pay to subcontractors
   d. Shipping and freight costs you pay to receive products
   e. All of the above

9) _______If you use subaccounts in the Chart of Accounts, it's OK to put some transactions in the main account and the rest in the subaccounts.
   a. True
   b. False

10) ______Your Expense accounts should be set up:
   a. To exactly match IRS tax forms
   b. With big "bucket" accounts to accumulate similar transactions, to keep it easy
   c. With granular detail so that you can run detailed reports
   d. Either B or C

11) ______Meals and Entertainment includes:
   a. Business meetings over a meal
   b. Coffee on the way to work
   c. Going out to lunch during your break

12) ______ You can use an "Ask My Accountant" Other Expense for transactions you don't know what to do with:
   a. True
   b. False

13) ______ You can only get to the Chart of Accounts from the Accounting > Chart of Accounts navigation bar:
   a. True
   b. False

14) ______ You should add to the Chart of Accounts every time you don't see a place to put a transaction:
   a. True
   b. False

15) ______ If you have redundant accounts in your COA, you must manually move each transaction into one of them before you delete the duplicated account:
   a. True
   b. False

16) ______ When you merge accounts, you have to reclassify all the transactions manually.
   a. True
   b. False

17) ______ When you delete an account:
   a. You can see it by toggling on "Inactive Accounts"
   b. It can't be reactivated
   c. It won't show up on your reports

18) ______ If you use Account Numbers:
   a. You should use standard numbering
   b. You can toggle them on and off
   c. They help you work with accountants and accounting departments
   d. All of the above

Answers: Matching: D, J, M, B, K, L, F, A, G, H, C, E, I
1) b, 2) b, 3) d, 4) d, 5) a, 6) c, 7) c, 8) e, 9) b, 10) d, 11) a, 12) a, 13) b, 14) b, 15) b, 16) b, 17) a, 18) d

Companion Course
SCAN ME
royl.ws/bootcamp

Want to learn more?

Deep Dive
SCAN ME
royl.ws/COA

The Products and Services List

The **Products and Services List** contains all the items and/or services you sell. When you first set up your QuickBooks Online file, it's very important to develop an organized, comprehensive set of items, for two reasons:

First, these are the entries that will show up on your Invoices, Sales Receipts, and Purchase Orders.

Second, when you run reports on your sales, you'll be able to determine which of your Products and Services are the most popular, and which have the best profit margin (which isn't necessarily the same thing!).

Your list can also have **Categories** to logically group similar items. Click the **More** button, then **Manage Categories** to create these groups. Be sure to assign each new Product or Service to one of the Categories.

Some people get confused as to whether to create this level of detail in the **Chart of Accounts** as Income, or whether to track the details using the Products and Services list.

Think of a clothing store.* You wouldn't want to see every item for sale in the **Chart of Accounts**! Instead, the COA would have Income categories for departments like Clothing, Shoes, and Accessories, because you *would* want to see these distinct revenue streams broken out on a P&L report.

The **Products and Services list** would then have Men's, Women's, and Children's departments (**Categories**), with further **Subcategories** for Shirts, Pants, Sweaters, Socks, etc. The actual items that get rung up at the register are assigned to these subcategories and point to the correct Income Account on the COA to tally their gross sales.

(*Note: in a real clothing store file, this level of detail would be in the shop's POS system, not in their QuickBooks file, but it's a good illustrative analogy. POS systems usually import Daily Sales Summaries to QBO instead of every single transaction.)

To set up your Product and Services List, select **Settings > Products and Services** or **Sales & Get Paid > Products and Services.**

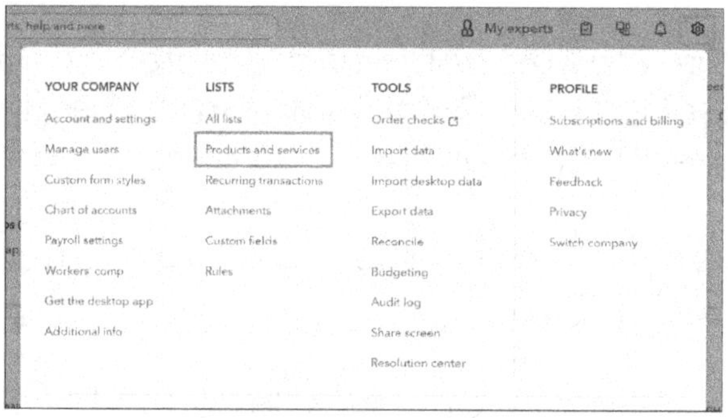

Using the same techniques described above in the Chart of Accounts section, you can customize this list by removing products and services you don't offer, adding your own, and arranging them into categories. You can change what columns show on this screen by clicking the little **List Settings gear** at the top right of the list.

There are four types of Products and Services in QBO: **Service Items, Inventory items, Non-inventory items,** and **Bundles.**

Services are non-tangible things you do for clients.

Inventory items are products that you sell, tracking the quantities on hand and the cost to purchase the items. These are only available in the Plus and Advanced versions of QBO.

Companion Course SCAN ME royl.ws/bootcamp

Want to learn more?

Deep Dive SCAN ME royl.ws/Products-Services

Non-Inventory items are physical products that you sell, but you don't use QuickBooks to track how many you have sitting on the shelf.

Bundles aren't actually separate products. A **Bundle** is a group of products that you always sell together. Bundles make it easy to enter multiple products on a Sales form in one step. Inventory products in a Bundle will reduce Inventory Assets as they're sold.

Creating a Service Item

Select **My Apps > Sales & Get Paid > Products and Services > New > Service**. The **Add a New Service** window opens.

Name the service. This is what you will choose off the list on each sales receipt and invoice. Each product or service must have a unique name.

If you have a code you use to track the item, enter it in the **SKU** field. If you have a picture associated with the service, you can upload it. This will be shown in the Products and Services list.

The **Category** allows you to group items together, similar to the Subaccounts we saw in the Chart of Accounts on page 48.

If you have **Classes** turned on, you will be able to assign a default Class to each product.

Check **I Sell This To Service To My Customers**. In the **Description** field, enter what you want your customers to see on your invoices and sales receipts. Type the most common text you would enter, so that you don't need to add it every time. If you like to include more detail, you can change it on each transaction. If it's never the same twice, you can leave it blank.

In the **Price/rate** field enter the default price. If you don't have a consistent price, you can also leave this blank to type it every time. Assign an **Income account** to track which of your Chart of Accounts category this falls under on the P&L report.

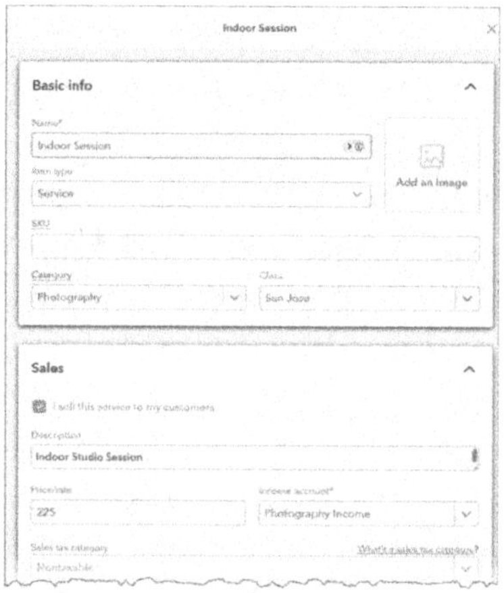

Select the **Sales Tax Category** to make the item **Taxable** or **Nontaxable.** If the service requires specific tax requirements for your state, click **View All Sales Tax Categories** and assign the correct scenario.

If you will hire a Subcontractor to perform this service on your behalf, you can do job costing!

Check **I Purchase This Service From A Vendor.** In the **Purchase Cost**, enter how much you pay the Subcontractor. In the **Expense Account**, assign this Service to your **Cost of Labor** account.

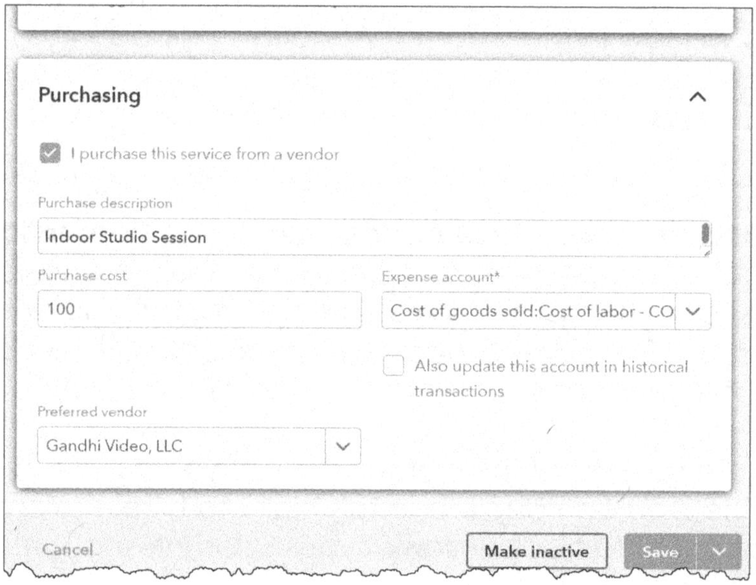

Creating a Non-Inventory Product Item

The next Item will be a **Non-Inventory Product**, which is a tangible product you sell, but that you don't track quantities on hand.

Select: **My Apps > Sales & Get Paid > Products and Services > New > Non-inventory item**.

Again, enter the Sales Information that appears on Customer receipts, with the correct Income account that tracks the money received.

If you buy these products for resale, set up the **Purchasing Information** by checking the **I purchase this product/service from a vendor** box. The **Cost** and **Description** you enter here will show on Purchase Orders, Bills, Checks, and Credit Card Expenses.

Enter the cost you pay for the products, and a **Cost of Goods: Supplies and Materials** category in the **Expense Account** field.

> *When you create a Product, link it to a Sales account to track your Income from it, and a COGS Account to track how much you spent on it. When the Item is used on an Invoice or Sales Receipt, it posts to these accounts automatically behind the scenes.*

Creating an Inventory Product Item

Inventory tracking is only available in the QuickBooks Online Plus and Advanced editions.

Head to **Account and Settings**. In the **Sales** section, turn on **Track inventory quantity on hand**. This allows you to buy and sell goods, tracking the sales and profit margin on each item.

If you sell products on an e-commerce website, consider managing your inventory from there, or use a 3rd party app that aggregates your inventory across multiple channels and syncs the data into QBO. That prevents you from tracking Inventory quantities and values in redundant systems. It also means that you can use QuickBooks Online Essentials, since you won't do inventory tracking in QBO at all.

Back in **Products and Services**, click the green **New** button. Choose **Inventory item**. The **Add a New Product** window opens.

Fill the top in the same way you would a Non-Inventory item.

QBO asks you to enter the **Initial quantity on hand** and the **As of Date**...but don't enter your current information! Since you probably have historic transactions to make for the product's purchases or sales, you won't be able to enter any transactions before this date!

Instead, enter in 0 quantity, and an **As of Date** MUCH earlier than the company Start Date. I usually enter in a date two years prior. The rest of Inventory item creation follows the same steps as **Non-Inventory products** above.

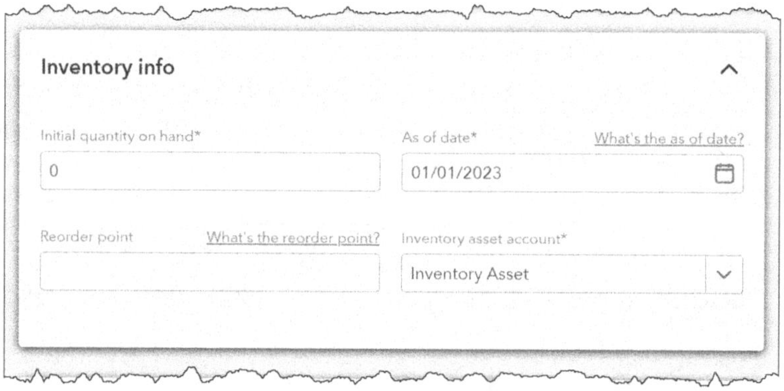

Be EXTREMELY careful here. Don't use today's date and quantity!

If you try to create any transactions involving your inventoried Products before the As of Date you entered in this window, QuickBooks Online will give you an error message and prevent you from proceeding.

ENTER A QUANTITY OF ZERO and ENTER A DATE LOOOOONG BEFORE YOUR FIRST TRANSACTION USING THE ITEM!

Companion Course
SCAN ME
royl.ws/bootcamp

Want to learn more?

Deep Dive
SCAN ME
royl.ws/Products-Services

Entering Inventory Quantities

After setting up your Inventory Items, it's time to enter the quantities. First, create any open Bills and Invoices as of the start date of your company file, as discussed in Setting Up the File on page 27. Then, use **+Create > Inventory Qty Adjustment** to true up the quantity as of the Start Date for your file.

If you don't have those numbers, get all your transaction history into QBO up to today's date, then use **Inventory Qty Adjustment** to update the quantities to current levels.

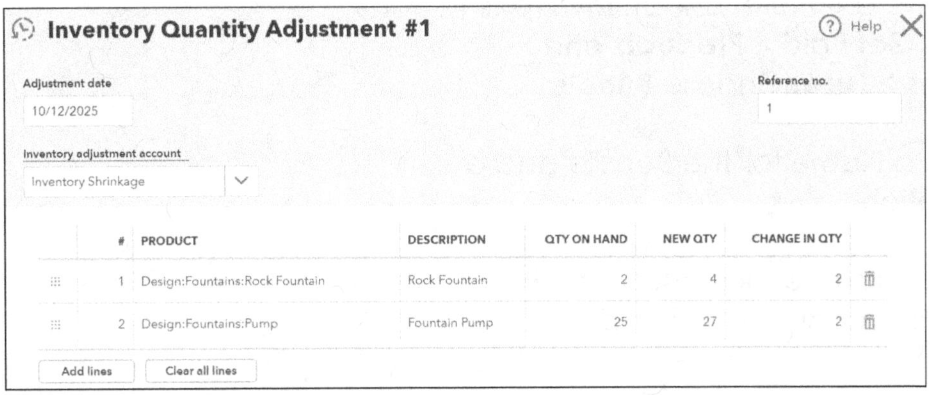

How Is Inventory Calculated?

When you buy Inventory Products, QBO stores their cost in **the Inventory Asset** account on your **Balance Sheet** (see page 171). That way, the original cost of the stock on your shelves is considered part of the value of your company.

When you sell the item, QBO automatically performs its magic behind the scenes. The original purchase cost is transferred from Inventory Asset to Cost of Goods Sold in your general ledger, showing that the value has left the building, and subtracting its purchase price from your Sales of Product Income on your Profit and Loss report.

QuickBooks Online calculates Inventory on a **First-in, First Out (FIFO) Basis.** If you buy five items at $1 and the next five items at $1.25, then sell six of them, your Cost of Goods will be $6.25 (5 at $1 plus 1 at $1.25).

Creating Bundles

After you've created all of your Products, you can group them together. That way, when you create an Invoice or a Sales Receipt, you can enter one item and have several show up automatically.

For example, when Craig installs a fountain, he always bills for the fountain, the pump, and the installation. By creating a **Bundle,** he can enter one product and the quantity. QBO will automatically populate the full list of items, calculate the grand total...and adjust his inventory!

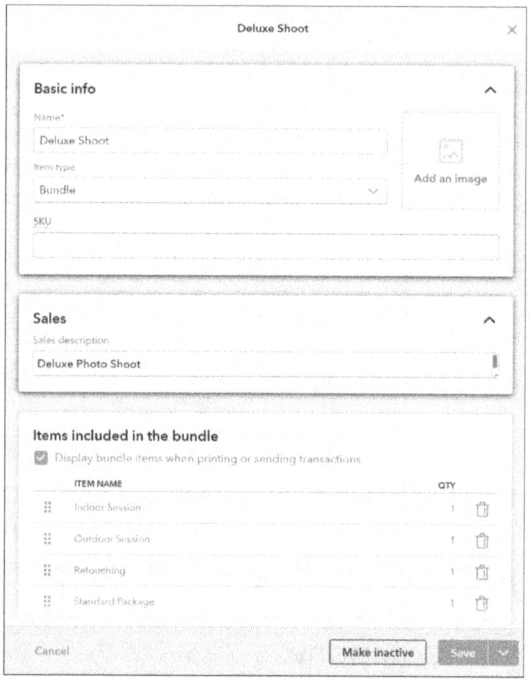

To create a **Bundle**, select: **My Apps > Sales & Get Paid > Products and Services > New**. Choose **Bundle**.

Create a **Name** for the Bundle and a **Description**.

In the bottom section, list all the items in the group, along with their quantities.

If you want the Customer's Invoice to show all the components, check the "**Display bundle components when printing or sending transactions**" box. If you only want the Customer to see the single Bundle Description, leave the box empty.

Click **Save and Close**.

QBO's Sales Tax Center looks to the Taxable status applied to each product and service. Be sure to apply the proper tax category to each one, including local tax rates.

Check Your Understanding: Products and Services

1) _______ Products and Services are:
   a. The items you enter on Invoices & Sales Receipts
   b. The items you purchase for resale
   c. The services you subcontract out to others
   d. All of the above

2) _______ Service items are:
   a. Tangible goods
   b. Intangible offerings
   c. Items you outsource

3) _______ If a Service cost is different every time, you can:
   a. Leave it blank
   b. Fill in a frequent value to save you a little typing
   c. Create a different Service item for each cost
   d. A & B

4) _______ If you buy and sell a product, you have to make two items for it, one for customers and one for vendors.
   a. True
   b. False

5) _______ Inventory controls are available in which version of QBO:
   a. Plus
   b. Essentials
   c. QuickBooks Lite

6) _______ Inventory item quantities should be entered when you create the Product, using the Start Date of the file.
   a. True
   b. False

7) _______ Bundles allow you to group items together without having to manually enter all the products and services each time.
   a. True
   b. False

Answers:
1) d, 2) b, 3) d, 4) b, 5) a, 6) b, 7) a

Classes and Locations, and Custom Fields

Classes, **Locations**, and **Custom Fields** are three methods of labeling your transactions so that you can analyze your company on multiple dimensions. Classes and Locations are features in QuickBooks Online Plus and Advanced, while Custom Fields appear in Essentials and higher.

These options provide an added level of detail, but they also require additional clicks in every transaction. You have to use them consistently to make them valuable.

The benefit is that you can run your Profit and Loss Report by Classes or Locations so that you can see multiple columns dividing out the income and expenses into useful groupings. Custom Fields can be used as filters in many reports.

Because these are freeform lists, label transactions with a system useful to your way of thinking, and the dimensions you want to analyze.

Keep in mind that these are meta-categories, an additional set of data that overarches your financial records. Set up your Chart of Accounts and Products & Services lists first. If you find yourself wishing you could replicate sections of these lists to track something separately, that's a sign that Classes or Locations would be useful.

Profit and Loss by Class

Account	Overhead	San Jose	Walnut Creek	Not Specified	Total
Income					
Discounts given	-	-	-	-115.00	-115.00
Photography Income	-	1,490.00	1,767.50	-	3,257.50
Sales of Product Income	-	155.00	3,189.93	-	3,344.93
Shipping Income	-	-	-	32.00	32.00
Total for Income	**-**	**1,645.00**	**4,957.43**	**-83.00**	**$6,519.43**
Cost of Goods Sold					
Cost of goods sold					
Cost of labor - COGS	-	665.00	-	-	665.00
Freight in - COGS	-	-	20.00	-	20.00
Supplies & materials - CO...	-	-	2,042.15	-	2,042.15
Total for Cost of goods sold	**-**	**665.00**	**2,062.15**	**-**	**$2,727.15**
Total for Cost of Goods Sold	**-**	**665.00**	**2,062.15**	**-**	**$2,727.15**
Gross Profit	**-**	**980.00**	**2,895.28**	**-83.00**	**$3,792.28**
Expenses					
Advertising & marketing					
Marketing	29.99	-	-	-	29.99
Social media	-	27.39	-	-	27.39
Total for Advertising & m...	**29.99**	**27.39**	**-**	**-**	**$57.38**
General business expenses					
Bank fees & service charges	10.00	21.00	-	-	31.00
Total for General busines...	**10.00**	**21.00**	**-**	**-**	**$31.00**
Insurance					
Business insurance	-	605.00	605.00	-	1,210.00

Classes

In **Account and Settings > Advanced** (see page 31), you can choose to assign Classes line-by-line, or once per transaction.

Always create an additional Class called **Overhead** and assign it to transactions that have nothing to do with any one Class, like company expenses.

- A landlord may use Classes for each property so that a landscaping bill can be divided up by addresses. Her P&L by Class would show the revenue and expenses for each property.
- A contractor may use Classes to divide reports into Residential and Commercial projects.
- Use Classes to track Net Income by revenue stream.

If you see **Not Specified** on your reports, it's because you didn't assign a line item to a Class when you created it, or because some QBO features like Discounts, Shipping, and Transfers don't have the ability to assign a Class.

Locations

QuickBooks Online Plus and Advanced have an additional way to slice-and-dice your data: **Locations.**

Locations are not available in QuickBooks Desktop, so if you are converting, you have a new dimension to implement!

Locations allow you to label each transaction with one classification that can be used on reports. Traditionally used when your business has more than one physical location, you can also use the feature to separate your data by Department, Division, Store, Business, Territory, or Property.

Turn on Locations in **Account and Settings > Advanced** (see page 33).

Locations can be used in conjunction with Classes. They work better on Balance Sheet transactions because the Location is associated with the source account (the "from" or the credit) behind the scenes in the transaction.

Custom Fields

Custom Fields are found in **Settings > Custom Fields.**

Custom Fields allow you to enter additional information in your income and expense forms to label your transactions so that you can search for and report on all related business activity.

They work best for non-financial activity regarding operations. Popular Custom Fields include PO Number and Sales Rep.

For example, if an organization holds fundraisers, it can create a Custom Field called Events to label all related income and expense transactions from each event, filter reports for any one of the events.

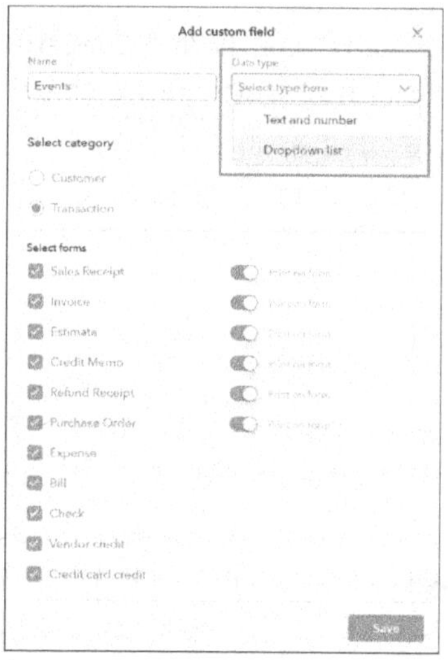

Custom Fields can include text and numbers, or you can choose off of drop-down lists (which help avoid typos).

They can be assigned to Customers and Vendors to track information about them, or on each sales & expense form to track information about the transaction.

They can be printed on your customers' copies, or hidden and only used internally.

QBO Lite has one Custom Field. Essentials and Plus provide four text-based Custom Fields. QBO Advanced has up to 48 fields, including an option to enter dates.

Check Your Understanding: Working with Classes, Locations, and Custom Fields

1) ______ Classes are used to:
   a. Group your transactions by tagging labeling
   b. Create a P&L report that breaks out certain categories
   c. Group your products and services
   d. A & B

2) ______ Classes can only be assigned to a transaction line by line, not by an entire transaction.
   a. True
   b. False

3) ______ Classes and Locations are only available in which version of QBO?
   a. Solopreneur
   b. Plus & Advanced
   c. Essentials
   d. QuickBooks Lite

4) ______ Which option allows you to include additional information on a form?
   a. Classes
   b. Locations
   c. Custom Fields

5) ______ Which option allows you to break your data up by address or department?
   a. Classes
   b. Locations
   c. Tags

Answers:
8) a, 9) b, 10) b, 11) c, 12) b

Part 2:

Using QuickBooks Online

Chapter 5: Customers

Now that your QuickBooks Online is set up, you're ready to do your favorite part of your business: working with customers and clients.

Known in the accounting world as **Accounts Receivable** or **A/R**, QBO gives you all the tools you need to track a customer from bid to invoice to payment to deposit.

Then, you can run reports about your clientele and their favorite products and services to analyze your success!

Sales & Customer Preferences

Start here to set your choices for Invoices and Sales Receipts. Select **Settings > Account and Settings > Sales.**

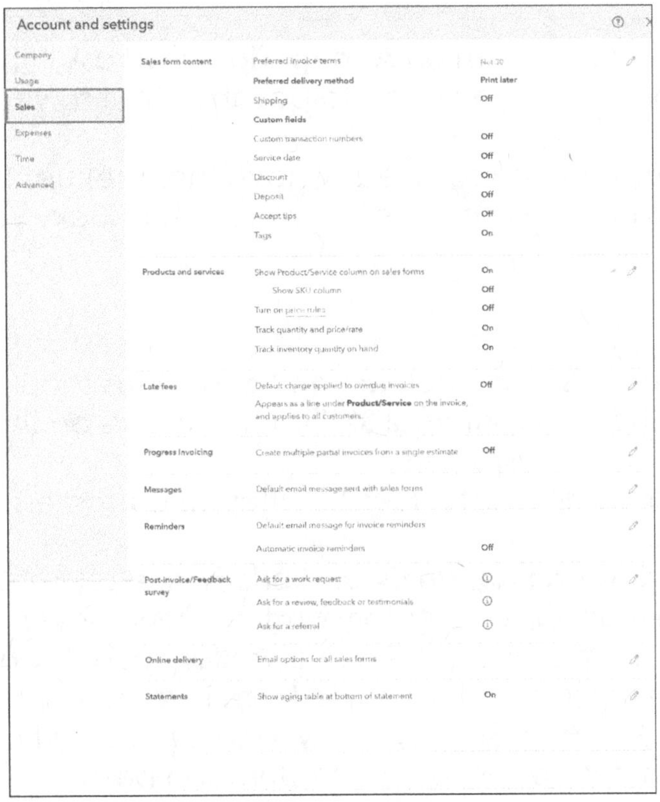

Sales Form Content

The Sales settings modify QBO for your specific company workflows. Click the pencil in the right column to change the content on your Sales Forms (Invoices, Estimates, and Sales Receipts):

- What are your **Preferred invoice terms**? Do customers pay at the time of service (Due on Receipt), or do they have 30 days to pay?
- Do you need extra fields on an Invoice for **Shipping** addresses, dates, and tracking numbers?
- Will you need any **Custom fields** to appear on each Invoice, to track your special needs?
- Do you have your own numbering system? If so, turn on **Custom transaction numbers**.
- Will each line item in the sale need its own date to itemize when it occurred? If so, turn on **Service Date**.
- Do you want to be able to apply discounts to a customer's invoice? If so, turn on **Discount**.
- Do you take deposits for work to be performed? If so, turn on **Deposit**.
- If you receive tips, turn on **Accept Tips**. It will ask if the tips are just for you (income), or if you need to pay them out to your staff (a liability).
- Turn off **Tags** unless you already have them set up. This feature is no longer available to new users. If you have it, lucky you!

Products and Services

- **Show Product/Service column on Sales Forms** should always be on.
- You can show your internal **SKU** item numbers on the Sales Form or hide them from customers.
- If you charge different prices to different customers, **Turn on price rules**.
- Leave on the **Track quantity and price/rate** columns.
- If you are managing Inventory and counting how many products you have in stock, turn on **Track inventory quantity on hand**.
    - You may see an option to track inventory for Sales Channels like Amazon, Shopify, eBay, and Etsy as part of the Commerce center. This feature is in beta.

Late Fees

If your customers chronically pay late, turn on Late Fees. You can charge a flat fee or a percentage of the invoice once, monthly, or daily. This setting can be turned on or off for each customer.

Messages

Customize your email communications with customers, including default email text. Edit the content to fit your style and branding.

Reminders

Use Reminders to automate your emails to customers about upcoming invoice due dates or alerting them when their payments are late. You can create up to three reminders before, on, and after the invoice due date.

This setting applies to all customers and cannot be toggled off for specific people. It's all-or-nothing.

Post-invoice/Feedback Survey

This section populates the Customer Hub (see page 110). After your customer pays their invoice, QBO will send an email asking them to rate your service. If they give you 4 or 5 stars, it asks when the customer would like to work with you again, request a testimonial, and suggest referrals to their friends and colleagues.

If you receive a 3-star rating, it will ask for feedback so you can improve your services.

Be sure to set the frequency of the rating request to once or twice a year so that you don't pummel them with emails every time you work together!

Online Delivery

When sending an invoice, should the custom see all the line items in the email, or just the date and total? You can choose to attach a PDF as well.

Statements

When sending customs summary statements showing their transactions for the year, choose whether to list each transaction as a single line, or to include all detail lines.

QuickBooks Payments

After you turn on **QuickBooks Payments Merchant Services** so that your customers can pay you by ACH or credit card, a new section will appear in the left sidebar. This is where you will set your default payment types, map the accounts, and access your statements.

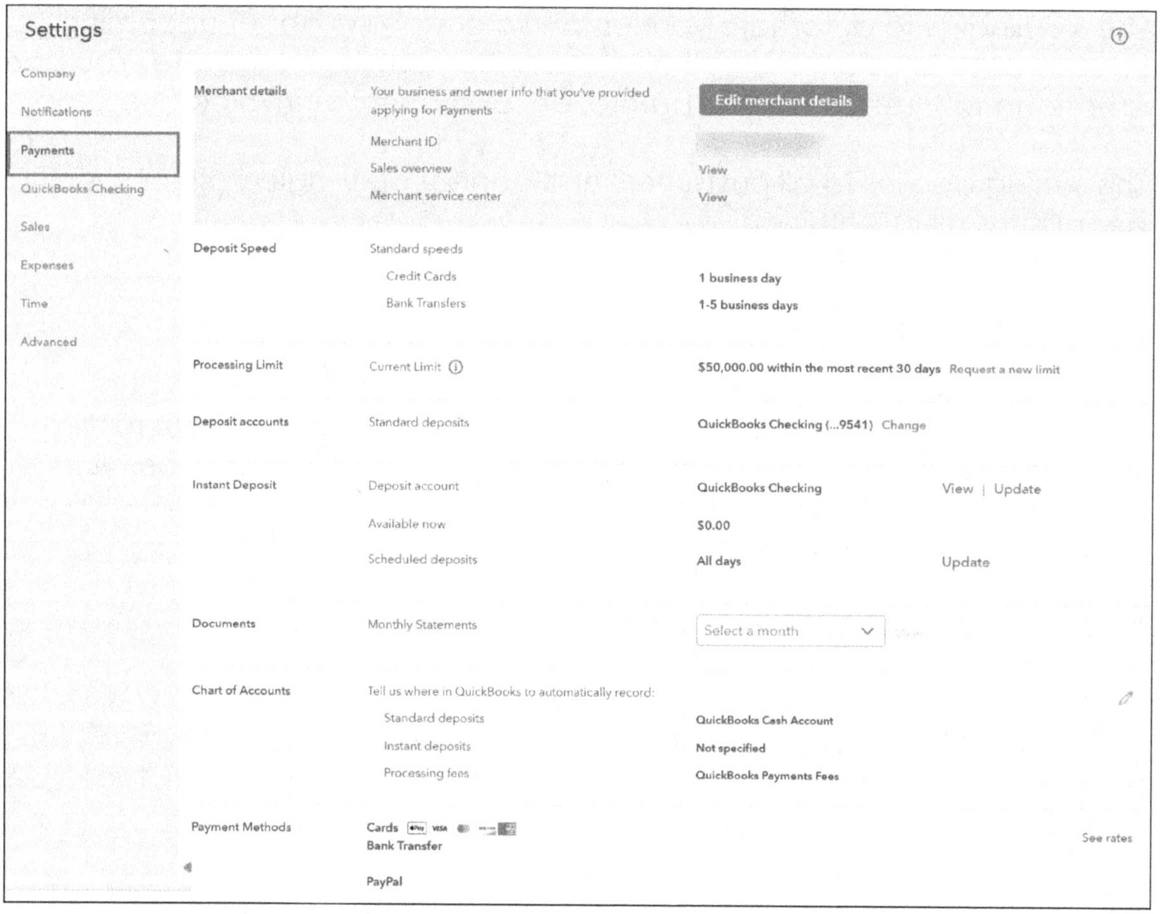

The Sales Center

To open the **Sales** screen, select **My Apps > Sales & Get Paid > Sales Transactions**.

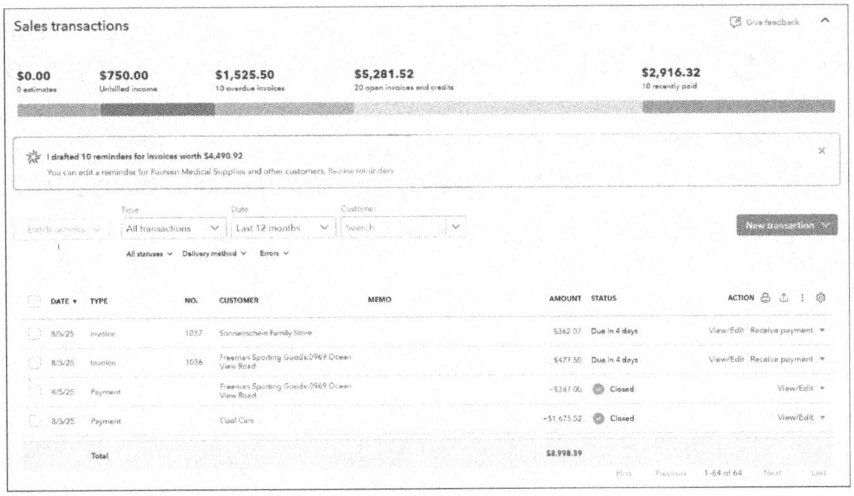

The multi-colored bar is called a **Money Bar**. Click on each of the colored boxes to filter the transactions to view open Estimates, Unbilled Income (see page 120), Overdue Invoices, Open Invoices, and Recently Paid sales.

This **Money Bar** is one of the reasons it's important to make Invoices and Sales Receipts for customer sales transactions, and not just pull in deposits through the Bank Transactions feed (see page 154). Revenue entered in QBO by Deposits instead of forms will not show when filtered with the Money Bar!

To see all the transactions again, click the colored bar again.

There are additional filters to see transactions only of specific types, in a date range, or for a specific customer. Below the filters don't miss the little dropdowns to specify the transaction's Status, Delivery Method, or transactions with email delivery or merchant processing errors.
Keep an eye out for the **AI Payments Agent** helping you with cash flow. It will suggest sending reminders to delinquent customers and setting up late fees.

The Customer Center

To open the **Customers** screen, select **My Apps > Customer Hub > Customers.**

To **Search** for customers, use the filters above the grid. The magnifying glass allows you to search by name, company name, and phone number.

You can also choose which information fields show in the grid. Click on **Customize** at the top right of the grid to select the fields you would like to see.

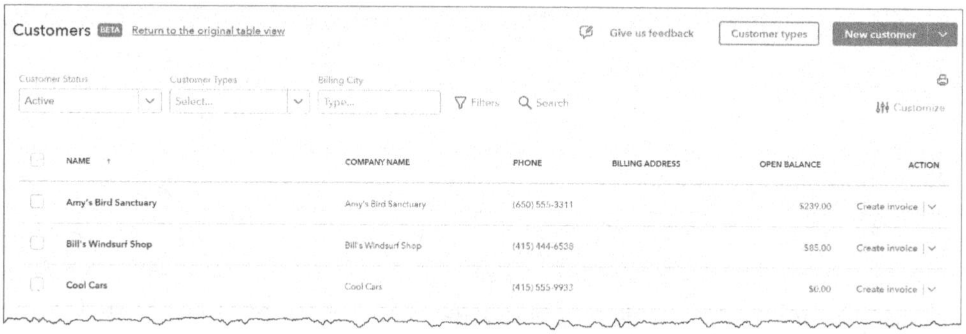

To **Print** your customer list you can click the **Printer** on the right, but you're better off heading to the Reports and printing a **Customer Contact List** from there.

Adding Customers

In the Customers Center

Select **New Customer**. Fill in the Customer's information.

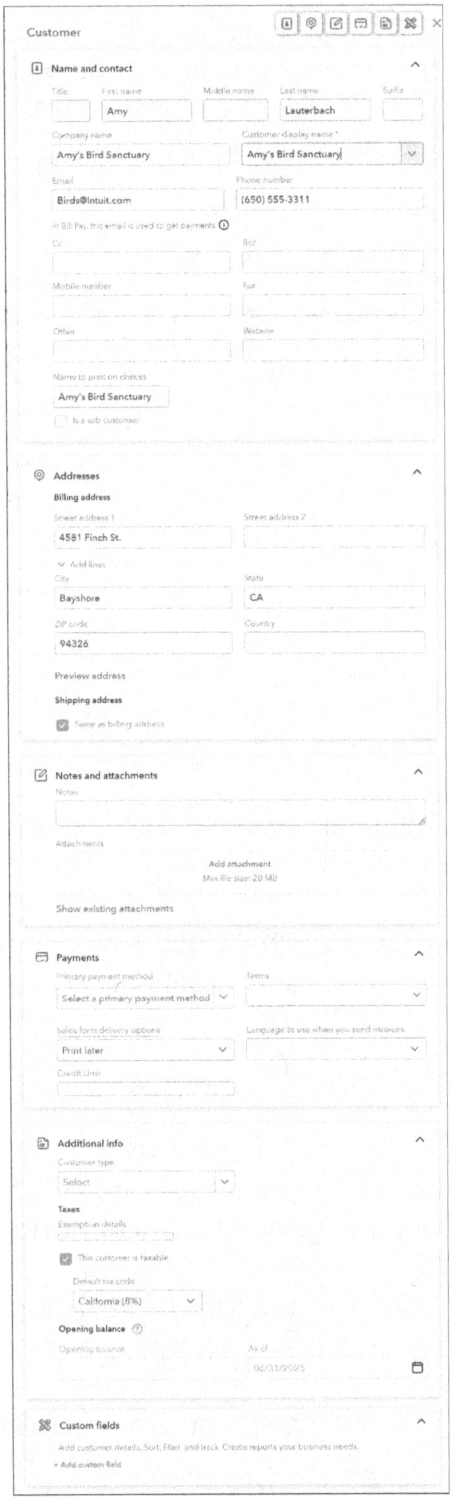

If you perform services for several departments within a company, or do several projects for a client, make each one a **Sub-Customer** of the larger organization. You can either bill each one independently, or send a cumulative bill to the larger organization (select **Bill with Parent**).

While that option is great for subcontractors who work on multiple jobs under one contractor, you may also consider using the **Projects Center** instead. Once you turn on **Projects** in **Account and Settings**, you'll have a one-stop shop to track job costing and project profitability. QuickBooks Desktop doesn't have anything like it!

Enter the customer's **Payment Information**. Store credit card or ACH info here to run automatic payments using your QB Payments Merchant Services account. After you type in sensitive information, it is replaced with asterisks for security. To stay PCI compliant, be sure not to save a customer's credit card information *anywhere* other than here, not even on your company's hard drive or on paper. If you've turned on **Price Rules**, use the **Customer Type** for custom pricing.

Use the **Taxes** section to set defaults if the customer will be charged or exempted from **Sales Tax**.

Adding New Customers As You Go

If you need to add a new Customer while already creating a new transaction, QBO offers you the opportunity to add a new one right in the Payee dropdown.

Using the Notes

The **Notes** area in the Customer Details card allows you to store information about your customers.

This is an excellent place to track phone calls and other correspondence. The box shows on the customer's main screen.

Including the date in your note helps you figure out if the comment is still relevant or outdated.

Generic Customer Names

If you run a retail business where don't need to import customer names, like a shop with a Point of Sale (POS) system or an e-commerce website, create generic customer names.

Instead of adding every single customer to the system, this allows you to track customers by type instead of by name.

For example, you could call them "Walk In Customers" and "Online Sales." This gathers all those sales in one Customer transaction list.

Hoot Tip! If you are going to use generic customer names, but it would be handy to be able to match a Sales Receipt with the client, use a **Custom Field** (see page 68). Create an extra field called "Customer Name" for their real name, giving you a place to search for it in case you ever need to look up this particular sale again in the future.

Merging Customers

You may occasionally discover you have the same customer entered more than once. Maybe you have them listed under both a company name and contact name, or maybe you made a typo.

It's easy to combine two accounts into one, just like we saw in the Chart of Accounts on page 50. There are two methods you can use: the **Merge Contacts** tool, or update the **Display Name**.

Merge Contacts

Open the customer you don't want to keep. Click the drop-down arrow next to the Edit button in the upper right corner, and choose **Merge Contacts**.

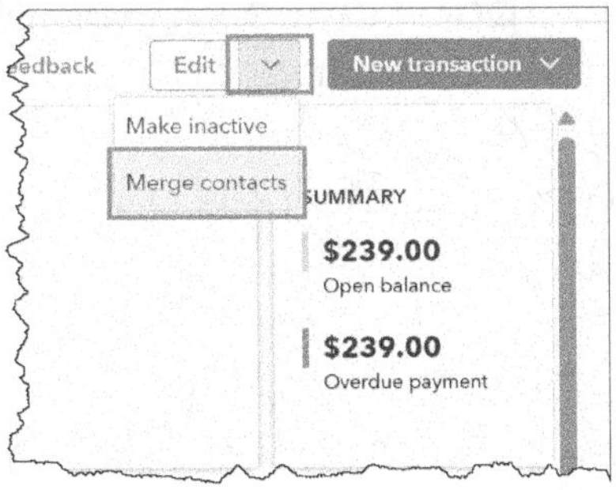

Select the customer you DO want to keep, then click the green **Merge Contacts** button.

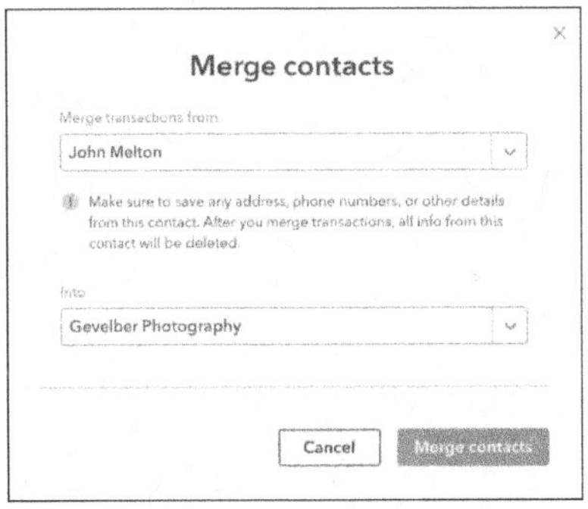

Display Name

You can also manually merge two customers by making sure that **Display Name** is the same in both cards.

When you change the Display name in the customer you don't want anymore, QBO will ask if you want to merge the customers. When you say yes, all the transactions from the edited account will move into the target account, and the edited account is inactivated.

If the address or contact information is different on the two cards, the information on the card ***NOT*** being edited is what will be saved! Be sure to merge the company with less information.

Deleting and Inactivating Customers

There is no true "Delete" of a customer (a lot of things in QBO say "Delete" that are only inactivated). To **Delete** a customer, open it by selecting the **Edit** button and click **Make inactive**. They will no longer appear on your lists, but historical transactions will still show up on reports.

To view inactive customers, back in the Customers list you can select **Inactive** on the **Customer Status** dropdown.

When running reports, deleted customers and their transactions still show up, so there's no data loss.

In the rare instance that you don't want to include Inactive/Deleted information on reports, exclude them by customizing the report and adding a filter for Active Customers.

Common Customer Workflows

Here are the QBO workflows typically used to manage customers:

1. Do your customers pay at the time of service?

Sales Receipt → Create Bank Deposit

2. Do your customers pay later, make multiple payments, or pay several invoices at once?

Invoice → Payment → Create Bank Deposit

3. Do you make Estimates & Bids?

Estimate → Progress Invoice → Payment → Create Bank Deposit

Notice that the last step of each is to make your **Bank Deposit**. That's when you combine today's cash & checks and take them to the bank, or your merchant services company batches the credit card and ACH payments for the day. These totals must MATCH the **Bank Transactions feed**.

As a best practice, deposit all your customer payments to **Undeposited Funds or Payments to Deposit**, and be sure to read page 94 to make your daily deposits.

Do not "Add" Deposits through the Bank Transactions feed.
You'll duplicate your Income!

Creating Sales Receipts

Enter a **Sales Receipt** when you are paid immediately for your products or services. If you've already received the money and are recording the sale after the fact, this saves you a step over the two-step process of creating an Invoice (see page 86) and Receiving Payment (see page 91). Both steps occur on this one screen.

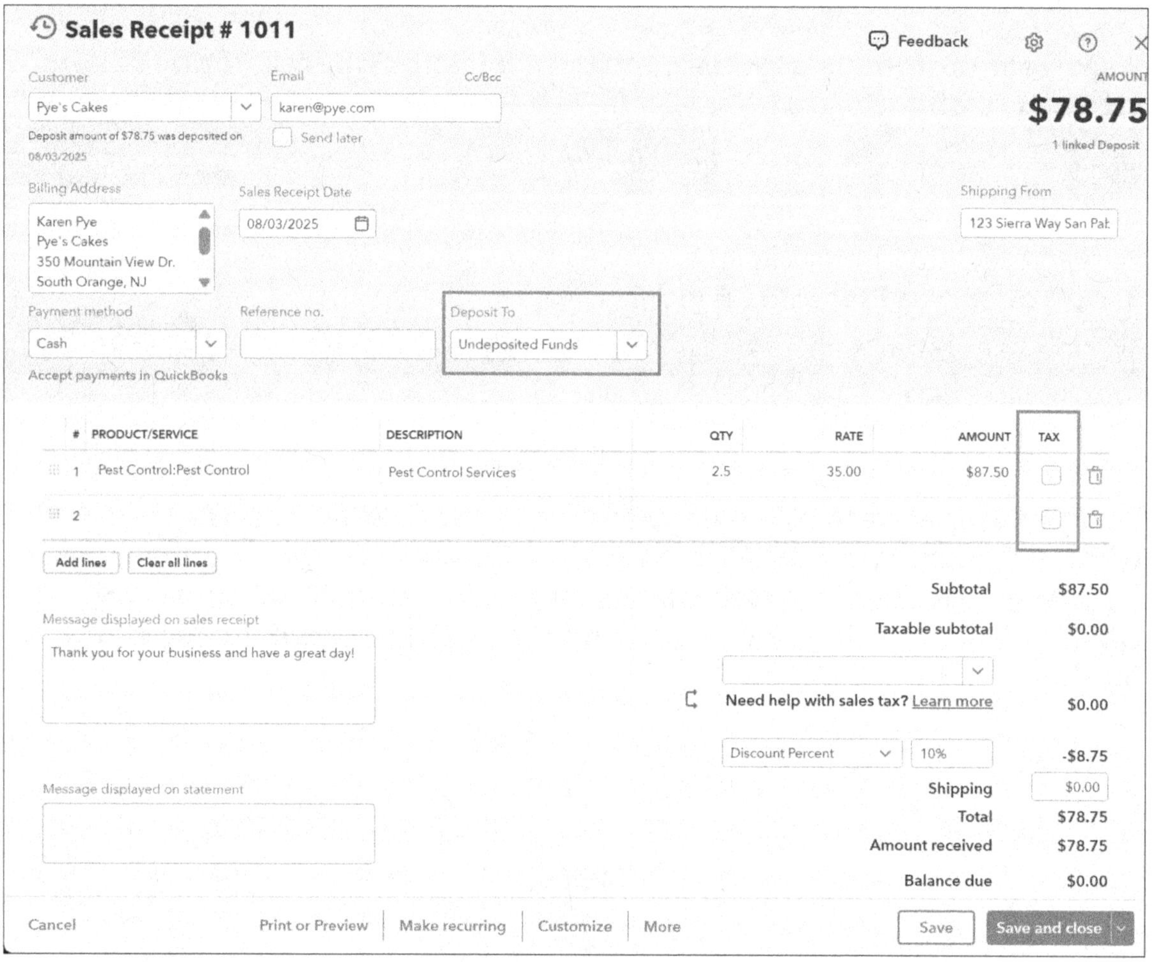

Select **+Create** > **Sales Receipt**, and the **Sales Receipt** form opens.

Enter the sales information, including **Customer, Date, Product/Service, Description, Quantity, and Rate**. Make sure appropriate items are marked as **Taxable**.

If you have **Discounts**, **Deposits**, and **Shipping** turned on (see page 73), include those amounts.

If you are using **Classes**, and **Locations**, add them too.

After you've added all these details and confirmed the total, choose the **Payment method**.

In the **Deposit To** field, always use **Undeposited Funds / Payments to Deposit**, so that the income will be grouped with other sales that day. At the end of the day, all cash/check and credit card payments can be combined and deposited using **Bank Deposits** (see page 94). Even if you deposit all your sales individually, the Bank Transactions feed looks here first, so you don't have to change workflows according to the type of payment.

Click **Save and send** to email the Sales Receipt, **Save and New** to immediately add another one, or **Save and Close** when you're done.

If you run a cash-based retail business and only want to track total sales instead of entering every transaction, create one Daily Sales Receipt to gather all your sales for the day in one step.

Creating Invoices

Invoices are used to record services you have provided, and the customer is going to pay later.

Select **+Create > Invoice,** and the **Invoice** form opens.

Use the drop-down menu to enter the **Customer** name.

Adjust the **Terms**, **Invoice Date**, and **Due Date** as needed.

Use the drop-down to fill in the **Product/Service** field. Or just start typing and your choices will narrow down.

Select **Save and Close** or **Save and send** to record the transaction.

E-mailed invoices are sent as attached PDFs, so that they cannot be altered by the recipient.

If you are signed up for QuickBooks Payments Merchant Services, your emailed Invoice will have a **Review and Pay button** allowing your customers to pay you by credit card or bank ACH. When they do, QBO will create the payment, mark your Invoice as paid, and batch the deposits for you…easy peasy.

> QuickBooks Payments Merchant Services fees are ***competitive or better*** than Square. Not only that, but because you will spend less time managing Square and PayPal fees, it will take you less time to use.
>
> If you are interested in that service, please contact us, and we'll get you set up at a discounted rate. Every penny counts!

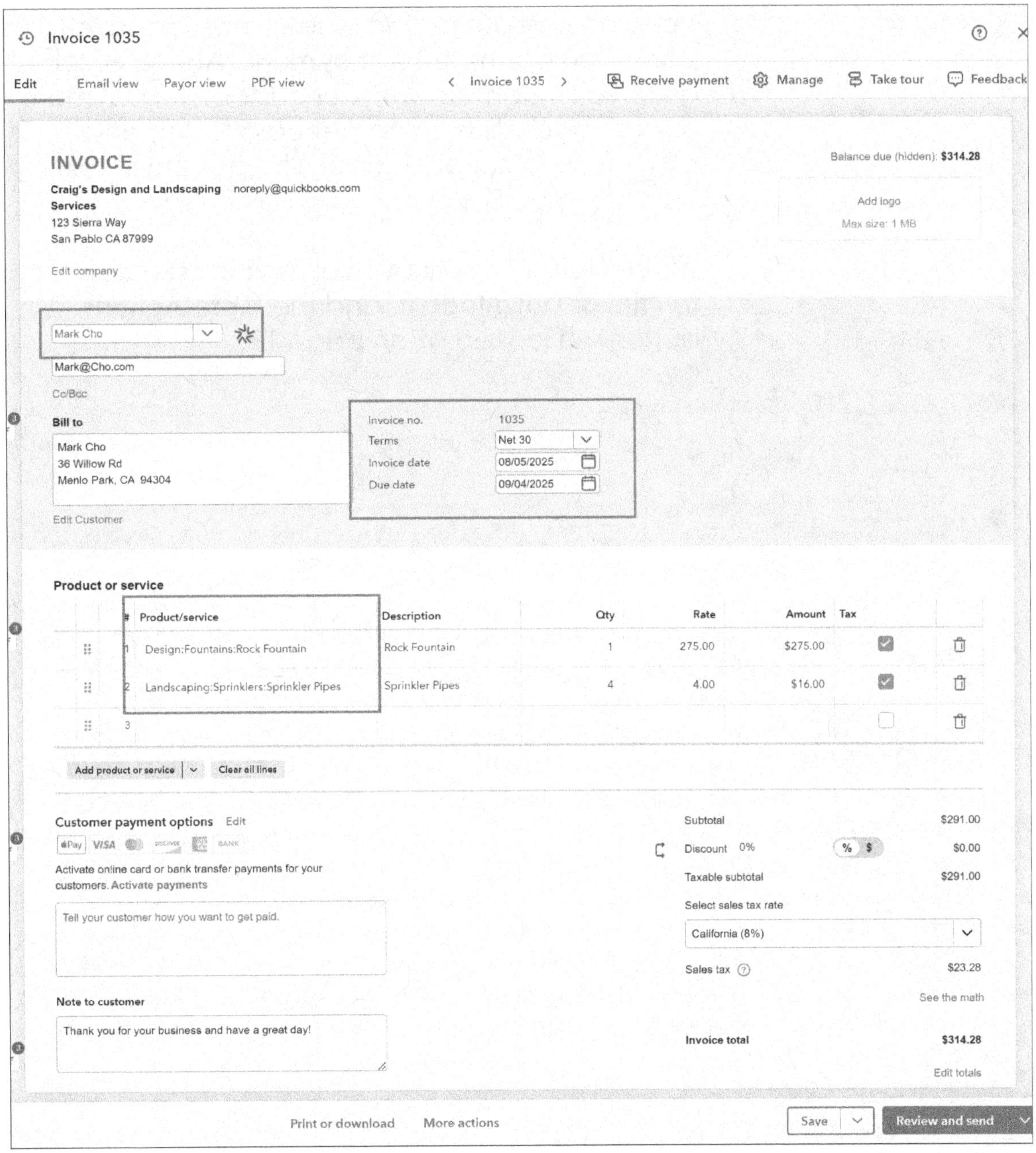
Invoice 1035
Edit
Email view
Payor view
PDF view
Invoice 1035
Receive payment
Manage
Take tour
Feedback
INVOICE
Balance due (hidden): $314.28
Craig's Design and Landscaping Services
noreply@quickbooks.com
123 Sierra Way
San Pablo CA 87999
Add logo
Max size: 1 MB
Edit company
Mark Cho
Mark@Cho.com
Cc/Bcc
Bill to
Mark Cho
36 Willow Rd
Menlo Park, CA 94304
Edit Customer
Invoice no. 1035
Terms Net 30
Invoice date 08/05/2025
Due date 09/04/2025
Product or service
Product/service Description Qty Rate Amount Tax
1 Design:Fountains:Rock Fountain Rock Fountain 1 275.00 $275.00
2 Landscaping:Sprinklers:Sprinkler Pipes Sprinkler Pipes 4 4.00 $16.00
3
Add product or service
Clear all lines
Customer payment options Edit
Activate online card or bank transfer payments for your customers. Activate payments
Tell your customer how you want to get paid.
Note to customer
Thank you for your business and have a great day!
Subtotal $291.00
Discount 0% $0.00
Taxable subtotal $291.00
Select sales tax rate
California (8%)
Sales tax $23.28
See the math
Invoice total $314.28
Edit totals
Print or download
More actions
Save
Review and send

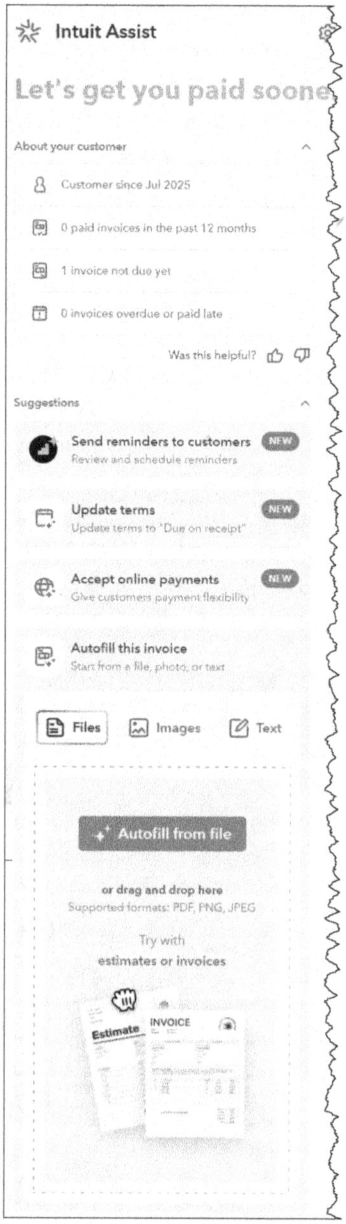

Keep an eye out for the blue sparkle in the left pane. This opens the **AI Payments Agent**, which gives you insight about your customer's payment habits, suggests ways to get paid faster, and allows you to Autofill invoices by pasting in text, uploading a PDF, or importing an image.

At the bottom of each invoice you'll see buttons to **Print or Download** it, and the **More Actions** button we looked at on page 19.

Managing Invoices

The **Manage** button opens a panel on the right side to update the invoice's settings.

Changes made here apply to just this invoice, although there are links to update each section's defaults.

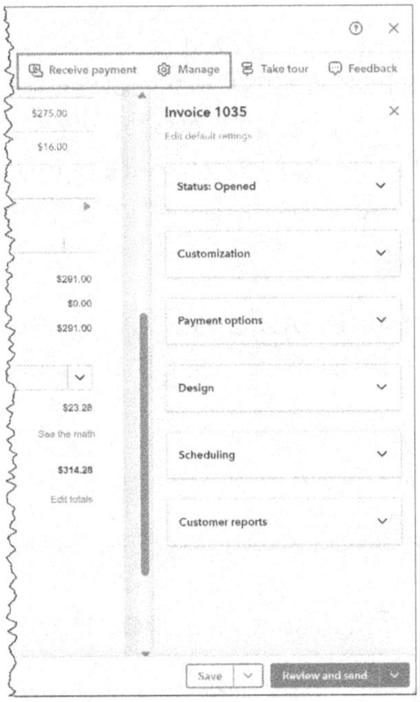

Status

View an invoice's *Activity*, including when it was sent, when it was opened, when it was viewed, and when its payment was deposited.

Customization

This section turns on and off a variety of fields on your invoices. This gives you the flexibility to create custom invoices for each of your customers.

The ***Customization*** section turns on and off fields including *Ship To*, *Invoice Number*, *Invoice Date*, *Due Date*, *Terms*, *Service Date*, *Product SKUs*, *Custom Fields*, and more. You even click **Edit Labels** to rename them.

Suggestions

Suggestions appear when there are open transactions related to that customer, such as estimates or unbilled time and expenses. You can add one or all of them to your invoice.

Payment Options

The ***Payment Options*** section allows you turn on and off your *QB Payments* on a case-by-case basis. You can allow payment by credit card, ACH bank transfer, PayPal, Apple Pay, and Venmo. You can also turn on *Tips*. You also have options to include or hide your *Invoice Totals*, *Deposits*, *Discounts*, and *Shipping Fees*.

If you turn off all QB Payments options, customers can still pay online and pay the merchant fees themselves, but the rate they are asked to pay is much higher.

Design

Choose your font and accent color to match your branding.

For more control, you can still use the legacy ***Other Templates***, which are also found under the Settings gear give you full control over your layout. However, the new Invoices perform best when using the default "Modern" settings.

When using **Modernized Templates**, you can preview your clients' experience by clicking on the *Email View*, *Payor View*, and *PDF View* in the upper right.

Scheduling

This section gives you the opportunity to turn the invoice into a template called a **Recurring Invoice**. Invoices may be scheduled to be created and even emailed automatically.

Recurring Payments adds the ability for these repeating invoices to be paid automatically. The customer is invited to enter their own credit card or ACH information, and pre-approve all future payments.

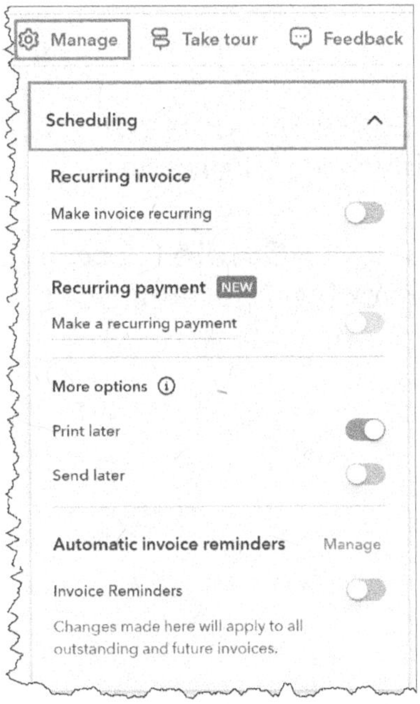

This section also controls invoice ***Reminders***. There are three options to automatically send reminders to your clients: before they are due, on their due date, and after the due date passes by without payment. Click the **Manage** link to customize these further, controlling the number of days as well as the messaging.

Note that this automation applies to ALL invoices, not just for this particular transaction.

Customer Reports

This handy shortcut instantly opens convenient reports filtered for that customer, including **Open Invoices** and **All Transactions**.

Emailing Income Receipts

Click on the **Business Feed**, the Intuit Assist icon in the left rail. One of the features you'll find on the right is an **Autofill** assistant. Here you can drop PDFs and images with sales documentation that you can turn into invoices.

It also offers you the option to forward emails into QBO. Use the email address provided, or customize it to make it shorter. The Business Feed will display all emails you forwarded, allowing you to turn the receipts into sales receipts and invoices.

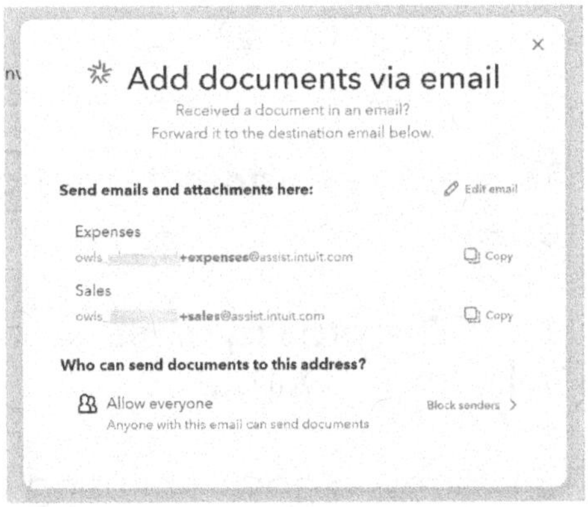

Receiving Payments

Customers can pay invoices in full, make partial payments, or pay several invoices at one time.

Select **+Create > Receive Payment**. Note that you can also click the **Receive Payment** button in the top right corner when you have an invoice open.

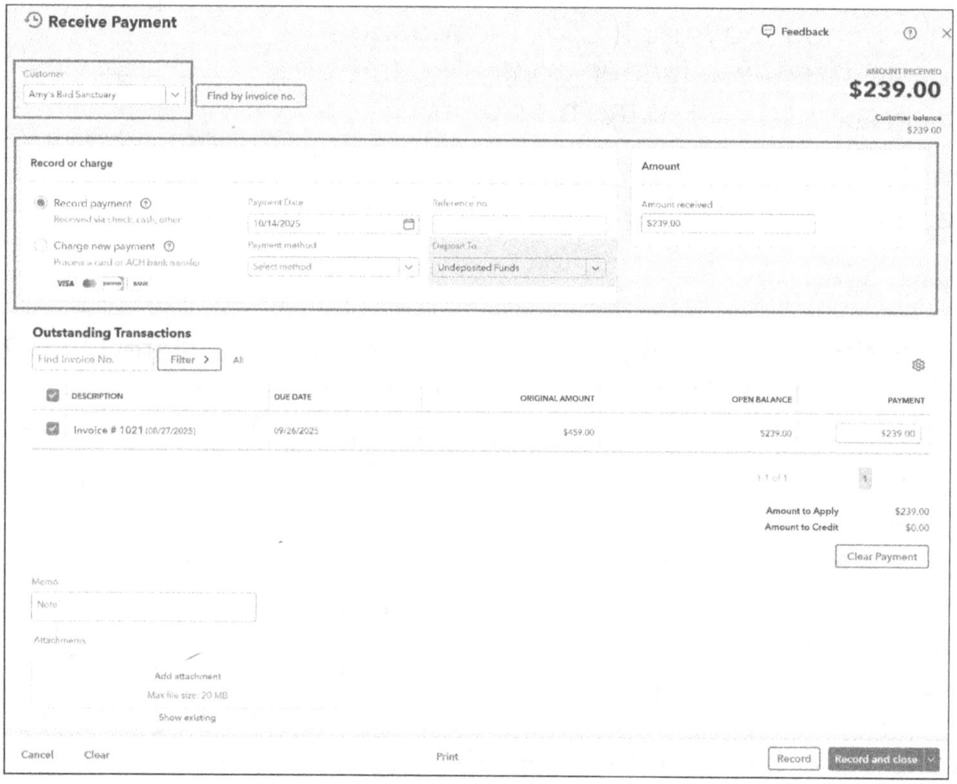

Choose the **Customer** paying you. Enter the **Amount** of the payment you received.

Select **Record Payment** if you are taking the payment outside of QuickBooks Online.

To process a payment using **QuickBooks Payments Merchant Services**, select **Charge New Payment**. Enter the **payment information**. You can process merchant services right from this window, and store the information for future use. When you choose Credit Card as the payment type, you'll see an **Enter Credit Card Details** button. If they choose to pay by ACH, select **Check** and you'll see a place to enter their bank account info.

Be sure to deposit all payments to **Undeposited Funds/Payments to Deposit**, NOT to your checking account.

The customer's **outstanding invoices** and their **balances** appear in the Payment window. QuickBooks Online automatically enters the payment **Amount** in the **Payment** field.

When you have multiple invoices to pay, confirm that amount is correct on every line, just in case there's an underpayment, overpayment, or you have the wrong invoice checked.

In the case of an overpayment, a **Customer Credit** will be created to apply to a future invoice (see page 105).

Select **Charge and Close** or **Record and Close** to record the payment.

You'll see all the customer's outstanding invoices on the list. **IT IS INCREDIBLY IMPORTANT** that you place a checkmark next to the actual Invoice you're paying against, and verify the dollar amount.

Otherwise, QuickBooks Online will pay off invoices automatically from the oldest to newest.

This will cause a cascading error. It will look like multiple payments have been applied to multiple invoices, invoices will appear partially paid, and the amounts will never match up.

QuickBooks Payments

When you accept credit card payments and ACH from customers, QuickBooks Payments Merchant Services allows you to email invoices with **Review and Pay** buttons so that your customers can pay online.

This is less labor-intensive than using a third-party payment like PayPal or Square.

You can also save the payment info to use again in the future, or automate **Recurring Payments**. This sets an invoice to recur on a schedule; your customer enters their own payment information securely and authorizes future automatic payments.

To sign up for QuickBooks at wholesale rates, please visit https://completebusinessgroup.com/royalwise-solutions/

Creating Estimates

Estimates work exactly like Invoices, but are used for bids before a job starts. **Estimates** are non-posting, meaning that they allow you to create a quote for a job, without it being reported as income in your system.

Select **+Create** > **Estimate**.

Fill out the **Estimate** the same way as you would an Invoice and send them to your customer for approval. When you land the job, open the Estimate and use the **Convert to Invoice** button to copy all the information into an Invoice.

Make any **Change Orders** or adjustments to the scope of the job in this new Invoice, or add a second Estimate with the changes.

Don't waste your time starting a blank invoice for an accepted bid...simply convert the Estimate! When it transforms into an Invoice, the Estimate closes automatically.

If you don't land the job, be sure to change the Estimate's **Status** to Declined. Your list of Estimates should be limited to real pending projects.

Progress Invoicing

Progress Invoicing allows you to charge your customer in stages, either for specific Products and Services, or milestone percentages.

Turn on Progress Invoicing in the **Settings > Account and Settings > Sales > Progress Invoicing** (see page 73).

When you click **Convert to Invoice**, you have the option to invoice the full amount, a percentage of the balance, or specific line items.

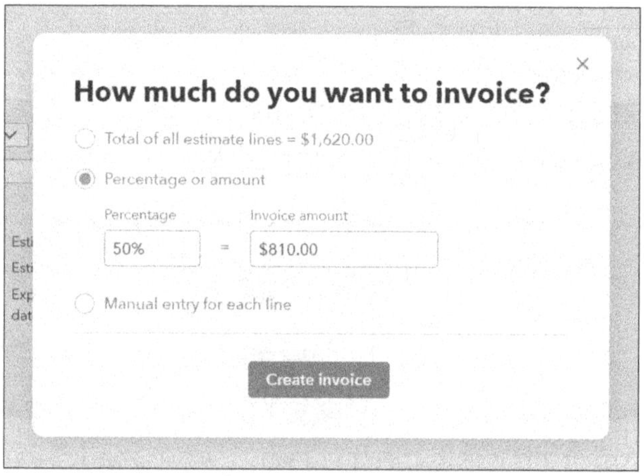

When you reopen the Estimate, you easily see how much of the original Estimate has been fulfilled and how much invoicing is still to come.

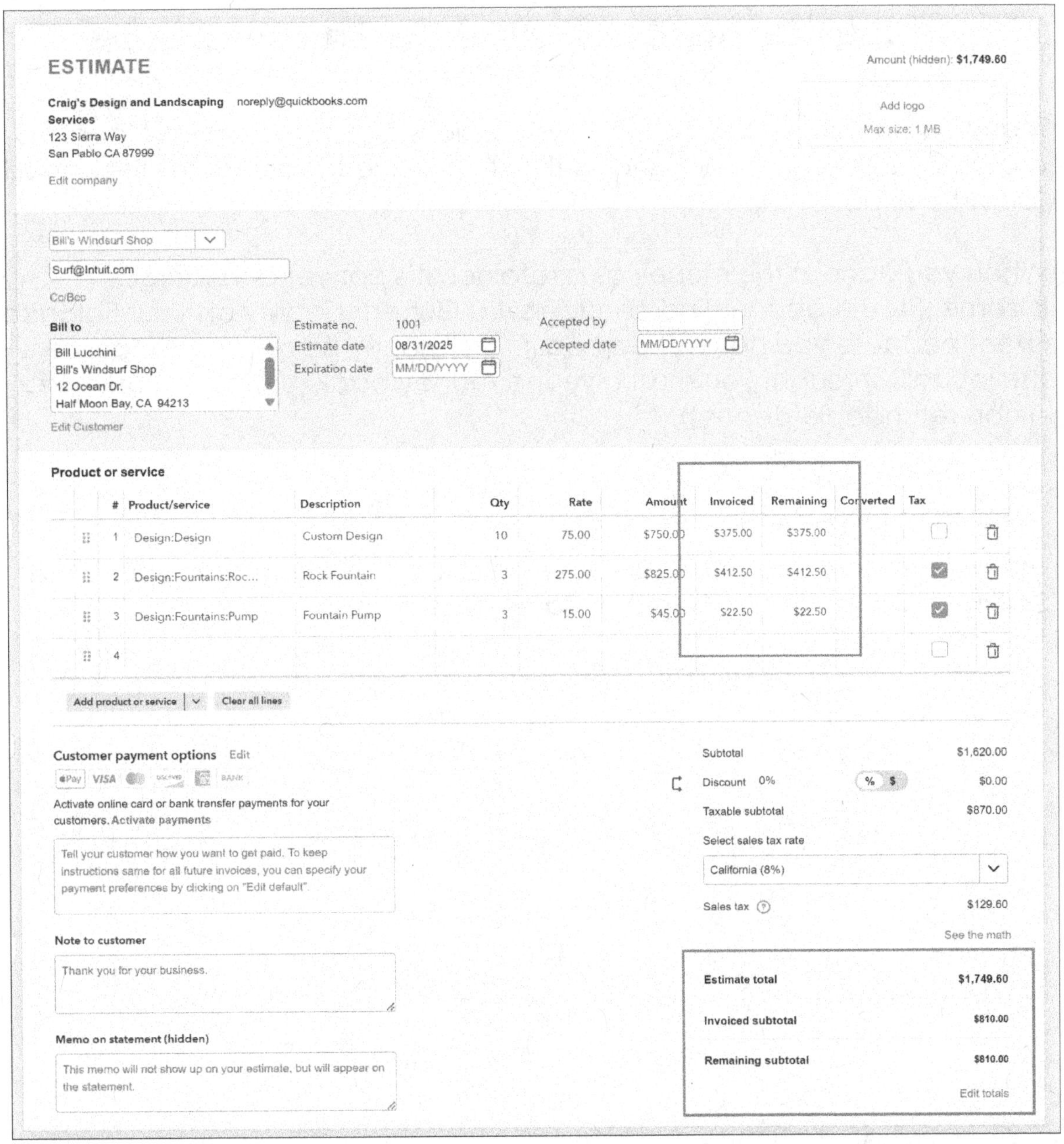
ESTIMATE
Amount (hidden): $1,749.60
Craig's Design and Landscaping Services
noreply@quickbooks.com
123 Sierra Way
San Pablo CA 87999
Edit company
Add logo
Max size: 1 MB
Bill's Windsurf Shop
Surf@Intuit.com
Cc/Bcc
Bill to
Bill Lucchini
Bill's Windsurf Shop
12 Ocean Dr.
Half Moon Bay, CA 94213
Edit Customer
Estimate no. 1001
Estimate date 08/31/2025
Expiration date MM/DD/YYYY
Accepted by
Accepted date MM/DD/YYYY
Product or service
Product/service Description Qty Rate Amount Invoiced Remaining Converted Tax
1 Design:Design Custom Design 10 75.00 $750.00 $375.00 $375.00
2 Design:Fountains:Roc... Rock Fountain 3 275.00 $825.00 $412.50 $412.50
3 Design:Fountains:Pump Fountain Pump 3 15.00 $45.00 $22.50 $22.50
4
Add product or service
Clear all lines
Customer payment options Edit
Activate online card or bank transfer payments for your customers. Activate payments
Tell your customer how you want to get paid. To keep instructions same for all future invoices, you can specify your payment preferences by clicking on "Edit default".
Note to customer
Thank you for your business.
Memo on statement (hidden)
This memo will not show up on your estimate, but will appear on the statement.
Subtotal $1,620.00
Discount 0% $0.00
Taxable subtotal $870.00
Select sales tax rate
California (8%)
Sales tax $129.60
See the math
Estimate total $1,749.60
Invoiced subtotal $810.00
Remaining subtotal $810.00
Edit totals

Taking Deposits on Work to Be Performed

Many companies take Deposits when a bid is accepted, both to confirm a customer's commitment and so that they have the resources they need to start the job.

When you accept this money as a retainer, it's not yet considered income. Proper accounting considers it a Current Liability on your Balance Sheet because you haven't earned it. The money is not yours, because if the job falls through, you must give the money back (unless you asked for a non-refundable deposit).

Turning on Deposits

The first step is to turn on the Deposits field. Go to **Settings > Account and Settings > Sales.** Turn on **Deposits. Save** your changes.

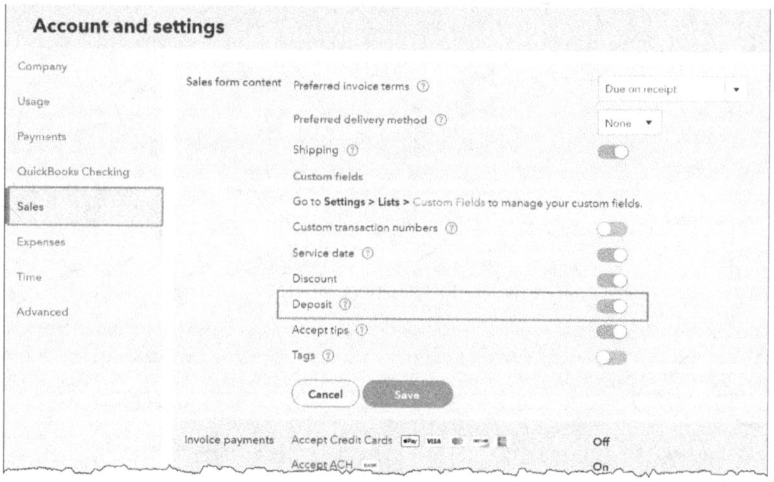

If you took the money externally

This works best when you *have already received the Deposit money* and are ready to create your Invoice. It counts the deposit as income instead of a liability, like an initial payment.

Create a new Invoice **(+New > Invoice)**, or open an existing invoice for the project. In the **Deposit** field on the bottom right, enter the amount of money you received.

A new pane opens on the right. Enter the **Payment method** used, and where you're putting it (**Undeposited Funds/Payments to Deposit** is best). The customer's deposit has been counted as Income, and the remaining balance remains on the Invoice for future payment.

The payment itself is waiting in Undeposited Funds to be matched to the Bank Transactions feed.

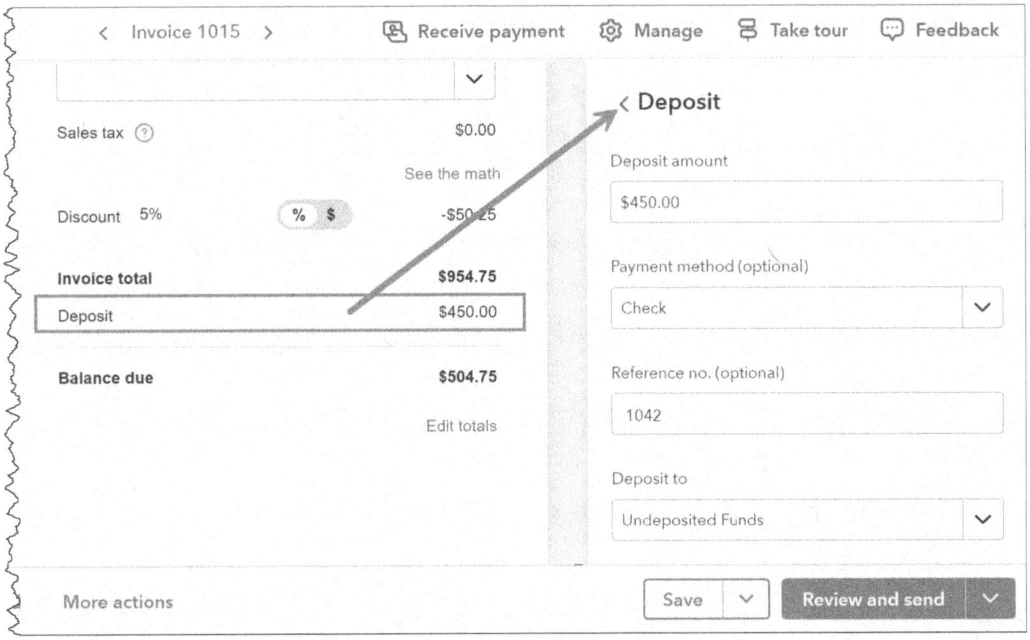

Using QBO's Built-in Deposits Feature

This works best when *you are sending your customer an Estimate, and they will put down their deposit upon approval*. You will send this payment request using **QuickBooks Payments**.

Create a new Estimate (**+Create > Estimate**) or open an existing estimate for the project. In the **Deposit** field on the bottom right, enter the amount of money you they will pay to start the project.

When you fill in an amount, a **new pane appears** on the right. Confirm the **Payment methods** you want the customer to use.

Note that if the deposit is for more than $2,000, you may see an option for **Customer Financing**, which will invite the customer to apply for a QuickBooks Loan or Line of Credit through Credit Karma, one of Intuit's other business services.

Click **Review and Send**. When they receive the Estimate, the customer will pay the deposit online, or they can send the payment separately. The remaining balance remains on the Estimate for future conversion to an invoice.

The Deposit will be held on the Balance Sheet in a Customer Deposit (Liability) account. When you convert this Estimate to an Invoice, QBO will automatically apply the deposit to the invoice and turn it into income.

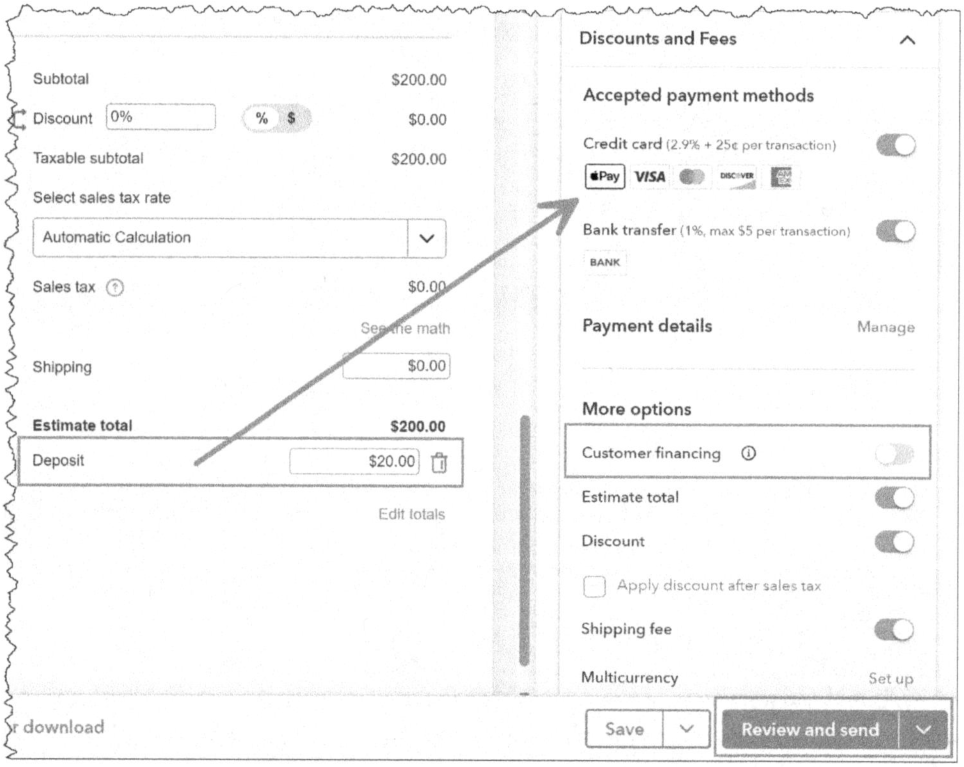

Bank Deposits and Undeposited Funds

After you have taken a Payment, but before you've put the money in the bank, those payments accumulate in the **Undeposited Funds** account.

In some QBO files, this account is called **Payments to Deposit** instead, but it functions exactly the same way.

Undeposited Funds or **Payments to Deposit** is like the cashbox where you keep all your cash and checks until you take them to the bank. It's where QBO holds daily sales until you physically make your deposit, and until Merchant Services batches credit card transactions into your bank account.

By putting every payment in this account, the Bank Transactions feed can find and match them. If several Payments get deposited together, this is where YOU batch them manually to match your statement.

It's important to empty out this account by depositing your cash & checks, and grouping your credit cards. This account should be empty ($0) except for transactions pending at the bank.

If your Balance Sheet indicates that you have a lot of money in Undeposited Funds, this may be a PEBCAK!

It is ***EXTREMELY*** important to group transactions in the same way the bank combines them.

There's no bigger waste of time than hunting down a deposit on your bank statement that doesn't match the amount shown in your QBO checking register!

When you go to the bank, itemize the checks on the deposit slip so that you have a reference. ***Better yet***, use your bank's smartphone app to deposit checks, so that each one is processed individually. Then your deposits will always match!

To properly record your Deposits, select **+Create > Bank Deposit**. The **Bank Deposit** window opens. The pending transactions are displayed.

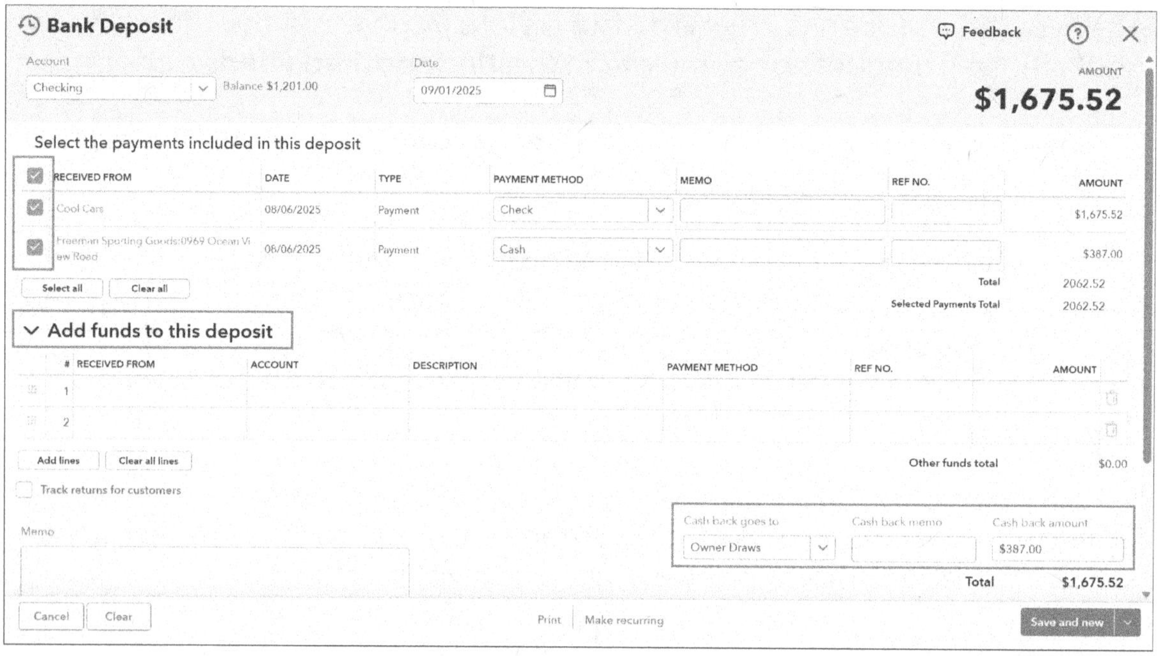

Confirm the **Account** where the Deposit will post. Make sure the **Date** reflects the date the money will physically be deposited at the bank. Check off the **Payments** that will be combined in the deposit.

Use the **Add Funds to this Deposit** area below for additional money added to the deposit if it's not sales-related (for example, a rebate check from your insurance company). Note that this area can also be used to deduct PayPal merchant service fees (see page 103).

If you pocket the cash a customer paid you instead of depositing it into the bank, use the **Cash Gack Goes To** at the bottom of the screen. Choose your **Owner Draw/Distribution Equity** account. If you're putting it in **Petty Cash**, you can select that here. This field deducts any cash you're keeping from the total amount going into the bank.

Click the **Print** button to print a deposit slip or summary report. Confirm that the total matches what is being deposited into the bank, then click **Save and Close**.

QuickBooks Payments Deposits

QuickBooks Online has its own built-in merchant services, with rates competitive to Square and PayPal.

One of the benefits that saves a lot of hassle is that QBO will close paid invoices, batch daily credit card and ACH transactions, and match Deposits on your behalf. You don't have to lift a finger!

Monitor the status of these deposits from the **My Apps > Sales & Get Paid > QuickBooks Payouts** tab.

In this screen you can see which individual transactions were grouped together, when they hit the bank, and how much the fees were.

If the money is still on its way, you can see the estimated date of arrival.

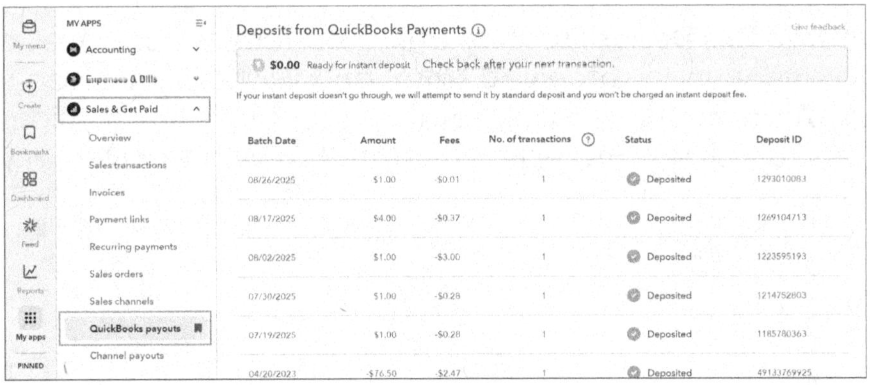

PayPal and Square

If you are using an third party merchant services company like PayPal or Square, they always deduct their fees before the money hits your bank.

This is challenging and confusing because you can never directly match the amount of your sale to the deposit.

PayPal and Square have connections within QBO's Integration Transactions to make entering their sales much easier. They import your sales and deduct your PayPal and Square fees automatically.

Importing Sales Totals from Third Party Systems

If you are importing sales from an e-commerce website, they also deduct their fees before the money hits your bank.

To compensate, create a **Sales Receipt**. You can create one for every single sale, but many people just enter daily, weekly, or monthly sales summaries.

In the sales receipt, use the grand total for the product or services sold. Then subtract additional lines for the fees so that the Sales Receipt's total matches the bank.

Alternatively, you can import the Sales Receipts for the full amount of the sales, then subtract the fees in the Bank Deposit **(+Create > Bank Deposit)**.

Check off the total sales for the day to match the payout reports.

In **Add Funds to This Deposit** section at the bottom, enter the eCommerce company vendor under **Received From**, and your eCommerce fees account. In **Amount**, *subtract* the total fees for those transactions. The total on the Deposit will now equal the **Net** that you received in your bank account.

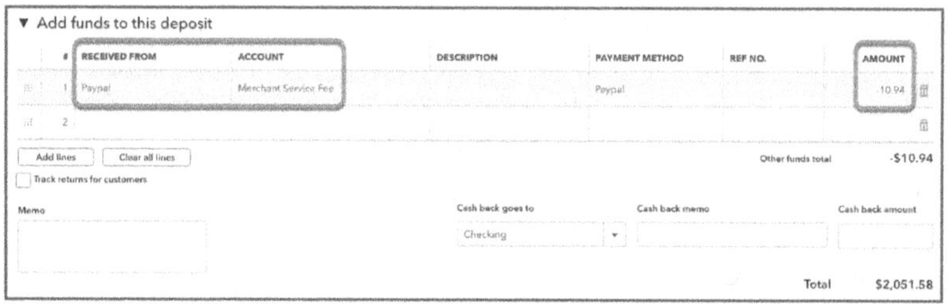

If you don't take this step, and just pull in the net payment from the Bank Transactions feed, you are underreporting your income and reducing eligible tax deductions. It may not seem like a big deal because the amounts wash, but your sales reports are wrong...and so are your taxes! If you apply for a loan, you will have underreported your gross income, and your numbers won't look as good as they could!

Companion Course
SCAN ME
royl.ws/bootcamp

Want to learn more?

Deep Dive
SCAN ME
royl.ws/e-commerce

Credit Memos

Credit Memos are used when you are refunding a customer, but retaining the difference as a store credit to be applied to a future purchase. If you are giving them the money back, see **Refunds** on page 107.

Issuing a Credit

Select **+Create > Credit Memo.**

Note that you can also click the **More Actions** button at the bottom of an invoice to choose **Create a Credit Memo** and turn the invoice into a credit for that sale.

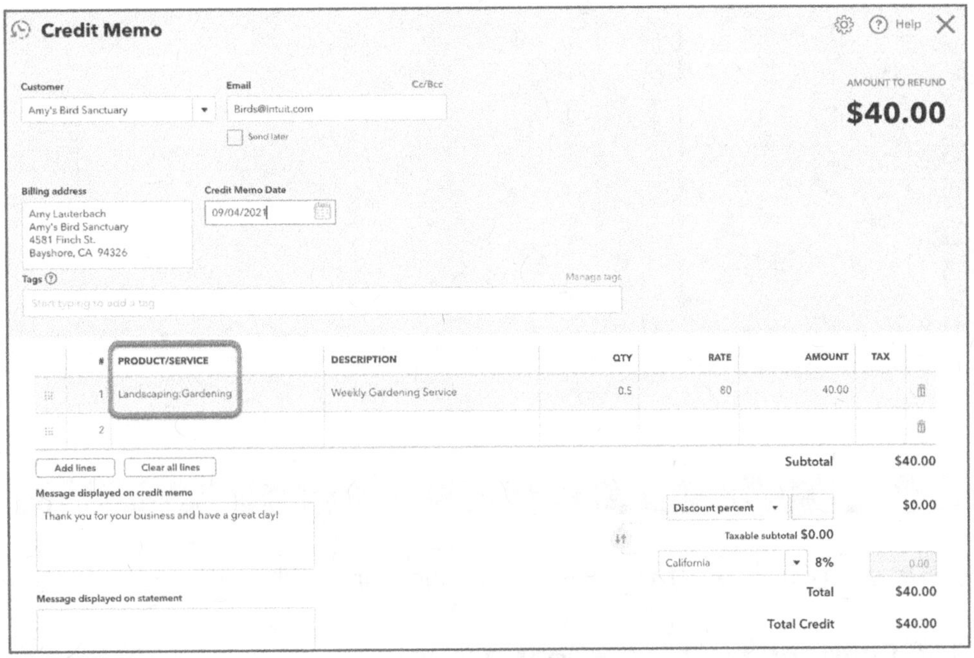

Fill in the **Product/Service** for the same Product or Service you had originally invoiced, so that your sales totals are accurate in your reports.

This Credit will now be available to apply as a payment the next time you **Receive Payment** on an Invoice.

Applying Credits

Outstanding credits are applied when using **Receive Payment** to close an Invoice. They cannot be used with Sales Receipts. The credit reduces the amount owed on the invoice, and pays off any remaining balance in full.

Select **+Create > Receive Payment.**

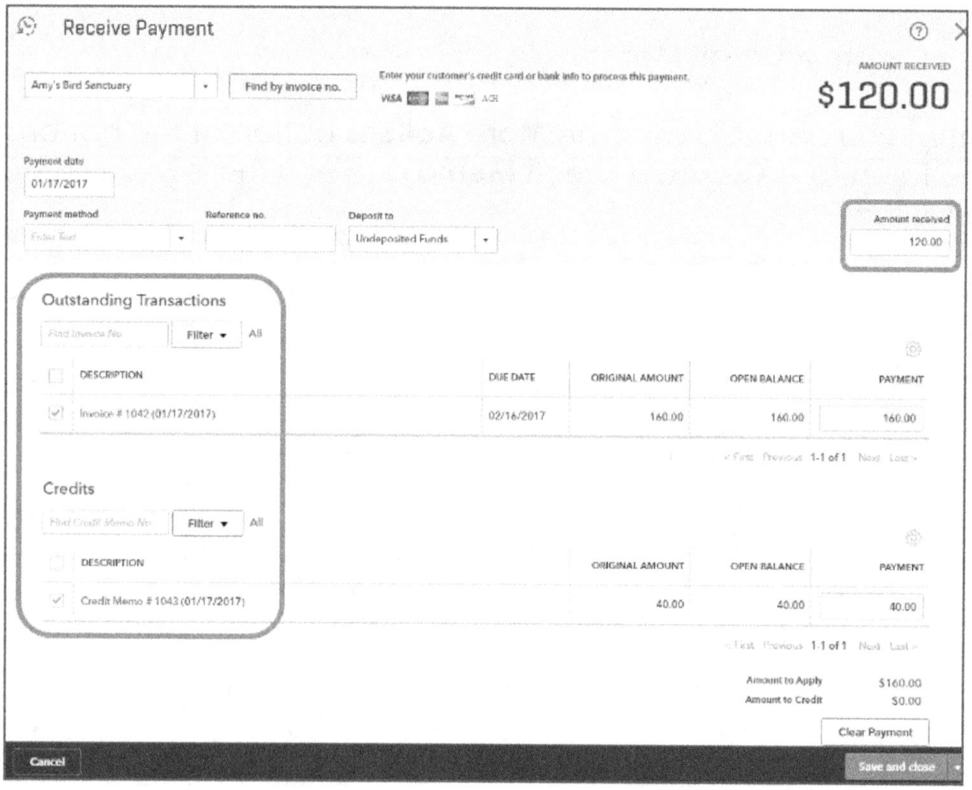

Choose your customer. Their open transactions will appear.

In the top **Outstanding Transactions** grid, check off the Invoice being paid.

Check off the **Credit Memo** at the bottom.

Look back at the Invoice. Correct the **Payment** box to equal the Credit if no additional money will be paid at this time. If the remainder is being paid now in full, the **Payment** should equal the **Open Balance**.

In the **Amount received** box at the top right, verify the amount of the actual money being charged.

In this example, the $40 credit on account is applied to the invoice for a total of $160, paying the original Invoice in full. The actual payment is received for the remaining $120.

Note that you don't have to accept payment at this stage. If you want to apply the Credit Memo to pay down the Invoice but wait until later to receive the Payment in full, make sure the two Credit and Invoice Payment lines are equal, and that the total Amount Received for the transaction is $0.

Creating Customer Refunds

How you process a Refund depends on what you are refunding. If you are giving a refund for a product or a service, it's pretty straightforward. If you're refunding a Credit your customer has on account, it's slightly more complex.

Refunding a Product or Service

You can't initiate a Refund from the New Transaction button in the Customer's detail window for some reason; it's only on the +Create button!

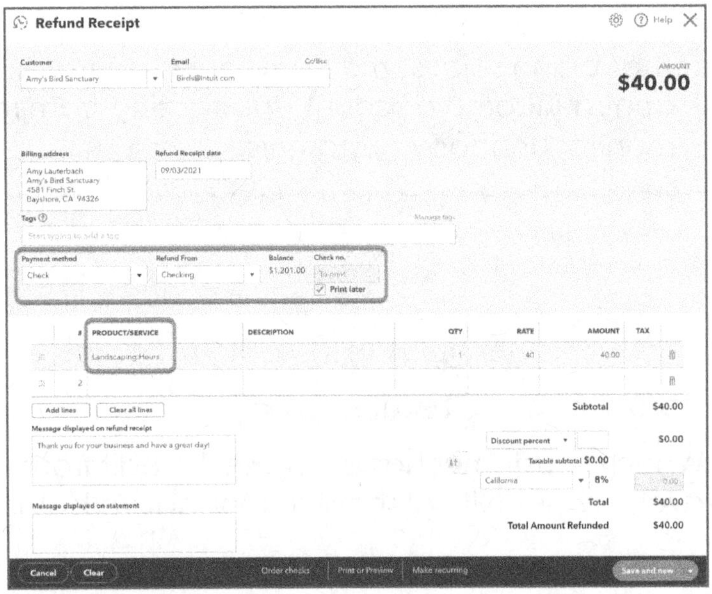

Select **+Create > Refund Receipt**. Choose your customer. Fill in the same line items from the original sale.

If they paid by credit card using QB Payments, you can refund directly back to the same credit card. Select the card type in the **Payment method**. Verify their credit card details. When you save the form, the refund will be processed and deducted from your next Bank Deposit batch.

To refund QB Payments made by ACH, you'll need to reimburse them by sending a check. Choose **Check** in the Payment Method, then fill in the **Check no.** or click **Print later**. Send the check to the customer.

For any other form of original payment, you can't actually process the refund through this form, and you'll need to use your original payment system. Create this Refund and enter *Undeposited Funds/Payments to Deposit* in the **Refund From** field. When you process your payment in your third-party system, it will be available to Match in the Bank Transactions feed or to be batched with a Bank Deposit.

Be sure to choose the same Product/Service that was originally charged. You want to reverse the income that you made from the original sale. A major ***PEBCAK*** is to use a separate Expense account like "Refunds."

That being said, some companies do track refunds in a separate contra-income account (subtracting from revenue) so they can monitor unhappy customers.

Refunding a Credit Memo

When a customer has an unused credit from a Credit Memo or overpayment, it will show as a negative balance. If instead of applying it as a payment on a future sale, you decide to give them back the money, perform these steps:

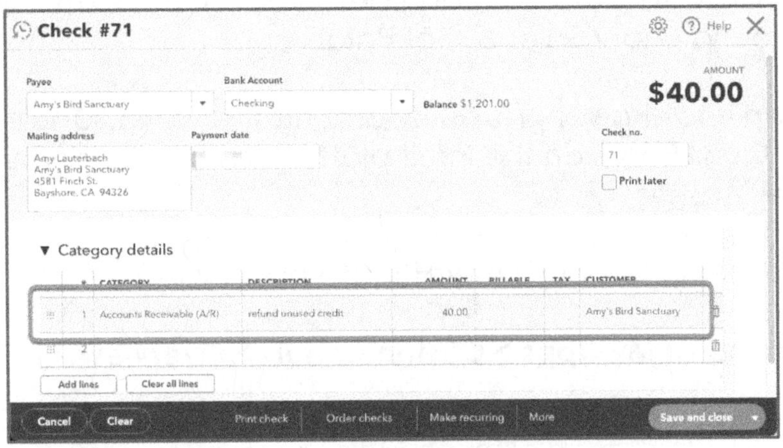

First, create the appropriate Refund, Expense or Check transaction for the payout according to the method of payment you are using for the refund.

Instead of refunding the product/service, use **Accounts Receivable.** Assign the Customer name to the line item. **Save and Close** the expense or check.

Next, create a **Receive Payment** for the customer. Check off the **Refund Payment** at the top in Outstanding Transactions, and the Credit Memo at the bottom under **Credits.** The balance will now be $0 for the payment.
This brings the customer's Accounts Receivable to $0 as well.

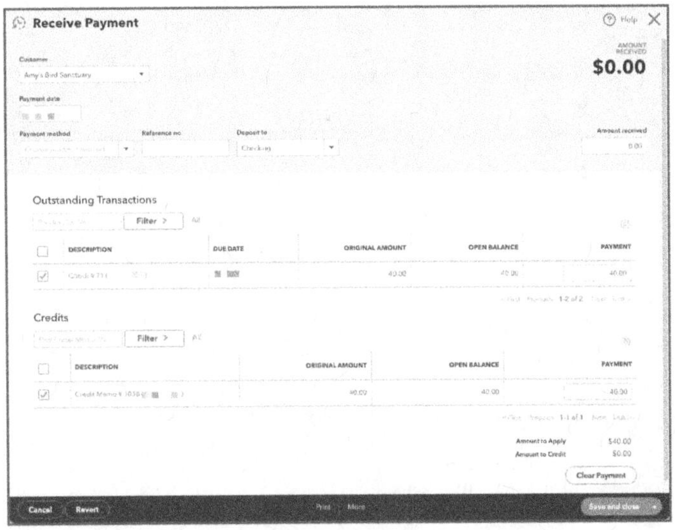

The Customer Hub

This feature is new to QBO and still in beta testing. The Customers center used to be found under Sales & Get Paid!

Intuit's mission is to "Power prosperity around the world." Their intention is to leverage QuickBooks on the Intuit platform to help business owners increase their cashflow.

The new features in the Customer Hub do exactly that!

The Hub is found at **My Apps > Customer Hub > Overview**.

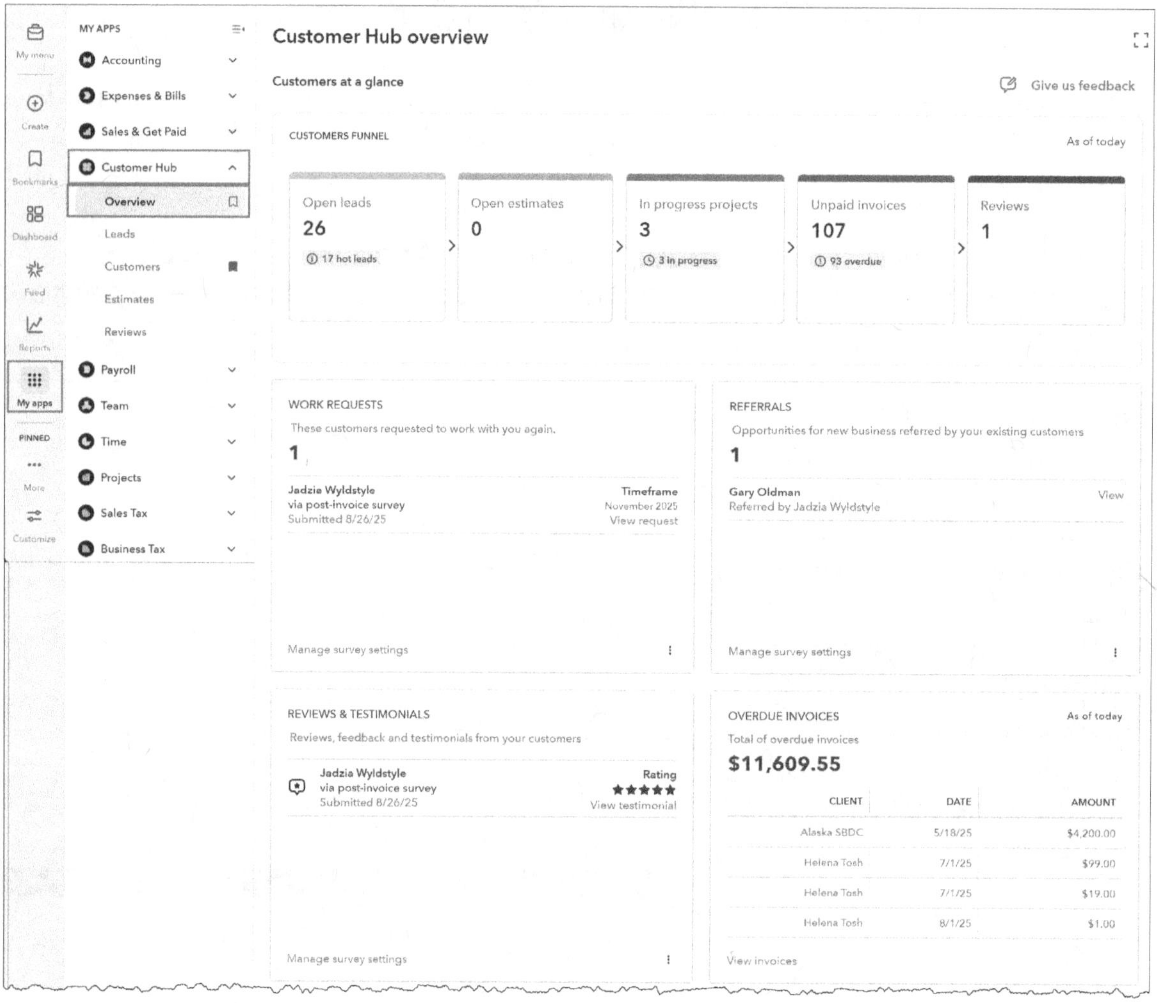

Overview

The settings to control these customer communication options were discussed on page 75.

Each of these areas leads to a full management screen. Now you have Customer Resource Management (CRM) software built right into your accounting software. This makes it easy to nurture leads and turn them into customers.

1. Customers Funnel

View your customers in a pipeline from Lead to Estimate to In Progress to Invoiced to complete.

2. Work Requests

It costs much more to gain a new client than it does to reach out to existing clients.

When a customer pays an invoice, send them a satisfaction survey. The form includes an opportunity for the client to tell you when they want you to contact them again in the future.

This primes the client to expect a call from you at their request so that you don't feel like you're bugging them.

It also sets you up nicely for repeat business and reminds you to follow up.

3. Referrals

Happy clients are glad to share you with their friends and family! This qualifies the referral so that you're not cold calling strangers.

4. Reviews and Testimonials

The satisfaction survey asks your customer to rate you on a scale of 1 to 5 stars. If they give you a 4 or 5, it asks them to leave you a review. These are great social capital for your email newsletters, website, and social media posts!

If they only rate you 1-3, it will ask for feedback so that you can improve your services.

5. Overdue Invoices

Stay on top of your cashflow by making sure your clients pay you promptly!

Leads

QuickBooks on the Intuit platform includes a Leads center. Connect your Gmail or Outlook email account. QBO will use its AI Customer Agent to locate emails with genuine client conversations, surfacing them so that you can easily nurture the relationship and turn the inquiries into jobs.

You can also add Leads manually.

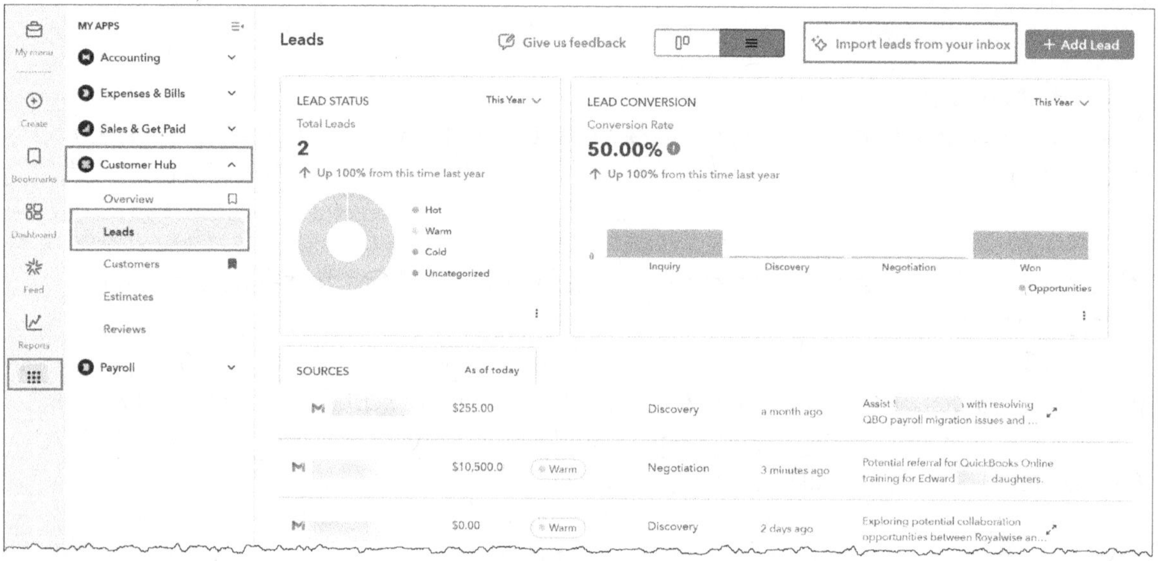

Each lead is tracked by temperature (cold, warm, and hot).

Assign a value to each engagement to prioritize the most lucrative opportunities.

Track the conversion status pipeline from Inquiry to Discovery to Negotiation to Won.

Turn leads into Customers in QBO in just a few clicks!

Check Your Understanding: Working with Customers

The Customer Center

1) _______The colored bar at the top of the Sales Center is called the:
   a. Filter bar
   b. Money bar
   c. Activity bar
   d. Action bar

2) _______If you filtered the Invoice list to just see Open Invoices, be sure to:
   a. Clear the filter to see everything again
   b. Send reminders to everyone immediately
   c. Receive payments on all of them at once
   d. Hit the Back button on your browser

3) _______Which way can you NOT sort your Customer list:
   a. Open balance
   b. Customer name
   c. Company name
   d. Phone number

4) _______You can only see your Customers listed in ascending order.
   a. True
   b. False

5) _______If you want to print your Customer list, the best way to do it is
   a. Using the little button with a printer on it
   b. Using your browser's Print option
   c. Exporting to Excel
   d. None of the above

6) _______If you don't see all of a Customer's transactions:
   a. They've been deleted
   b. You're in the wrong screen
   c. You have a filter applied
   d. Look in the Vendor Center

7) _______My Customer list has fields I don't want to see, and others are missing
   a. Go up to the Settings > Account and Settings
   b. Use the Customer center's List Gear choose the fields you want to see
   c. There's nothing you can do
   d. A & B

Sales Settings

8) ________ Sales settings are found here:
   a. Settings > Account and Settings
   b. Settings > Account and Settings > Sales
   c. The Customer Center

9) ________ The Service Date field tracks:
   a. The date each line item was performed
   b. The date on an Invoice
   c. A & B

10) ______ Most people don't need to turn on the Product/Service column on their Sales Forms.
   a. True
   b. False

11) ______ Track Quantity on Hand turns on:
   a. A Quantity field on your sales forms
   b. A Quantity available popup when you create a Sales Form
   c. Inventory counts for your products & services
   d. All of the above

12) ______ Progress Invoicing can be found in:
   a. QBO Lite and Essentials Suite
   b. It's not a feature in QBO
   c. All versions of QBO
   d. QuickBooks Online Plus and Advanced Suites

13) ______ QuickBooks Payments is the only merchant services built into QBO.
   a. True.
   b. False.

14) ______ When you send an email to a customer:
   a. You can include the details in the message
   b. You can attach a PDF
   c. You can send the customer to a payment portal
   d. All of the above

15) ______ The report sent to a customer that includes a list of all recent transactions and the open balance is called a:
   a. Sales Receipt
   b. Invoice
   c. Statement
   d. History

Adding New Customers

16) ______You can add new Customers:
   a. In the Customer Center
   b. On the fly in an invoice
   c. By importing them from Excel
   d. All of the above

17) ______The main designation that identifies the customer in the system is the:
   a. First & Last name
   b. Company
   c. Display name as
   d. Print on check as

18) ______Enter each customer's default tax rate in the:
   a. Notes area
   b. Tax info section
   c. You can't; you have to change it in each transaction
   d. A & B

19) ______Credit card numbers can be stored:
   a. Automatically
   b. Securely
   c. At the customer's risk
   d. At your risk

20) ______Customer sub-jobs are billed to:
   a. The main customer
   b. The job
   c. Either one
   d. Both

21) ______If you have a retail store and don't want to enter every Customer, use:
   a. Sub-customers
   b. Customer jobs
   c. Generic Customers
   d. Inactivate when they're done

Managing Customers

22) ______Deleting customers removes them from the system permanently.
   a. True
   b. False

23) ______Deleted customers still show up on historic reports:
   a. True
   b. False

24) _______ If you have a customer in the system twice with two different names,
   a. You must pick one to delete
   b. You can merge them
   c. You can keep both

25) _______ When merging customers, change the one that has:
   a. The least accurate address
   b. The fewest transactions
   c. The incorrect name
   d. Any of the above

26) _______ If you try to merge and it doesn't work, here's what's wrong:
   a. You have 3 of the same customer
   b. The transactions are stopping it from working
   c. The names don't exactly match
   d. A & B

Invoices and Sales Receipts

27) _______ Sales Receipts are used for:
   a. Recording sales that are already paid in full
   b. Recording sales with partial payments
   c. Recording sales that you haven't been paid for yet
   d. A & B

28) _______ New Invoices can be made from:
   a. +Create > Invoice
   b. New Transaction button on the Customer screen
   c. The dropdown on the far right of the Customer center
   d. All of the above

29) _______ As a rule, you should Deposit your Payments to:
   a. The Bank account
   b. Undeposited Funds/Payments to Deposit
   c. Inventory Assets
   d. All of the above

30) _______ Partial Payments:
   a. Get really confusing
   b. Need to be attributed to the correct Invoice
   c. Aren't a good idea
   d. Should always be applied to the oldest Invoice

Refunds and Credit Memos

31) ______Refunds can be made from:
   a. The New Transaction button on the Customer screen
   b. The dropdown on the far right of a Customer's transaction
   c. +Create > Refund Receipt
   d. A & C

32) ______Refunds can be NOT made using:
   a. The original credit card that was charged
   b. A different credit card than was charged
   c. A check
   d. The cash drawer

33) ______All of these are true about a Credit Memo, except:
   a. They are similar to an Overpayment
   b. They need to go back to the same Product or Service used originally
   c. They can be automatically applied to the next Sales Receipt
   d. They can be automatically applied to the next Payment

Making Bank Deposits

34) ______When you receive a payment from a customer, you should Deposit it right into the checking account.
   a. True
   b. False

35) ______The account that holds all your payments before you batch them is called the:
   a. Bank Transactions feed
   b. Undeposited Funds or Payments to Deposit
   c. Accounts Receivable
   d. B & C

36) ______Additional transactions that can be added to a Deposit include:
   a. Additional checks not related to customers
   b. Money in your cash drawer
   c. Money you deduct from a bank deposit
   d. All of the above

37) ______It's crucial that the money you deposit exactly matches the slip from the bank teller or ATM.
   a. True
   b. False

Answers:
1) b, 2) a, 3) d, 4) b, 5) a, 6) c, 7) b, 8) b, 9) a, 10) b, 11) d, 12) d, 13) a, 14) d, 15) c, 16) d, 17) c, 18) b, 19) b, 20) c, 21) c, 22) b, 23) a, 24) b, 25) a, 26) c, 27) a, 28) d, 29) b, 30) b, 31) c, 32) b, 33) c, 34) b, 35) b, 36) d, 37) a

Chapter 6: Vendors

(Accounts Payable)

This chapter covers the topics associated with **Accounts Payable** or **A/P**, which refers to the money you owe -- your company's Expenses and Liabilities. QBO's A/P features increase with your QBO version. QuickBooks Lite and Essentials have Bills. Plus and Advanced allow for job costing.

Expenses Preferences

Click **Settings > Account and Settings > Expenses > Edit**.

Bills and Expenses

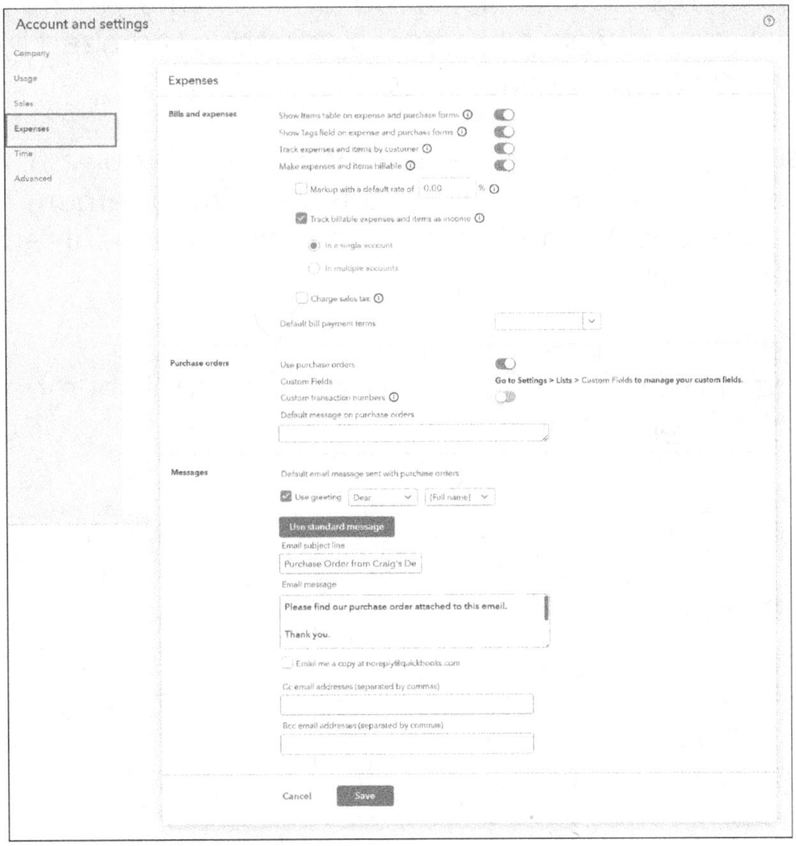

1. Show items table on expense and purchase forms
When products are bought for resale, Expense forms will have two grids: the top for overhead costs like Shipping, and the lower for the products and services themselves.

2. Show Tags field on expense and purchase forms
Turn this off. Tags are no longer available for new users. If you have an older file and were previously using Tags, keep it on! Lucky you!

3. Track expenses and items by customer
This is important for Job Costing and tracking profitability. If you want to see not just how much income you received from a customer, but also how much you spent providing their services, this allows you to assign a customer to every expense. That way you can monitor your net profit, not just your total revenue, customer by customer.

4. Make expenses and items billable
Used when you want to pass on a reimbursable charge to customers for a Product you purchased, subcontracted labor, or time you put into their job. This option allows those expenses to appear as itemized lines on Invoices. You can set a default rate for **Markup**.

You can also track that reimbursement as Income if you wish. Most businesses turn this option on, which posts the reimbursement to Billable Expense Income. If you don't turn it on, the reimbursement reduces the expense category itself.

5. Default bill payment terms
Are most of your Bills Due on Receipt, or after a certain number of days? Net 15 and Net 30 are common.

Purchase Orders

Purchase Orders allow you to order products from a vendor, have them sent to you, and then pay later. This allows you to track inventory you have on order, or contracts with subcontractors.

HOOT TIP

Go to any Expense, Bill, or Check. Note that sometimes the **Item Details** table is collapsed, so you may not even notice it. Click the triangle to the left and it will appear. This allows you to pay for products and subcontracted services.

Messages

Set up the default email message when you send Purchase Orders to your vendors.

The Vendor Center

Select **My Apps > Expenses & Bills > Vendors** in the left sidebar. The **Vendors** screen opens.

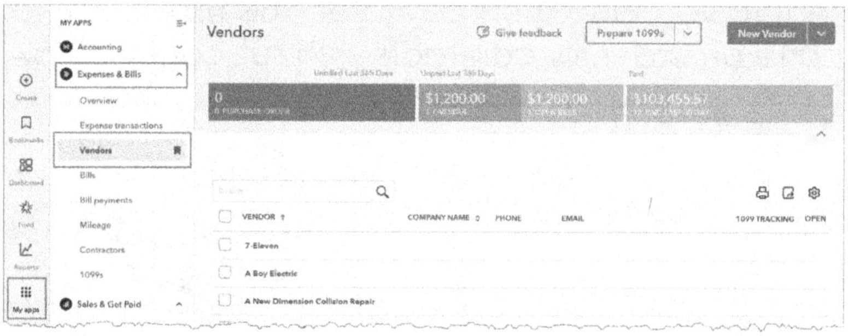

The colored bar at the top of the screen is called the **Money Bar**. Click on the different colored boxes to filter the Vendor List to see who has open Purchase Orders, Overdue Bills, Open Bills, and Expenses Paid in the last 30 days. After toggling through the filters, to view the complete list of transactions again, click the blue **Clear Filter / View All** link.

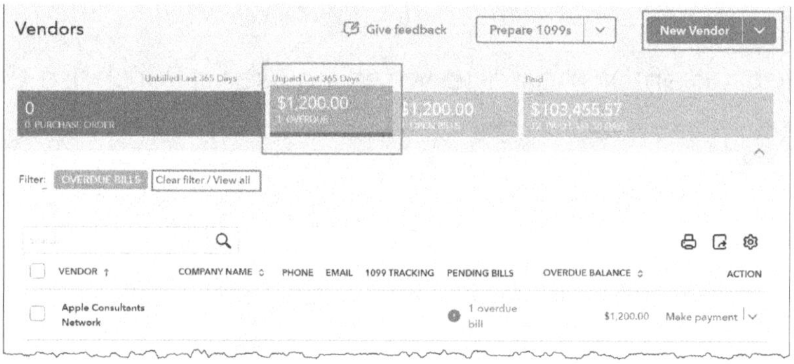

To **Search** for a vendor, use the box above the grid. Try searching by company name, contact name, and phone number.

You can also choose which information fields show in the grid. Click on the **List Settings gear** at the top right of the grid (as opposed to the big main Settings gear with QBO's tools) to select the fields you would like to see.

Check **Include inactive** to view vendors you previously inactivated.

The other two top buttons allow you to **Print** your Vendor List and **Export it to PDF or Excel.**

Adding a Vendor

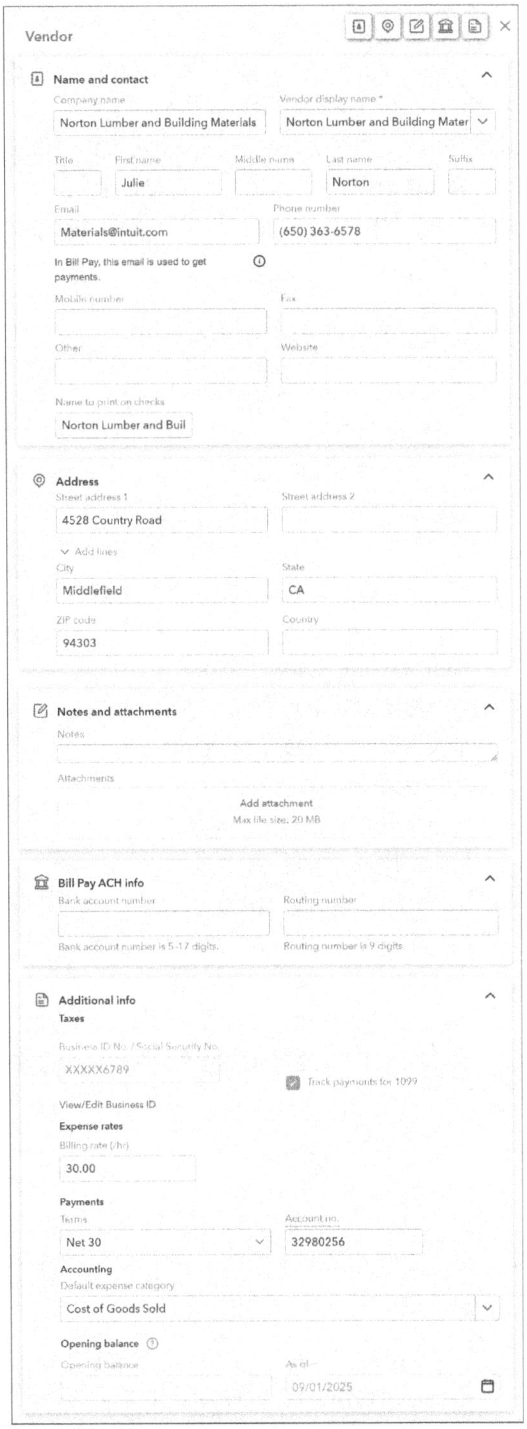

Using the New Vendor Button

Click the **New Vendor** button on the right to add a Payee to your list.

Enter the **Company Name**, contact's **First Name** and **Last Name, Email, Phone, and Website** for the new Vendor.

Select the **Vendor Display Name*** you want to see on your lists. This is also the unique identifier for the payee.

Complete the **Address Info** if needed.

In the **Bill Pay ACH Info** section you can securely save their payment information to pay them through QBO's **Online Bill Pay**. If you don't have it, you can ask for it the first time you send them a payment, and it may appear automatically if they're part of Intuit's **Business Network.**

If the Vendor is eligible for a 1099, enter the SS# or EIN# in the **Additional Info** section and check **Track payments for 1099**. QuickBooks Online will then filter all payments for 1099s at the end of the year.

If they have a standard **Billing rate** and **Terms**, you can enter them here. The **Account no.** field is your account number with them.

You can also set a default **Expense Category** that will autofill when you create a new expense or bill.

If you later stop working with this Vendor, click **Make inactive** so they don't show up on your lists anymore. Your history remains intact, and all transactions will still show up on reports.

As You Go

Vendors can also be added on the fly in the middle of a transaction by clicking on the **Add new** option at the top of any transaction's **Payee** field.

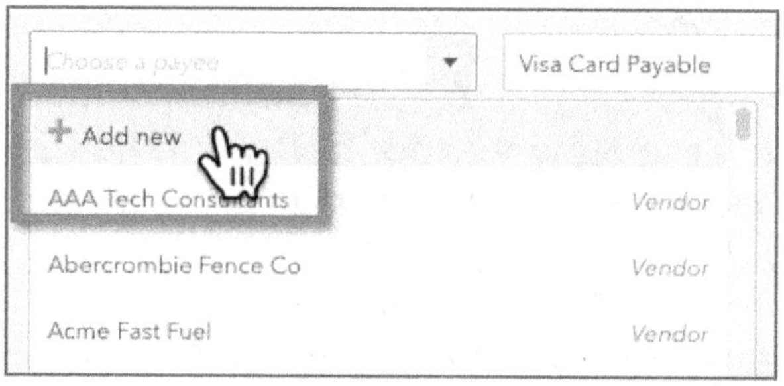

Generic Vendors

Just like we saw with creating Generic Customer Names on page 80, the same holds true with **Generic Vendors**. You may not need the name of every restaurant you've ever eaten at, every gas station you've ever been to, or every parking lot in town.

Instead, add these Vendor accounts: Restaurant, Gas Station, Parking.

Because the Bank Transactions feed still includes the original Payee in the Bank Detail line, you don't lose the true vendor information, and you don't clutter your Vendor list.

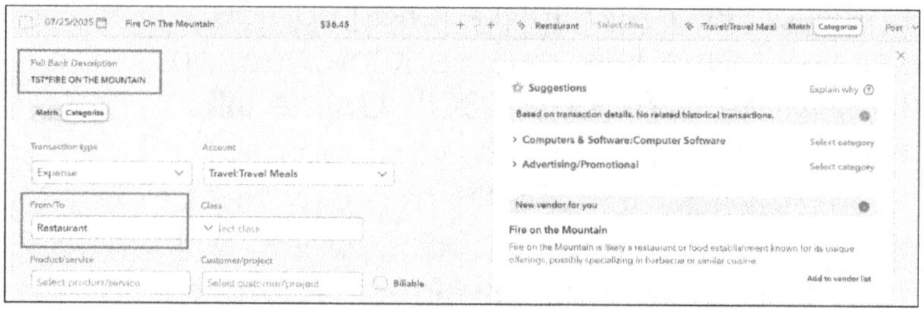

Be sure to annotate the transaction's Memo with details so that you have a record of the business purpose.

> **HOOT TIP**
>
> When it would be helpful or necessary to track the true vendor for operations, this shortcut would not be appropriate. For example, if you order in catered lunches for your staff, you should use the actual restaurant name for the Payee.

Working with the Vendor List

Click on a **Vendor** from the **Vendors List** to open their Details card.

To update the Vendor's Details, click the **Edit** button in the upper right corner.

Leave comments about the Vendor in the **Notes** area. Notes are also available inside the Edit window.

Select **New transaction** to enter a transaction for this Vendor.

Each row also has a selection of **Actions** on the lower right.

If you need more room on the screen, collapse the **Vendor list** on the left.

Common Vendor Workflows

Here are the QBO workflows typically used to manage vendors:

1. Do you pay at the time of purchase?

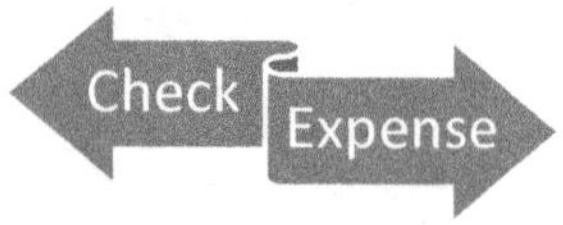

Enter a Check or an Expense.

2. Do you pay later, make multiple payments, or pay several bills at once?

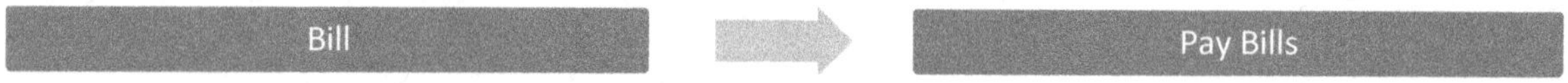

3. Do you order Products?

You have additional workflow options that provide data for additional reports, including Product Profitability and Job Costing. These are turned on in **Settings > Account and Settings > Expenses** (see page 119).

1. Do you order Inventory Items?
Use the bottom **Item Details** grid for any sales-related purchases.

2. Do you do Job Costing?
Assign the **Customer** name on the right.

3. Do you pass on the expense to the Customer for reimbursement (time and materials)?
Check the **Billable** box. Later add the expense to the customer's next invoice.

HOOT TIP

Note that there are two grids on each Bill, Check, or Expense:

The top one, **Category details**, posts directly to the Chart of Accounts. The bottom one, **Item details**, tracks your purchases for Products and Services. These may be tangible items you sell, or subcontracted services you hire.

Entering Bills

Enter Bills when you owe money to a vendor that you're not going to pay immediately. Use this workflow to track what you owe so that you can plan your cash flow based on the Bill's **Due Date**.

> HOOT TIP
>
> You don't need to enter a Bill if you're just paying an expense in full the moment you receive it in the mail. Instead, save a step by entering a check or credit card Expense, discussed starting on page 132.

Creating Bills

Select **+Create > Bill**.

Fill in the **Vendor, Date, Amount,** and the **Category Details**.

If the Bill is for products or services received, use the **Item Details** section instead, and list the products.

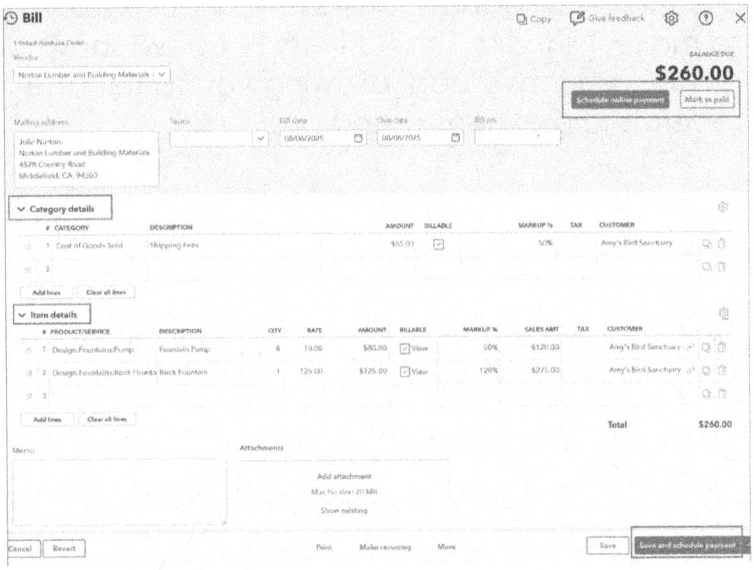

If you would like to store a PDF of the original invoice from the vendor right in the transaction, add it as an Attachment.

Choose **Save and Close** or **Save and New**.

Purchasing Inventory Items

If the Bill is for **Inventory Items**, be sure to use the bottom **Item Details** section instead, and list the products. Again, if the Item Details table doesn't show, click the tiny triangle to its left. If there is no tiny triangle, see **Expense Settings** on page 119.

Using the AI Agent Panel to Create Bills

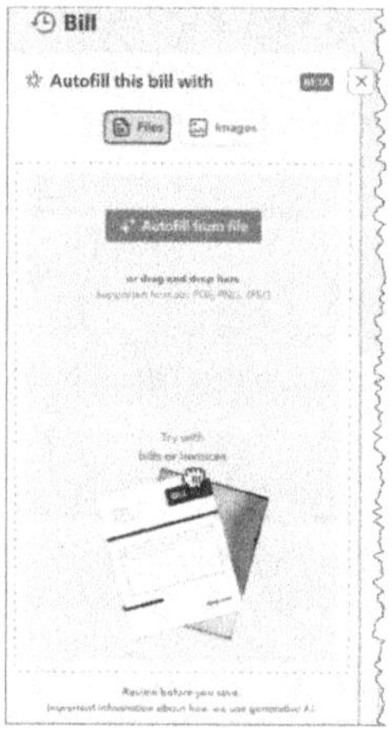

On the left of every Bill is one of the AI Agents with a blue sparkle. Click on it to open a pane that allows you to import PDFs and images. QBO will use optical character recognition to try to fill in the Vendor, Date, and line items. This feature is new and may speed up your process but will not get it right yet.

The document you upload will be saved as an attachment.

Emailing Receipts

Click on the **Business Feed**, the Intuit Assist icon in the left rail. One of the features you'll find on the right is an **Autofill** assistant with another box similar to the one in the Bill.

Just as we saw in the Sales section on page 91, it offers you the option to forward emails into QBO. Use the email address provided, or customize it to make it shorter. The Business Feed will show all emails you forwarded, allowing you to turn the receipts into expenses and bills.

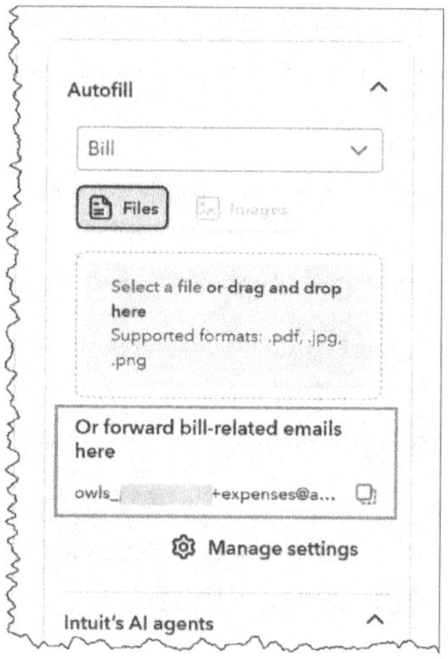

Paying Bills

Online Bill Pay

QuickBooks Online can pay your bills electronically, right inside the software.

When you click **Save and Schedule Payment** in the green button or **Schedule Online Payment** at the top, it opens the **Online Bill Pay** integration.

You can also get to the **Pay Bills** screen from the **+Create** button or **My Apps > Expenses & Bills > Bill Payments**.

You can pay vendors by direct deposit or have QuickBooks send a physical check. Your payees get to decide!

All payments by ACH are completely free. If you send a check, there is a nominal fee, but it's cheaper than buying checks, lining them up in the printer, signing them, and mailing them!

You can fund the payments from your checking account, or using a credit card for a small fee.

Depending on how many bill payments you make, this service may be free or there may be a monthly charge.

Using Online Bill Pay means you never need to handwrite or print a check ever again! It also saves you from entering the payments twice in an external payment system and again in QBO.

Mark as Paid

When you're ready to pay an outstanding Bill using any other payment method than QBO's Online Bill Pay, open it and click **Mark as Paid** in the upper right corner.

Enter the **Bank/Credit Account** you're using, the date, and check off all the Bills you're paying with that payment. Click **Save and Close**.

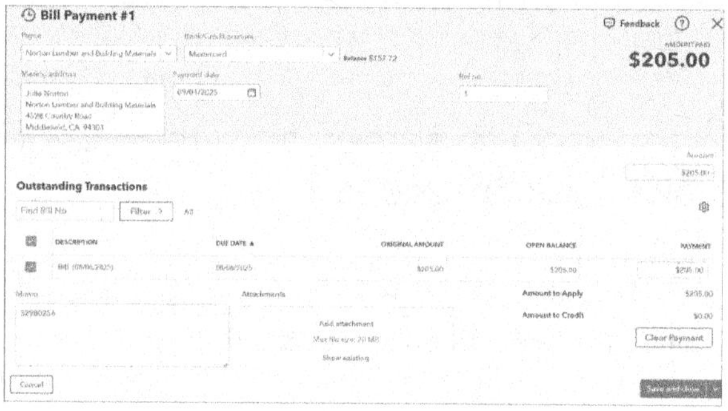

If you're paying several Bills all at once, instead choose **+Create > Pay Bills**.

Select the **Payment account** you're using to pay the Bills. Verify the **Payment date**.

Check off the Bills you are paying. Verify the amounts in the Payment column. If you are making a partial payment, adjust the amount here.

If you're paying by Check, select whether it will be printed or hand-written by clicking **Print later**.
Enter the **Starting Check Number** for the first check.

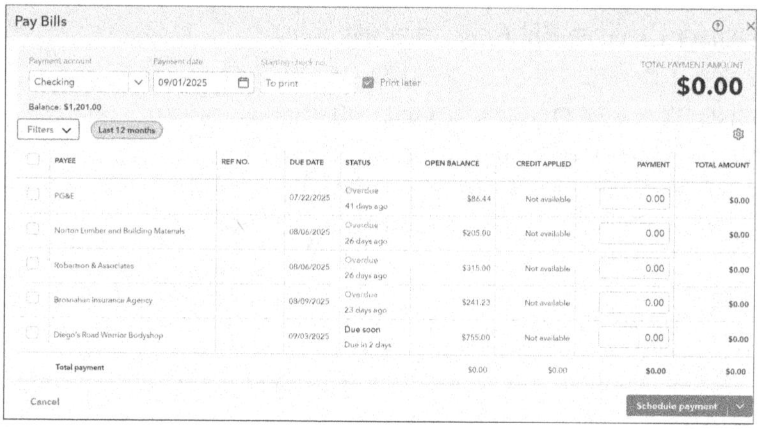

If you're Printing your checks, click the **Save and Print** button. Otherwise, change the button to **Save and Close**.

The Business Network

Intuit is rolling out a means of connecting QuickBooks users together. By activating the Business Network in **Settings > Account and Settings > Advanced**, you can connect your business with your vendors and clients.

Enter your ACH info to get paid by your customers. You'll be able to pay your vendors through Online Bill Pay if they've entered theirs.

In the future, when you create an invoice, it will appear as a bill in your clients' QuickBooks automatically. When you create a bill, it will appear as an invoice in your vendors' QuickBooks.

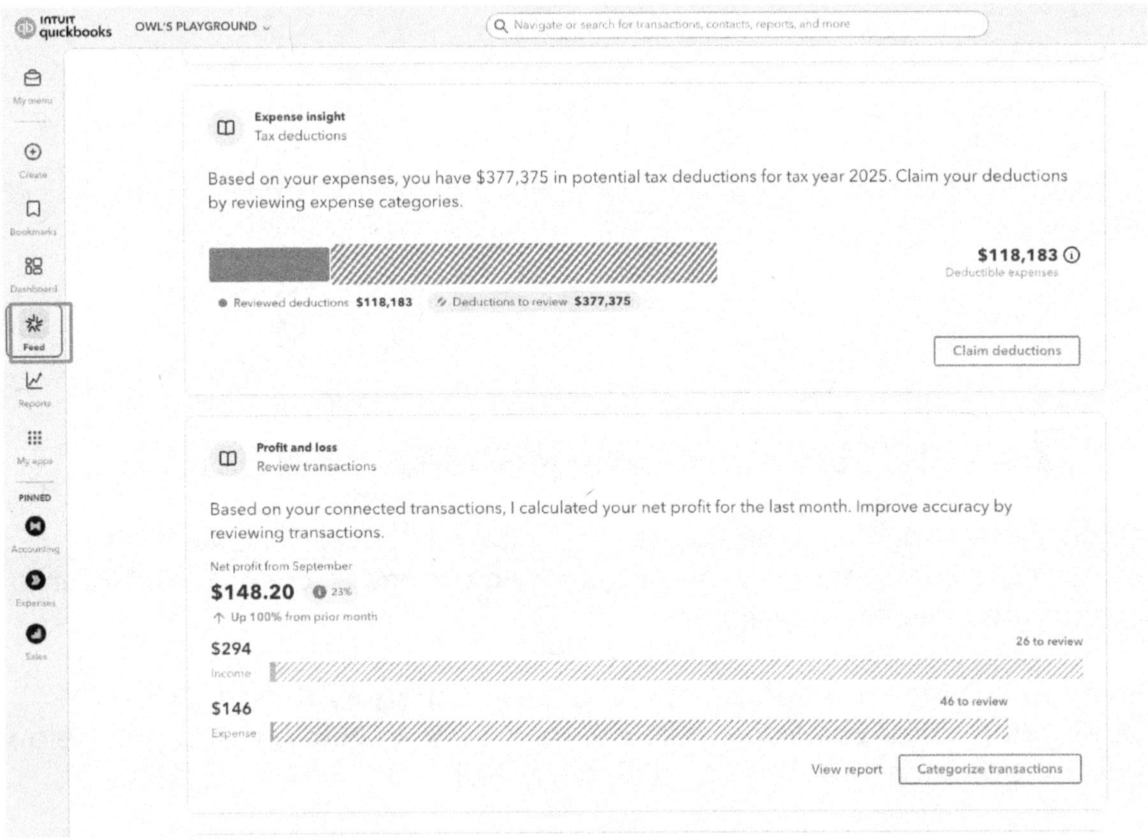

Writing Checks

OK, yes, some of us still write checks! On paper! And send them in mail!!!

Creating a New Check

Select **+Create > Check.**

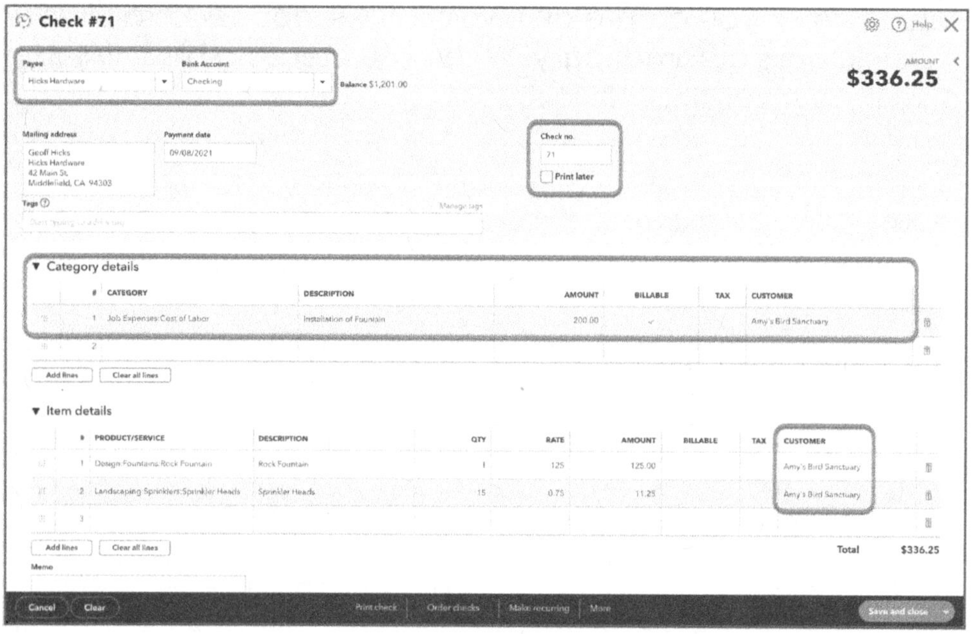

Choose a Vendor from the **Payee** drop-down list. Next to it, verify the correct Checking account. Enter the **Check Number**, or click **Print later** to queue the check to be printed.

If you're paying for a business expense, use **Category Details**. *If you're buying Items that you track as inventory,* use **Item Details** in the grid below (click the little arrow to its left if it's collapsed).

Optional: If you want to associate this expense with a specific customer so that you can do job costing (track how much you spent for a customer), enter the **Customer** name on the right of the transaction.

If you want to invoice that customer for the expense, **put a check in the Billable column**. You'll then add this cost to their next Invoice. *Do not check this unless you want a customer to directly reimburse you!*

Printing Checks

Printing checks saves a lot of time versus writing them by hand. Be sure to purchase QuickBooks-compatible check stock.

There are several ways to get to the **Print Checks** dialog box:

- All of the Expense and Check forms have a **Print Checks** button at the bottom.
- Click **+Create > Print Checks.**
- Print from the **Expenses Center**.
- When looking at a check on a Vendor's Transaction List, click **Print Check** in the Action column on the far right.

Print Checks Setup

The first time you print checks, you'll get a **Print Checks Setup** window.

Choose whether you have **Voucher Checks** or **Standard 3-up** checks.

Print a sample on plain paper, stack it with your pre-printed check stock, and hold it up to the light to see how the two align. Use QBO's tools to adjust the placement by dragging the grid to for the check amount. ***You may have to try a few times to get your settings right.*** When you're done, click **Yes, I'm finished with setup.**

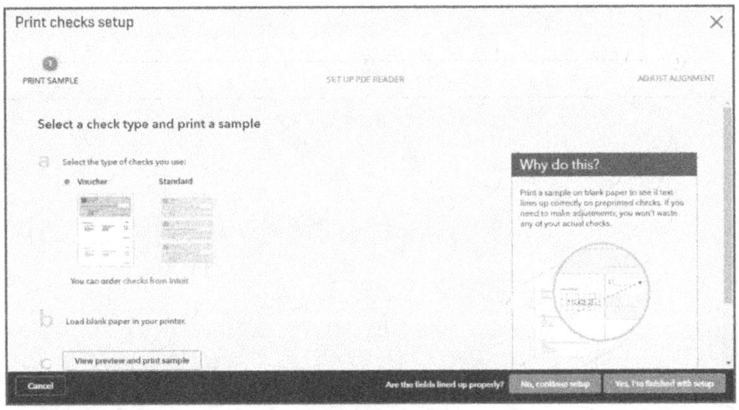

Printing the Checks

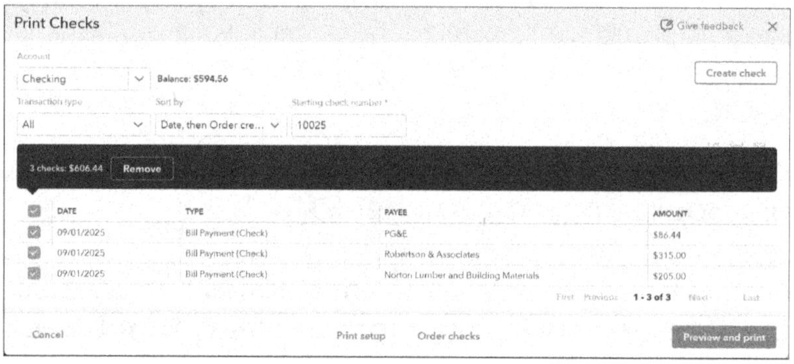

Enter your **Starting Check Number**. If you're using 3-up checks, use the **On first page print** box to specify how many checks are on your first page.

Load the check stock into your printer's manual paper tray. Note that most printers will print a single check, but for some the paper size is too small and will jam your printer.

Click **Preview and Print**. Then click **Print** again.

Your browser's printing window appears. Select your desired options.

Experiment, because sometimes you may get better results by clicking "**Print Using System Dialog**" and using your computer's settings instead.

Managing Expenses

The **Expenses** option is an all-purpose window accommodating almost all forms of payment, including credit cards, debit cards, and cash.

Select **+Create > Expense.**

Entering **Expenses** works exactly like creating a check, except there is no check number. There is a free-form **Reference number** box instead.

Note the **AI Accounting Agent** blue sparkle on the left. If you have a PDF or image you can use it to autofill some of the expense details.

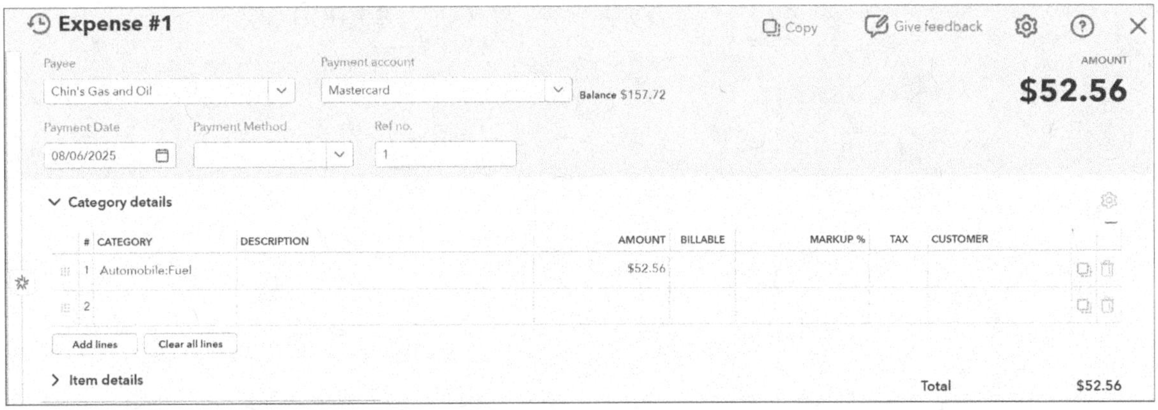

As before, if you're buying **Inventory** products, open the **Item Details** grid at the bottom of the screen.

Paying Credit Card Bills

Credit Cards should be connected in the Bank Transactions Feed to import all expenses. Be sure to only connect business cards and not personal cards.

When you pay your credit card bill, use **+Create > Pay Down Credit Card**. This ensures that you create the expense transaction properly.

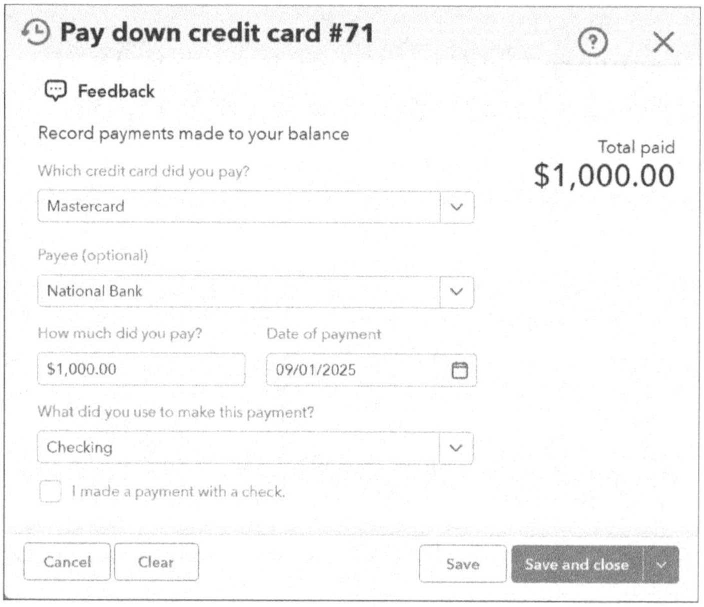

NEVER itemize your charges in an Expense form to make a credit card payment.

Individual charges should be imported by connecting your credit card to the **Bank Transactions** feed.

If you're still typing in a list of expenses using an adding machine to compile expenses for food and gas...you're old school! And you're wasting a lot of time.

Companion Course

SCAN ME

royl.ws/bootcamp

Want to learn more?

Job Costing Expenses

Are you doing Job Costing or running profitability reports? The following features are part of QBO Plus and Advanced, and are turned on in **Account and Settings** (see page 119).

If expenses are incurred while serving a customer, be sure to put the **Customer/Project Name** in that blank on the right.

If you are passing the cost on to the customer for reimbursement, check the **Billable** box. The next time you create an invoice for that customer, the expense will appear in the drawer on the right, ready to be added to the invoice.

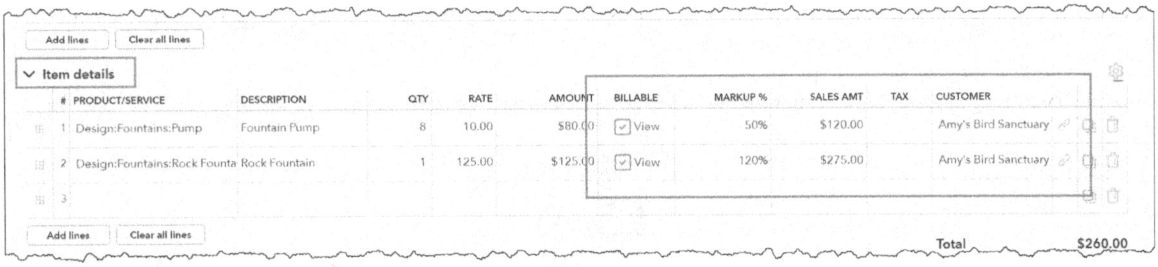

If you set up the **Markup** in the **Account and Settings**, QBO will even calculate the Markup automatically for you when you create an invoice (you can, of course, adjust the markup amount each time). You also have the option to show or hide the markup when you invoice your customers.

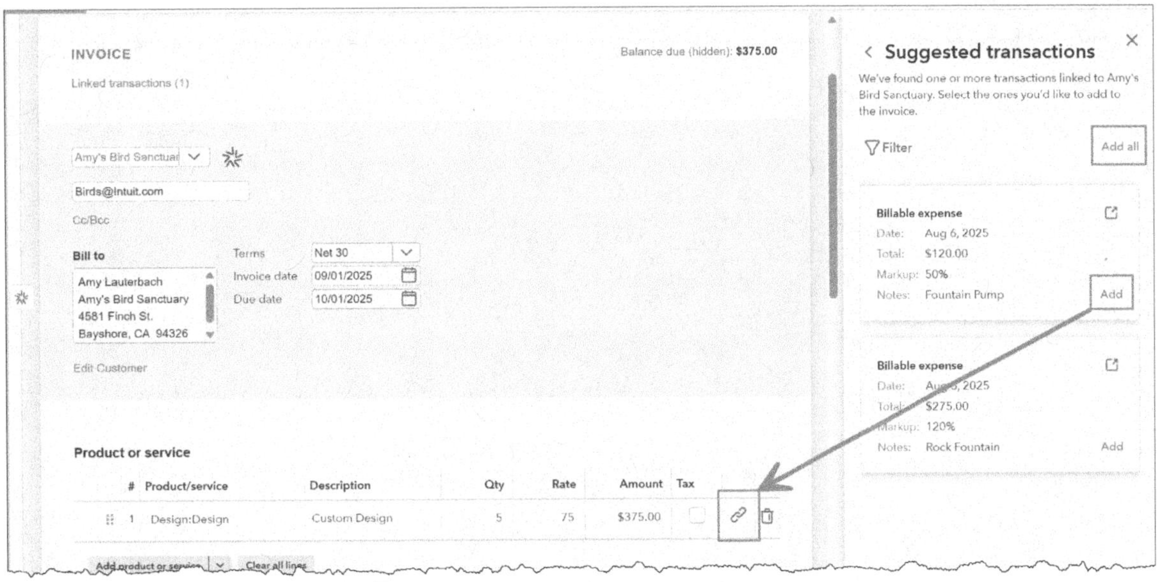

Vendor Refunds

When you are given a **Refund** on services you received or items you returned, it's important to apply the refund directly to the account used for the original purchase. If you bought a product, be sure to get a refund for that product!

In other words, if you bought office supplies and return a box of pens, you want your Profit & Loss report to only show the total you truly spent on your office supplies. If you used an Office Supplies account for the purchase, refund to Office Supplies. If you used a Product/Service called Pens, refund to Pens.

How you process the return depends on the form of payment.

Be sure to choose the same Product/Service that was originally charged. You want to reverse the expense that you made from the original purchase. A major ***PEBCAK*** is to use a separate Expense account like "Refunds," unless you have a specific need to track returns separately.

Crediting a Credit Card

If you paid by credit card, use **+Create > Credit Card Credit** to put the money back on the card.

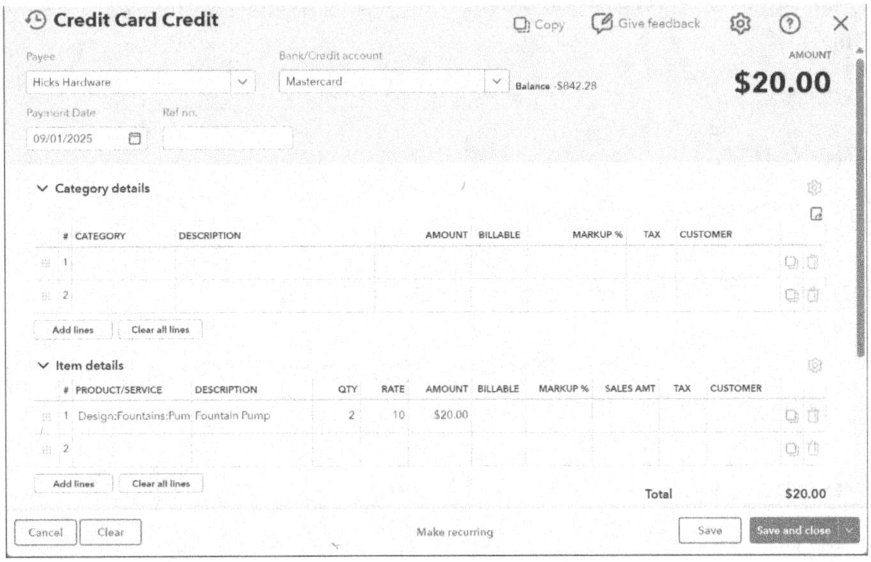

Cash or Check Refunds

If you receive money back from a vendor and they refund you using **Cash** or **Check**, receive that money through the **Bank Transactions** feed (see page 178), or by including it in the **Add Funds to This Deposit** area on a **Bank Deposit** (see page 154).

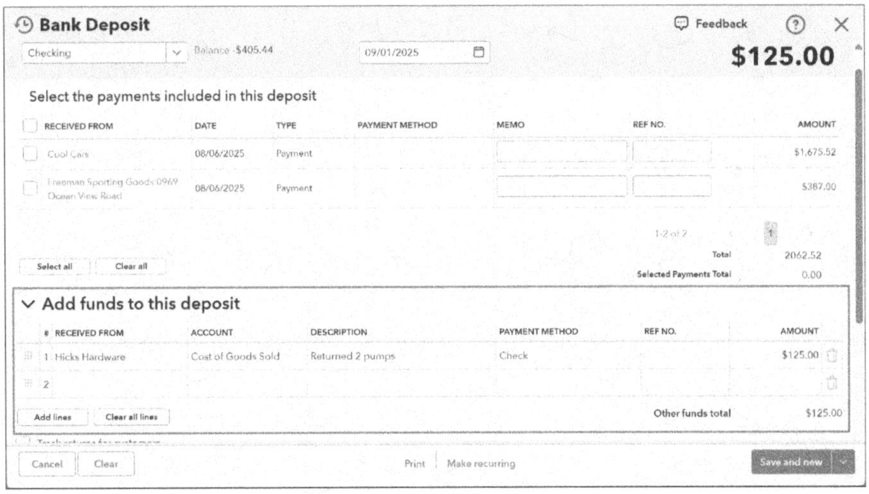

Issuing Vendor Credits

When you receive a credit from a vendor to apply towards your next purchase, create a **Vendor Credit** to keep that amount on file to apply to a future bill.

Create the Credit

Select **+Create > Vendor Credit.**

Enter the information just as you would for a **Bill**.

Note that you should credit either the **Category** that matches the original purchase, or the specific **Item** that you are returning.

Select **Save and Close** or **Save and New** to record the transaction.

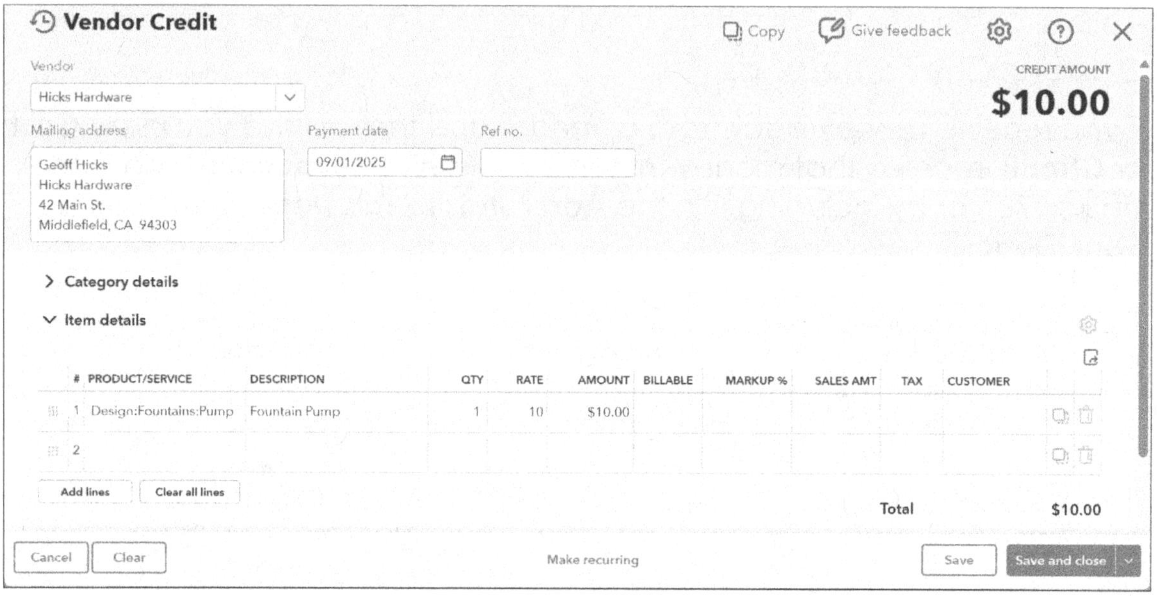

Applying Vendor Credits

By default, QBO will apply any **Vendor Credits** directly to your next bill payment automatically. You'll only have to pay the remaining balance.

Note that Credits only work when you make a payment to a Bill, not when you run a Check or create an Expense.

What if you do not want to apply the Credit yet?

You'll need to turn off QBO's **Automation** settings for applying credits.

This default is set in **Account and Settings**, as we saw on page 33.

Select **Settings > Account and Settings > Advanced > Automation.**

Turn off **Automatically Apply Credits.** Click **Save.**

Before you pay a Bill, you will now have to apply the credit manually.

Use the **Pay Bills** screen as we saw on page 128.

In the **Bill Payment** screen, look at the **Credits** section at the bottom. Check off the **Vendor Credit** that you wish to apply to the open Bill.

Fill in the rest of the Bill Payment as before. As we saw before with Applying Credit Memos on page 106, it's easiest to work from the bottom up.

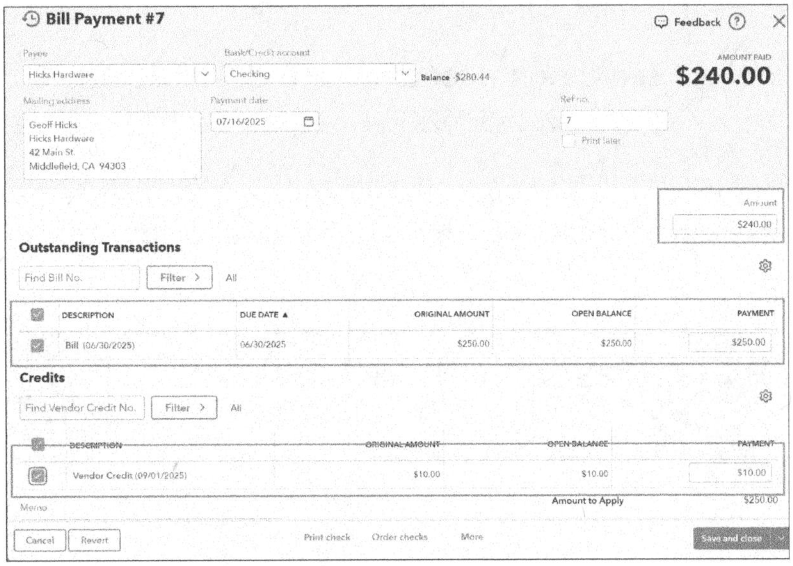

Employees and Contractors

The **Payroll** section under My Apps on the left navigation pane is where you'll find **Employees, Contractors,** and **Benefits** tools.

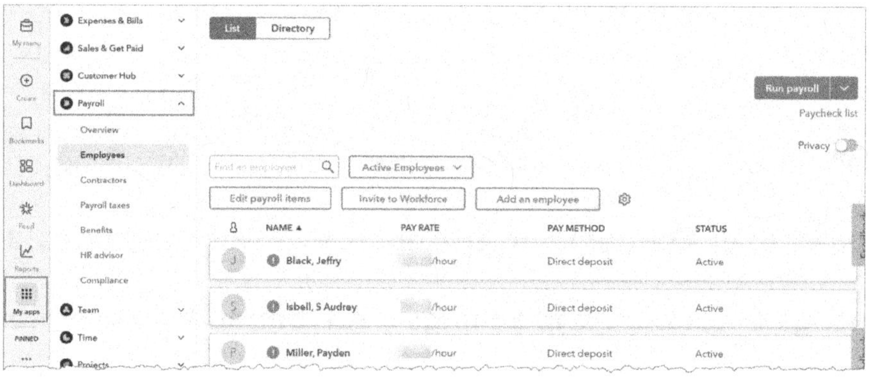

Employees

The **Employees** area is where you go to run **Payroll**. With **Full-Service Payroll**, Intuit takes care of everything for you. You report the hours, and Intuit will run the checks, pay the taxes, and file your monthly, quarterly, and annual reports.

Enroll by clicking the green **Get started** button. If you enroll through your trusted ProAdvisor, you can get discounted payroll.

Find a local ProAdvisor at www.findaproadvisor.com...

...or visit our self-serve portal for discounted QuickBooks Software at https://completebusinessgroup.com/royalwise-solutions/.

Payroll is not covered in this book because every state has its own requirements, but we do have a video course about it:

1099 Contractors

If you have independent workers who don't qualify as employees, QuickBooks Online considers them **Contractors**.

According to federal tax laws, a Contractor is a vendor you pay for business-to-business services. They are either self-employed or an LLC. S-Corps are exempt.

In January, you must send all your qualified contractors **1099 Forms**, and submit a 1096 to the IRS. To be eligible, you must have paid them more than $600 using a payment method that directly impacted your checking account. In other words, cash and check payments or personal apps like Venmo are included. Payment involving credit cards and other merchant services are exempt.

It's a good idea to have every independent contractor you employ fill out a W-9 form as soon as you hire them. That way you won't have to chase them down for their addresses and Social Security Numbers or EINs in a filing deadline panic. You can store this info in the Vendor's Details.

The **Contractors** tab makes this easy to manage. You can access the Contractors center from both Expenses and Payroll in the My Apps menu.

Click the **Add a Contractor** button. QBO will send the vendor an online W-9 form to fill out electronically.

Click the **Pay Contractors** button to pay contractors for their services using QBO Payroll.

In January, click **Prepare 1099s** to send 1099s to your contractors and submit your forms to the IRS. If you are a QBO Payroll subscriber, there is no extra cost for this service.

QBO's 1099 Wizard
royl.ws/QBO1099
Scan me

Check Your Understanding: Working with Vendors

Expenses Settings

1) ________ Expense settings are found here:
   a. +Create > Expenses
   b. Settings > Account and Settings > Expenses
   c. The Vendors Center

2) ________ The "Show Items table on expense and purchase forms" option is
   a. Sometimes Off by default
   b. Crucial if you pay for any of the Services or Items you sell
   c. Frequently still hidden under a triangle on the forms
   d. All of the above

3) ________ "Track expenses and items by customer" allows you to:
   a. Do job costing
   b. See who purchases are for
   c. Filter expense reports by customer
   d. All of the above

4) ________ Billable items and expenses should ONLY be used if you incur an expense, and the customer will reimburse you for that specific purchase later.
   a. True
   b. False

5) ________ The default Markup will show on a customer Invoice:
   a. On a separate itemized line
   b. On the same line, invisible to the customer
   c. There's an option that will give you the choice

6) ________ In QBO Plus, Custom Fields show up:
   a. On your Vendor screen
   b. In your Purchase Orders and Bills
   c. Optionally on your printed forms
   d. B & C

7) ________ Purchase orders:
   a. Allow you to buy products for specific customers
   b. Add items to inventory
   c. Count as Accounts Payable
   d. A & B

Adding New Vendors

8) _______You can add new vendors:
   a. In the Vendor Center
   b. While creating an Expense
   c. By importing them from Excel
   d. All of the above

9) _______The main designation that identifies the vendor in the system is the:
   a. First & Last name
   b. Company
   c. Display name as
   d. Print on check as

10) ______If you have a standard rate that you always pay for a vendor, add it to the _____ field:
   a. Billing rate (/hr)
   b. Opening balance
   c. Markup
   d. A & C

11) ______You shouldn't actually enter anything into the Opening balance box.
   a. True
   b. False

12) ______The 1099 box only appears in this version of QBO:
   a. QuickBooks Lite
   b. Essentials
   c. Plus
   d. All of the above

13) ______Vendors are used in these transactions:
   a. Expenses
   b. Checks
   c. Bills
   d. All of the above

14) ______Generic Vendors are great for:
   a. Restaurants
   b. Gas Stations
   c. Parking lots
   d. All of the above

Cleaning up the Vendor List

15) ______ If you have a vendor in the system twice with two different names,
   a. You can pick one to inactivate
   b. You can merge them
   c. Either way is fine

16) ______ If you need to look at a vendor that has been deleted or merged:
   a. You can't
   b. Use the List Settings gear at the top right of the Vendor list and click Include Inactive
   c. Use the big Settings gear in the upper right of the screen
   d. B & C

Creating and Paying Bills

17) ______ Bills are used for:
   a. Writing checks for utilities
   b. Paying some time after you receive the notice
   c. Purchases when you pay in full
   d. All of the above

18) ______ If you're buying a product, or subcontracting a service, use this table:
   a. Category Details
   b. Item Details
   c. Either
   d. Both

19) ______ If you are paying for an overhead expense, use:
   a. Category Details
   b. Item Details
   c. Either
   d. Both

20) ______ You can pay off more than one Bill when you make a Payment.
   a. True
   b. False

Writing Checks

21) ______ If you don't see an Item Details section in the Check:
   a. Be sure the option is turned on in Account and Settings
   b. Click the triangle to its left
   c. A & B
   d. None of the above

22) ______To tell QBO you want to print a check instead of writing it manually:
   a. Enter in the check number
   b. Mark it as "Print Later"
   c. Choose Printer settings

23) ______If you print your checks instead of writing them manually, use the:
   a. Print Check button at the bottom of the Check
   b. Print Checks in +Create menu
   c. Print Check next to the check in the Vendor's transaction list
   d. All of the above

24) ______You have to order your checks from Intuit for them to print correctly.
   a. True
   b. False

25) ______QBO will remember your check numbers and how many are left on a 3-up page.
   a. True
   b. False

Working with Credit Cards

26) ______It's important to have separate credit cards for personal and business expenses because when you use one card:
   a. It makes your Owner/Shareholder Draw larger than it really is
   b. It's easy to separate transactions on your lists
   c. You can rack up Frequent Flyer Miles faster

27) ______When you return a product and get a refund on your credit card,
   a. Put the refund in a Credit Card Refund account in your Chart of Accounts
   b. Leave the money as an Unapplied Credit account
   c. Refund the money back into the Category or the Product/Service that it originally came from
   d. Any of the above

Vendor Credits

28) ______Vendor Credits can be applied to:
   a. Bills
   b. Credit Card Expense charges
   c. Checks
   d. All of the above

Billable Expenses

29) _______ Marking an Expense as Billable allows you to:
   a. Invoice a customer to get reimbursed
   b. Track an item from purchase through sale
   c. Mark up an Expense and track the profit
   d. All of the above

30) _______ Billable Expenses are not available in this version of QBO:
   a. QuickBooks Lite
   b. Essentials
   c. Plus
   d. Advanced

31) _______ The ability to mark expenses as Billable to a Customer is turned on by default.
   a. True
   b. False

32) _______ The ability to track expenses by Customer does NOT allow you to:
   a. Do job costing
   b. Track an item from purchase through sale
   c. Automatically invoice a customer for a product
   d. Run a report for Expenses by Customer

33) _______ Setting Default Markup prevents you from adjusting it on a Customer's Invoice.
   a. True
   b. False

34) _______ You can see your Unbilled Expense Activity:
   a. In the blue box in the Customer Center money bar
   b. In the blue box in the Vendor Center money bar
   c. On the Unbilled Charges report in the Report Center
   d. A & C

Summary

35) _______ If you need help setting up your Vendors, Products and Services, or purchasing settings, you should:
   a. Call QBO's Live Experts
   b. Ask your accountant or bookkeeper
   c. Watch our QBO Video course at http://royl.ws/bootcamp
   d. Call Alicia at 503-406-6550
   e. Any of the above

Answers:
1) b, 2) d, 3) d, 4) a, 5) c, 6) d, 7) a, 8) d, 9) c, 10) a, 11) a, 12) d, 13) d, 14) d, 15) b, 16) b, 17) b, 18) b, 19) a, 20) a, 21) c, 22) b, 23) d, 24) b, 25) a, 26) a, 27) c, 28) a, 29) d, 30) a, 31) b, 32) c, 33) b, 34) d, 35) e

Chapter 7: The Accounting Center

The hallmark of QBO that gives it such great return on investment is its **Accounting Center**. You'll save several hours of clerical work a week by using the Bank Transactions feeds, Rules, Receipts, Integration Transactions, and Recurring Transactions.

The Bank Transactions Feed

The **Bank Transactions feed** connects to the bank websites for your checking accounts, savings accounts, and credit cards. It becomes a central hub to see what transactions have cleared the bank that day.

By using it as your focal point, you'll know what work you need to do in your QuickBooks Online to stay up to date.

Any transactions you see here need to be either Matched to existing transactions, or Posted to your books. Your goal is to see zero transactions under each card.

This marvelous automation feature is found under **Transactions** in the Accounting section of My Apps. Finish each day here, as part of the **"Quick" in QuickBooks** on page 6.

While you do need to train it to import accurately, the Bank Transactions feed automates the time-consuming task of manually entering every single debit card and credit card charge.

It also helps you discover transactions you missed, or ones you created that never hit the bank.

Best practices for managing the Bank Transactions feed are covered in the sections below. Most important is knowing which transactions you can just enter using the feed, and which ones you still need to create using the QBO features throughout this book.

Setting up the Bank Transactions Feed

Banking works in one of two ways:

- *Direct Connect.* A direct connection to your bank or credit card company automatically pulls in all that day's transactions for your approval. It works with most bank accounts for free.
- *Web Connect.* Go to your bank's website and download the month's transactions, then import them into QuickBooks Online. This works just fine when your bank doesn't have a native integration, but is more labor-intensive.

To get set up, click on the **Link Account** button, then choose your bank. Log in with your bank's username and password. Map your business bank accounts to your accounts in QBO. Do not add your personal accounts.

Choose how far back you would like to import. If you're converting an existing file, you may just need the last month. If you're starting a new file, you may import a year or more.

If you need to go back further, go to your bank's website and download a .qbo or .csv export of the missing transactions. Use the drop-down arrow on the **Link Account** button and select **Upload From File**.

Repeat this step for all your business bank accounts and credit cards.

When connecting for the first time, the bank integration will create an already-reconciled Opening Balance Equity entry. This is helpful if you're starting from scratch, but most of the time it needs to be edited or deleted. Find it in the **Bank Register** (see page 51) to adjust it or remove it.

Companion Course
SCAN ME
royl.ws/bootcamp

Want to learn more?

Deep Dive
SCAN ME
royl.ws/bank-transactions

Clearing Out the Bank Transactions Feed

How the Artificial Intelligence Works

There's a 6-step process behind the scenes that determines how QBO's **Accounting Agent** categorizes transactions in the Bank Transactions Center:

1) Is there already an existing match for an unreconciled transaction for that dollar amount? Suggest it as a Match.
2) Is there an open invoice or bill for that dollar amount? Suggest this transaction to pay it.
3) Does it meet the criterion in any of your Rules? Apply the Rule.
4) Did you code a similar transaction in the past? Repeat it now.
5) Has any other company categorized a similar Bank Detail? The AI suggests out of its database.
6) If none of these steps trigger, the transaction is left as Uncategorized.

The Artificial Intelligence (AI) learns as you go, and will automatically suggest payees and categories for you. But you should never fully trust the automatic data.

The problem is that some banks only have generic bank descriptions. It will repeat the most recent Payee and Category throughout your Bank Transactions Feed, even if it's wrong.

Don't get fooled! Don't get confused. Don't get mad, either.
YOU are in control.
Just click on the transaction and change it to what it's supposed to be.

Finding Matches

QBO first looks for matching *unreconciled* transactions within a reasonable date range. Once a transaction has already been reconciled, it's no longer a candidate.

Since it's scanning for dollar amounts, it will even try to match to open Invoices and Bills!

1. Any transactions clearing the bank that you have already entered manually into your QBO will be ready to **MATCH**. This green **MATCH** is your holy grail, verifying you processed your transactions correctly.

2. If it finds more than one potential match, you'll see **# | Suggested Matches Found**. Click on the row and choose the proper matching transaction. Compare the dates and the Full Bank Description to decide which transaction is correct.

3. If you're 100% sure the transaction already exists, use the **Match** button to pull up a list of entries that have not yet been paired to the feed. If you had created two payments but they came through the bank as one, this Match tool allows you to combine them.

4. For transactions that don't match at all, you can edit and Post them or create them manually, depending on what type of entry it is. Use the instructions throughout this book to manually create these income and expense transactions, then Match them.

> *PEBCAK!* Transactions that have to do with customers, including **Deposits** and purchases of items from the Products and Services list, ***cannot simply be pulled in***. You have to create those invoices and purchases manually, and then Match them in the Bank Transactions feed.

Simple Expenses

Transactions for overhead expenses can usually be Posted through this Transactions interface. Here's how:

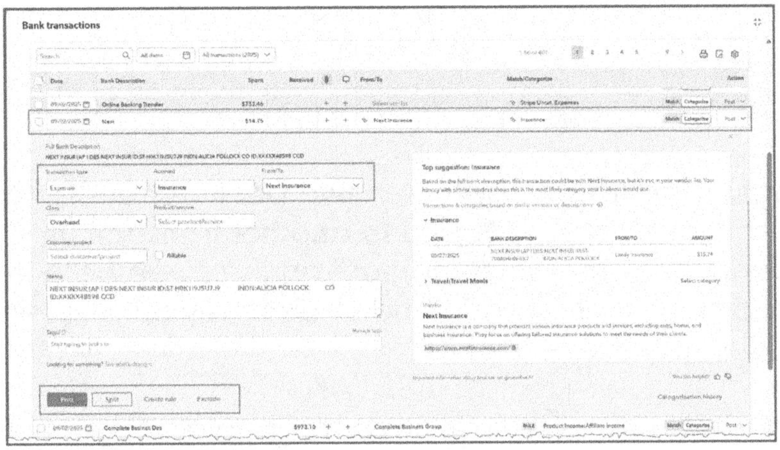

Click on one to edit it.

If it's a vendor who you'll use often, enter them in the **From/To** box. Don't skip this field! If you don't enter a Vendor name, the only way you'll find this transaction later is by drilling in through a report. It won't show anywhere in the Vendors Center.

The **Bank Description** shows you what the bank sees. When you click on the transaction, you can see the Full Bank Description with the exact detail from your bank's statement or website. This information stays with the transaction at all times for easy identification. Because you always have this data at your fingertips, you can create your own Vendor names.

If it's a one-off expense or a payee you don't want to accumulate in your Vendors list (like restaurants or gas stations), have two choices:

1. Create generic vendors like "Restaurant" or "Gas Station" that you can use for all similar suppliers (see Generic Vendor names on page 124 to make sure this is appropriate!).
2. Create a "Miscellaneous" vendor for one-off purchases

Next, enter the transaction's **Account**. Be sure to choose the right one, and be very sure not to leave it as **Uncategorized**! When done, select **Post**.

Product & Service Purchases

If you are buying a product that is on your **Products and Services** list (see page 56), don't just assign an Expense or COGS account inside the Bank Transactions feed. Use the **Product/Service** field instead of the **Account** field.

Transfers

If the transaction is a transfer between two bank accounts, QBO will display a green box that says **Paired to another transaction**. This indicates that QBO found the same dollar amount on the same date in two different accounts, one money in and one money out. Accepting either one will handle both in one click!

For other **Transfers** between bank accounts that don't auto-match, change the **Transaction Type** to *Transfer*. Once you categorize a Transfer on one side, it will Match the Bank Transactions feed on the other side. Be careful not to create two transactions, one money in and another money out. You can, of course, create a Transfer manually by following the instructions on page 177, then Match both sides.

Deposits

When you come to a **Deposit**, ***do not*** just "Add" it here, because it will skip all QBO's sales tracking features. **Deposits** must **MATCH** existing transactions with a green box, or you'll double your income!

When you see a Deposit on this list, that's your signal to go to **+Create > Bank Deposit** to gather the corresponding individual payments and sales receipts into a matching Bank Deposit (see page 94). As soon as you're done, QBO notices the new batched dollar amount and **Matches** the transaction. If you are tracking sales data in your POS or e-Commerce website, it may be OK to pull Deposits straight in using Post.

If you Post deposits instead of Matching them to existing Sales Receipts and Invoice Payments, you will DOUBLE your income on your P&L!

Companion Course
SCAN ME
royl.ws/bootcamp

Want to learn more?

Deep Dive
SCAN ME
royl.ws/bank-transactions

Bank Rules

Every time you process a new type of transaction, QBO learns from your history, so the next time it sees that same Bank Detail, it will update this entry automatically.

Instead of relying on QBO's artificial intelligence, use the **Rules** tab in the menu at the top of the screen. Here you can create your own Rules to categorize transactions. This feature is extremely powerful. You can specify criteria by bank account, bank detail, and amount. Assign your own Payee, Category, Class, and more.

My favorite part is at the very bottom. For routine expenses, turn on **Automatically confirm transactions this rule applies to**. QBO will skip the Bank Transactions feed and add the transaction straight to the register. No work for you at all!

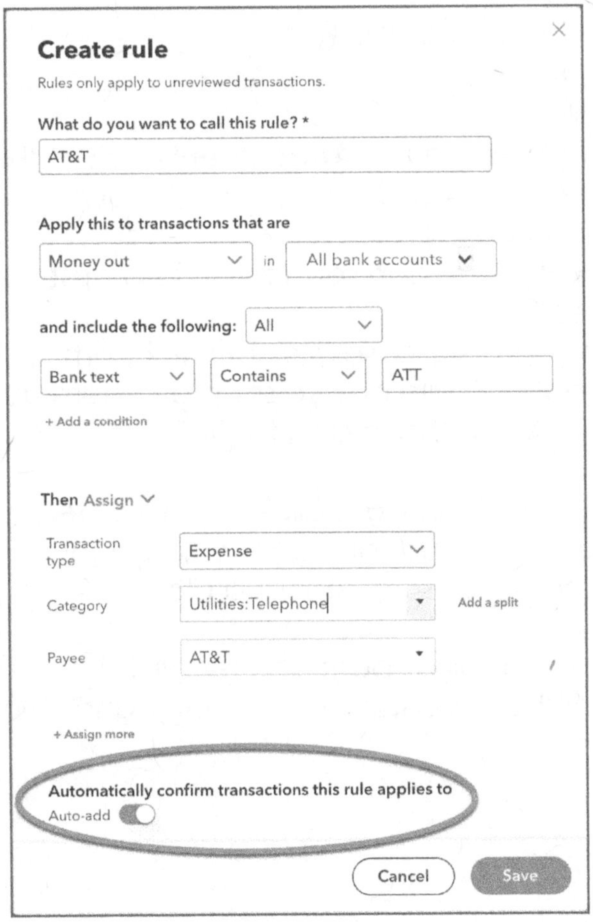

Receipts

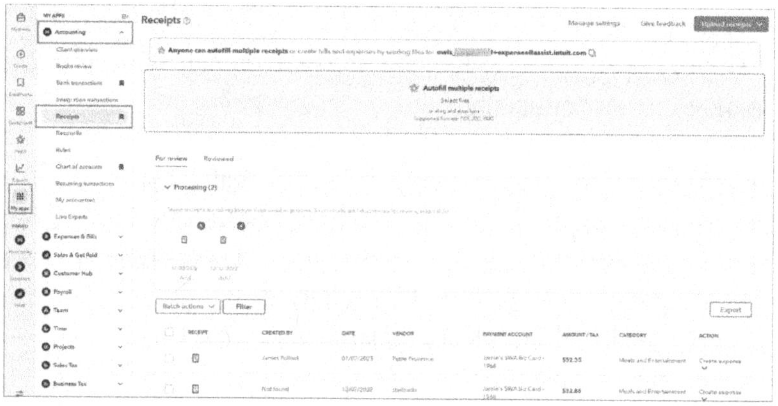

QBO makes it easy to import jpgs and PDFs of your receipts and attach them to your transactions. It works with the Bank Transactions feed as a 2-way street – no matter where you initially create the transaction, the other will find it and match the banking detail and the attachment.

There are several ways to import receipts:

- Visit the **Receipts** tab in the Bank Transactions center and drag them into the left box
- Upload them from **Google Drive**
- Drag-and-drop them into the **Intuit Assist** pane on the left of invoices and bills
- Drag-and-drop them into the **Attachments** box at the bottom of every form (or click on the paper clip and browse to where they're saved on your computer)
- Any registered QBO user can send them to a customized email address you create (yourcompanyname+expenses@assist.intuit.com)
- Use the QuickBooks mobile app to snap a picture using your phone, which instantly uploads the image to QBO

After you import each receipt image, click on it to categorize it. The date and amount usually autofill, although you should double-check these. Add the payment account, description, and class.

If QBO can find a match, it will append the receipt to the existing transaction. If you add the transaction, the Bank Transactions feed will match it when it clears.

Integration Transactions

Look in the **Integration Transactions** tab in the Accounting center for integrations with other websites and payment processors.

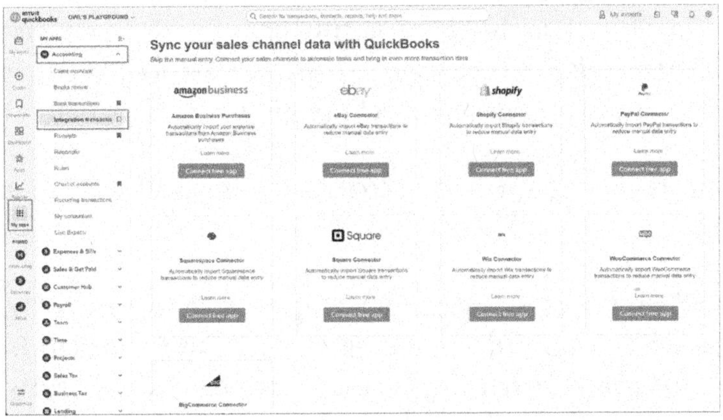

As of this writing, there are integrations with **Amazon for Business, PayPal,** and **Square. QBO Commerce** connections with Amazon Seller accounts, Shopify, Squarespace, eBay, Wix, WooCommerce, and BigCommerce are also accessed through this screen.

Amazon for Business displays your purchase details so you can see what you bought and which payment method you used, without logging into amazon.com in a separate window. You can enter new expenses right from here and match them to the Bank Transactions feed when they clear.

Some of the connections import individual sales with or without customer names. Some will map to Products and Services while others don't. Some only import daily sales summaries.

You will need to experiment with each one to see if it works for you.

If it doesn't suit your needs, there are alternatives from other third-party app developers under the Integrations button in the upper right of your screen.

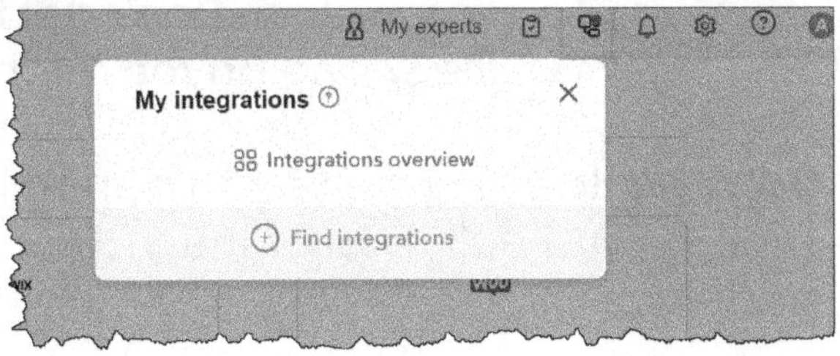

Troubleshooting the Banking Feed

Overstated Income: If your reports show that your income is WAY higher than it's supposed to be, it's probably because you have been clicking **Post** next to the deposits in your feed, instead of Matching them to existing customer Payments (see page 86) and Sales Receipts (see page 83) waiting in Undeposited Funds / Payments to Deposit.

Another red flag is a long list of old transactions in the **+Create > Bank Deposit** screen.

An easy way to find these duplicated Deposits is to run a Profit & Loss Statement, then drill down into the dollar amount for each Income category. Look for the transaction type "Deposit." That shows the money was categorized directly to the income account instead matched to existing transactions.

To fix a duplicated Deposit, click on it to **Edit.** Check off the transactions in the top half of the window that should have made up that total. Then click the **Trash Can** at the far right of the lower section with the accidental entry to remove it.

The total Deposit remains the same, so it's fine to do this even if the transaction has already been reconciled.

Incorrect Payee: A huge, inconvenient issue that you may come across is that some banks use generic bank descriptions like "Check." This causes Banking to autofill the From/To and Account with the most recent previous transaction. **Don't get fooled when you see an expense with the wrong payee**, or the wrong category assigned.

Don't panic! It's up to you to determine if these are correct or not. As you click on and edit most of the transactions you'll develop a feel for the patterns.

Companion Course — SCAN ME — royl.ws/bootcamp

Want to learn more?

Deep Dive — SCAN ME — royl.ws/bank-transactions

One Vendor, two types of Expenses: Sometimes one vendor might have two different types of transactions. For example, Intuit is my vendor for the subscription to my QBO account. Intuit is also the vendor for my Merchant Services Fees account. I must keep an eye on each transaction to be sure it gets filed appropriately.

This is where the custom **Bank Rules** come into play. I created two Rules, based on the Bank Text AND the amount of the transaction.

In each Rule, select **"All" of these conditions** so that both the Bank Text and the dollar amount are taken into consideration.

Intuit transactions under $15 are categorized as Merchant Services. Intuit transactions over $15 are Software.

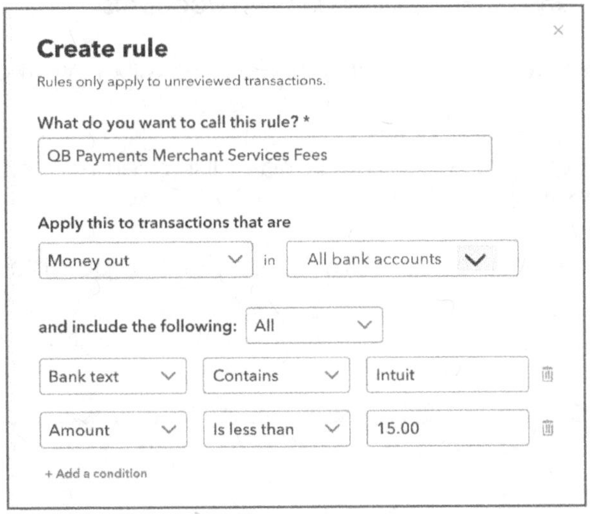

HOOT TIP

My Best Bank Transactions Feed Advice:

1. **Manually create transactions that involve Customers and/or Product & Services.** Enter your income using Sales Receipts and Invoice/Receive Payments. Be sure the Deposit To: field says Undeposited Funds / Payments to Deposit. Also, manually enter expense transactions for product purchases.
2. **Match all Income**: Use Bank Deposit to combine individual payments into lump sums that match the money going into the bank.
3. **Use Transfers**: Any time money is moving between bank accounts, use Transfer so that one transaction appears in both accounts.
4. **Use Pay Down Credit Card**: Using this feature will prevent a lot of data entry mistakes.
5. **Pull in other Expenses:** Go ahead and pull in overhead expenses, unless you need to attribute them as above.
6. **Create Rules:** Automate as many transactions as possible to reduce your data entry time.

Reconciliations

At the end of every month, your bank generates statements and either sends them to you through snail mail, or you can download them from the bank's website. You may also see a link in QBO's Reconciliation window allowing you to download them from inside the interface.

Reconcile is the feature in QuickBooks Online that allows you to match your transactions to the ones the bank has. Every month you'll reconcile your checking and savings accounts, credit cards, PayPal, Venmo, and loans.

Reconciling is a necessary process because it's your opportunity to double-check your accuracy. You'll discover transactions entered twice. You'll find transactions that you entered but that never happened in the real world. And sometimes you find money the bank took out of your account that you never knew about.

To reconcile your QuickBooks Online records against your bank statements,

Select **Settings** > **Reconcile**, or **My Apps > Accounting > Reconcile** in the left sidebar.

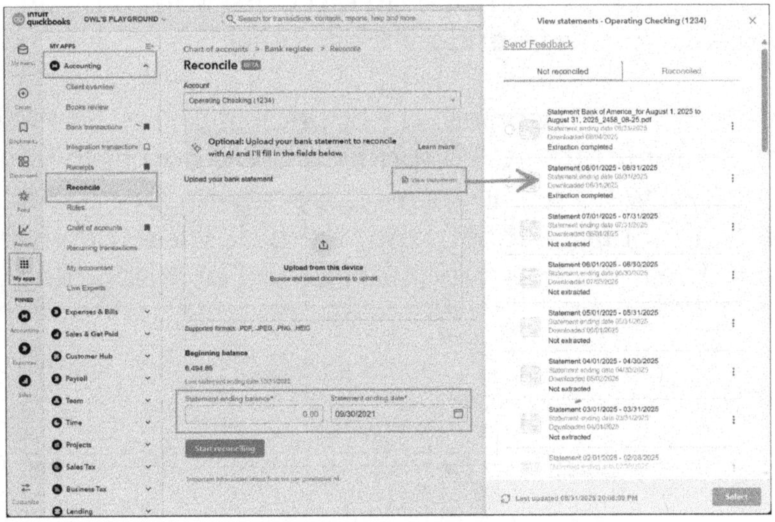

Select the **Account** from the drop-down list.

The **Beginning balance** automatically populates with last month's Ending Balance. It does this by adding up all the previously-reconciled transactions.

Some banks allow you to **View Statements** just by clicking the link. Not only will this open the statement for easy viewing, it will also populate the **Statement Ending Balance** and **Statement Ending Date** for you.

If your bank doesn't allow statement import, these fields won't autofill. Instead, download your statement from your bank and enter this information manually.

When reconciling credit cards, be sure not to enter the credit card's Payment Due date instead of the statement date!

PEBCAK!

If your **Beginning Balance** is wrong, it means you changed a transaction that was previously reconciled.

Don't panic! You do NOT need to unreconciled the previous month. That will make much more work for you!

Try repeating the previous month's reconciliation by re-entering last month's balance and ending date, and see if the problem fixes itself. Look for an extra transaction with an old date from a past period. Check it off, and your **Difference** will equal $0!

If that doesn't work, you can run a Reconciliation report that will show you changes. Even better, QBO suggests a **We can help you fix it** link to see changes that were made to your already-reconciled transactions. Keep an eye out for transactions that were deleted, or where you clicked the **R** status inside the register instead of reconciling properly.

Reconciling in Classic Mode

Select the green **Start reconciling** button, and the **Reconcile** window opens.

Companion Course SCAN ME *royl.ws/bootcamp*

Want to learn more?

Deep Dive SCAN ME *royl.ws/Reconciling-In-QBO*

If you have been using the Bank Transactions feed, sometimes it only takes a few seconds to reconcile the bank account. That's one of the reasons we love the Bank Transactions feed so much! In the old days, reconciling sometimes used to take hours.

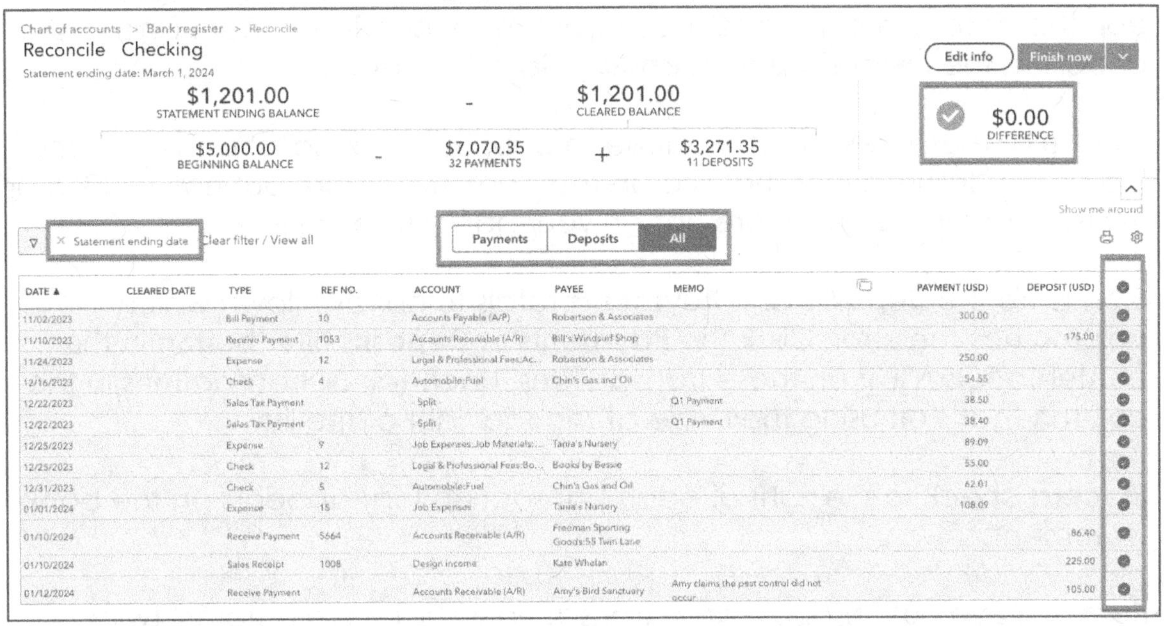

Your goal is to make the **Difference** at the very top right equal $0.

If the Difference is not $0, first double-check the **Statement ending date** and **Statement ending balance** to make sure you don't have a typo. If you made a mistake, click the **Edit info** button and fix it.

If that doesn't work, compare the **Deposits total** and the **Payments total** to your statement to determine which column is off.

Note that you can sort the transaction list by **Payment** amount and **Reference number** as well as date. Just click on the heading! Changing it to **Payment** amount makes it easy to scan the list for a particular dollar amount, and to look for duplicates. I frequently switch back and forth between sorts to speed up my matching process.

The next step in fixing the reconciliation is to look for a transaction or two that equals the Difference. If there is one, check or uncheck the circle, and you're done! I usually look at the transactions on the same day as the statement date – sometimes they aren't included until the following month.

The third troubleshooting step is to see if a missing transaction dated in the following month. Click the **X Statement ending date** link. All the rest of the transactions after the ending date will show up. Look to see if there's a transaction on this list dated the following month that really should have been in the current date range. If there is, click on the transaction and edit the date to move it into the current reconciliation screen. Finish by checking the **Reset statement ending date** link again.

If none of these steps work, it's time to pour through the list one at a time, looking for transactions that are on the bank statement but not in QBO, or transactions in QBO that are not on your bank statement.

Compare the **Deposits** and **Payments** totals to narrow down which column has the error. Click the **Payments** or **Deposits filter button** in the center to focus just on those transactions. Uncheck all transactions in the column that's off using the circle at the top right of the list.

Place a check to the right of each transaction that appears on the bank statement.

Keep an eye out for duplicated transactions that were entered twice, and delete one of them. Note that the transaction may reappear in the Bank Transactions feed, so you'll need to Match it properly or Exclude it.

Are there transactions on the statement that aren't in QBO? Sometimes that happens. Create the missing entry.

Do you have extra transactions that aren't on the statement?

1. If they're near the statement ending date, they may just not have cleared yet. You'll see them next month.
2. If they're checks that the payee hasn't cashed yet, that's fine, too. If they're more than 90 days old, though, you may want to reach out to the payee!
3. If they are duplicates of another transaction, decide which is correct, and delete the error.
4. If they just don't match anything, research them. Old transactions that aren't reconciled throw off your bank balance, your reports, and your taxes. Eventually you need them gone.

When all the transactions on the bank statement are checked and the **Difference** at the top right is $0.00, select **Finish now.**

When you finish a reconciliation, QBO will ask you if you want to view the Reconciliation Report.

You can find this report in the Reconcile Center's **History by Account** link, and in **Reports > For My Accountant > Reconciliation Reports**.

Craig's Design and Landscaping Services

Checking, Period Ending 09/23/2021

RECONCILIATION REPORT

Reconciled on: 09/23/2021

Reconciled by: Craig Carlson

Any changes made to transactions after this date aren't included in this report.

Summary	USD
Statement beginning balance	5,000.00
Checks and payments cleared (32)	-7,070.35
Deposits and other credits cleared (11)	3,271.35
Statement ending balance	1,201.00
Register balance as of 09/23/2021	1,201.00

Details

Checks and payments cleared (32)

DATE	TYPE	REF NO.	PAYEE	AMOUNT (USD)
05/26/2021	Bill Payment	10	Robertson & Associates	-300.00
06/17/2021	Expense	12	Robertson & Associates	-250.00
07/09/2021	Check	4	Chin's Gas and Oil	-54.55
07/15/2021	Sales Tax Payment			-38.50
07/15/2021	Sales Tax Payment			-38.40
07/18/2021	Expense	9	Tania's Nursery	-89.09
07/18/2021	Check	12	Books by Bessie	-55.00
07/24/2021	Check	5	Chin's Gas and Oil	-62.01
07/25/2021	Expense	15	Tania's Nursery	-108.09
08/07/2021	Bill Payment	7	Hicks Hardware	-250.00

Reconciling in the Modern Interface

If available, try the option to upload your statement. This new reconciliation process uses AI to highlight differences between your statement and your register. Note that this workflow is still in Beta and may look different in your file.

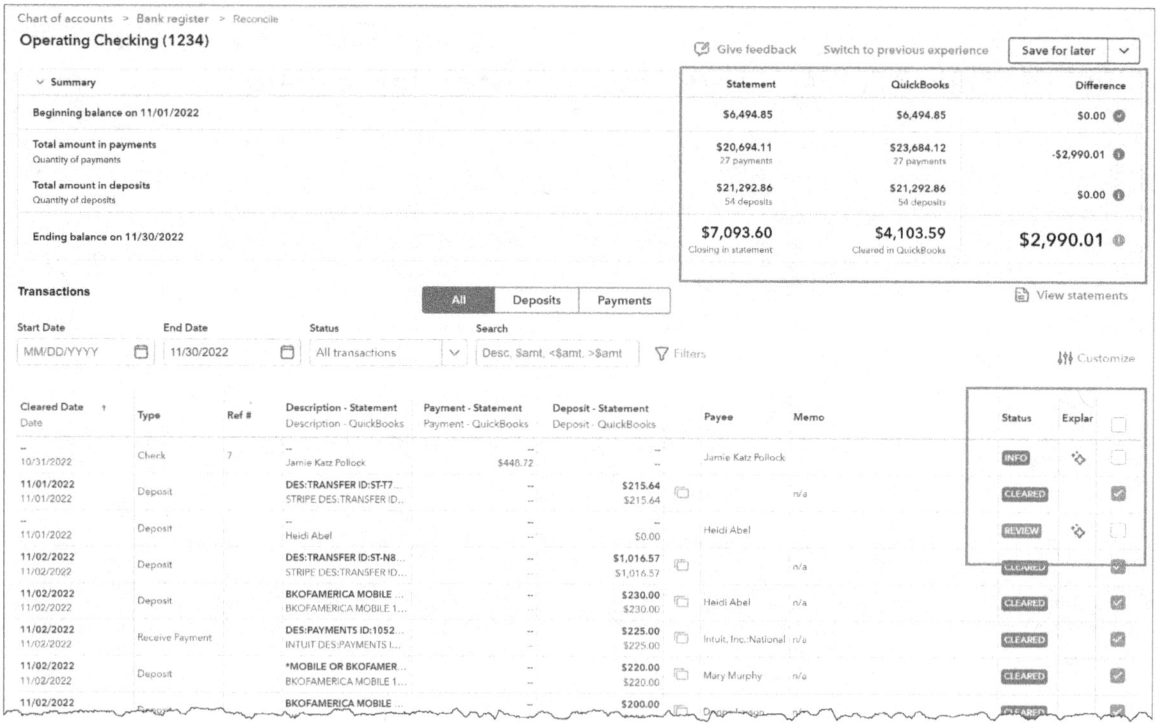

The **Summary** at the top tells you exactly where you're off.

Each row contains info both from your QuickBooks register AND from your statement so you can compare dates, descriptions, and dollar amounts.

The **Status** column calls your attention to transactions that don't match the statement, and the AI attempts to explain why.

Companion Course
SCAN ME
royl.ws/bootcamp

Want to learn more?

Deep Dive
SCAN ME
royl.ws/Reconciling-In-QBO

Check Your Understanding: The Accounting Center

Bank Transactions

1) _______It's OK to automatically pull in which of these transactions using the Bank Transactions feed?
   a. Straightforward expenses
   b. Checks
   c. Deposits
   d. Loan payments
   e. Transactions that must be connected to Customer jobs

2) _______The guidelines QBO uses to automatically classify transactions in your Transactions feed are called:
   a. Matching
   b. Transfers
   c. Rules
   d. Recognized

3) _______When transactions show the wrong Payee,
   a. Panic
   b. Change them manually
   c. It's because a previous Bank Detail was the same, and QBO is trying to help
   d. B & C

4) _______Deposits can't be pulled in automatically because:
   a. They have to match your grouped sales transactions
   b. You need Invoices and Sales Receipts to attach to customers
   c. You will duplicate your income
   d. All of the above

5) _______If you're having trouble figuring out your Transactions feed, you should:
   a. Watch our QBO Banking Course at http://royl.ws/bank-transactions
   b. Call Alicia at 503-406-6550
   c. Call QBO Live Experts
   d. Ask your accountant or bookkeeper
   e. Any of the above

Answers:
1) a, 2) c, 3) d, 4) d, 5) e

Reconciling

1) ________ Reconciling your bank accounts:
   a. Uses the Bank Transactions feed to pull in your transactions, so you know everything you did was right
   b. Verifies that you have the same transactions the bank has
   c. Only needs to be done a few times a year
   d. Can be done by changing the **R** status in the register

2) ________ Your Statement Ending Date is:
   a. The date your payment is due
   b. The last date in the date range of the statement
   c. Sometimes hard to find on a statement
   d. B & C

3) ________ If your Beginning Balance doesn't match last month's ending balance, the first step is to:
   a. Use QBO's We Can Help You Fix It tool
   b. Run a Reconciliation Change report and look for the changes
   c. Repeat last month's reconciliation and see if a stray transaction shows up that makes up for the difference
   d. Any of the above

4) ________ The very first step when reconciling is to:
   a. Double-check your date and ending balance to make sure you don't have a typo
   b. Check all the boxes and see if the difference is $0
   c. Get a cup of coffee – it's going to be a long afternoon
   d. Print out your statement so you have it on paper

5) ________ If your Difference is not $0, the first place to look to find the problem is:
   a. Look for a transaction for that amount
   b. The totals for Payments & Deposits to see which column has the issue
   c. Your bank's website
   d. Both A & B

6) ________ Choose the option that does not help you find the discrepancies:
   a. Sort the columns descending to ascending
   b. Refer to your bank statement
   c. Undo the previous reconciliation
   d. Sort by check number
   e. Sort by dollar amount
   f. Disconnect and reconnect the Bank Transactions feed
   g. Uncheck the "Hide transactions after the statement's date" box
   h. C & F

Chapter 8: Reports

This is where all your hard work setting up and using QuickBooks Online pays off. QBO's **Reports** allow you to interpret your data and glean all sorts of valuable insights.

What you get out of the **Reports** depends on what you put in. On one end of the spectrum is using QBO as a glorified checkbook: fast, simple data entry that gives you basic reports. On the other end of the spectrum, QBO is able to offer you detailed analysis like job costing and item profitability, if you take the time to enter more detail on each transaction.

You'll find your own happy medium that provides the level of analysis you want, considering the time you have available to do the work.

Each version of QuickBooks Online offers different reports. The QuickBooks Lite version has 20 reports, while the Plus version has over 100. Advanced has its own custom Performance Center with charts. Your accountant also has access to several additional financial reports.

Take a few minutes and look at all the reports in the **Report Center**. You'll find ways of exploring your data that you've probably never considered.

All reports can be customized and memorized so that you can slice and dice your data into useful information.

> The best way to learn about QuickBooks Online reports is visually. Please refer to our ***Running Reports to Analyze Growth*** video at http://royl.ws/Reports to see demonstrations of useful reports, and how to modify and customize them.

Profit and Loss Report

The **Profit and Loss Report (P&L)** details your sales and costs, showing you how much profit (or loss) you've made. It's discussed in detail on page 43.

Run this report monthly, quarterly, and annually. Customize it to include a Previous Year column to compare how you did last year!

Keep an eye out for the little Sparkle icons. These are QBO's Accounting Agent AI alerting you that something's unusual about one of the totals.

Click on the icon for insights into anomalies. Is it a data entry error? Is it a new trend in your company's activity?

Profit and Loss

Craig's Design and Landscaping Services

January 1-September 6, 2025

Account	Total
Income	
Design income	2,250.00
Discounts given	-89.50
Landscaping Services	**$1,477.50**
Job Materials	
Fountains and Garden Lighting	2,246.50
Plants and Soil	2,351.97
Sprinklers and Drip Systems	138.00
Total for Job Materials	**$4,736.47**
Labor	
Installation	250.00
Maintenance and Repair	50.00
Total for Labor	**$300.00**
Total for Landscaping Services	**$6,513.97**
Pest Control Services	110.00
Sales of Product Income	912.75
Services	503.55
Total for Income	**$10,200.77**
Cost of Goods Sold	
Cost of Goods Sold	405.00
Total for Cost of Goods Sold	**$405.00**
Gross Profit	**$9,795.77**
Expenses	
Advertising	74.86
Automobile	**$113.96**
Fuel	349.41
Total for Automobile	**$463.37**
Equipment Rental	112.00
Insurance	241.23
Job Expenses	[illegible]
Plants and Soil	353.12
Sprinklers and Drip Systems	215.66
Total for Job Materials	**$802.82**
Total for Job Expenses	**$957.89**
Legal & Professional Fees	**$75.00**
Accounting	640.00
Bookkeeper	55.00
Lawyer	400.00
Total for Legal & Professional Fees	**$1,170.00**
Maintenance and Repair	**$185.00**
Equipment Repairs	755.00
Total for Maintenance and Repair	**$940.00**
Meals and Entertainment	28.49
Office Expenses	18.08
Rent or Lease	900.00
Utilities	
Gas and Electric	200.53
Telephone	130.86
Total for Utilities	**$331.39**
Total for Expenses	**$5,237.31**
Net Operating Income	**$4,558.46**
Other Income	–
Other Expenses	
Miscellaneous	2,916.00
Total for Other Expenses	**$2,916.00**
Net Other Income	**-$2,916.00**
Net Income	**$1,642.46**

The Balance Sheet

A **Balance Sheet Report** shows you all the accounts that deal with your financing. It's discussed in detail on page 43.

Keep an eye out for the little Sparkle icons. These are QBO's Accounting Agent AI alerting you that something's unusual about one of the totals.

Click on the icon for insights into anomalies. Is it a data entry error? Is it a new trend in your company's activity?

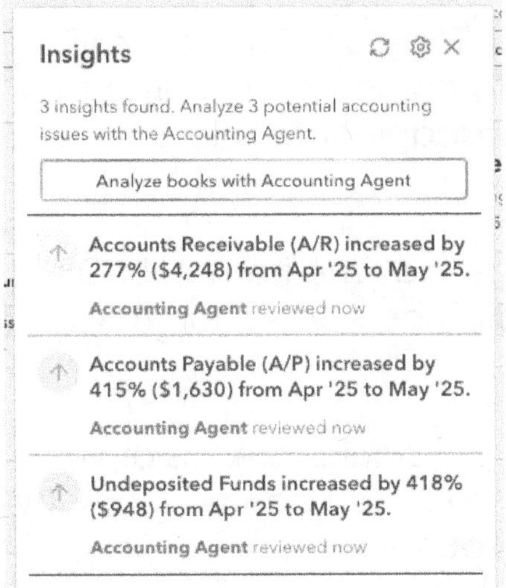

Balance Sheet
Craig's Design and Landscaping Services
As of September 6, 2025

Account	Total
Assets	
Current Assets	
Bank Accounts	
Checking	1,201.00
Savings	800.00
Total for Bank Accounts	$2,001.00
Accounts Receivable	
Accounts Receivable (A/R)	5,281.52
Total for Accounts Receivable	$5,281.52
Other Current Assets	
Inventory Asset	596.25
Undeposited Funds	2,062.52
Total for Other Current Assets	$2,658.77
Total for Current Assets	$9,941.29
Fixed Assets	
Truck	
Total for Truck	[illegible]
Total for Fixed Assets	$13,495.00
Other Assets	–
Total for Assets	$23,436.29
Liabilities and Equity	
Liabilities	
Current Liabilities	
Accounts Payable	
Accounts Payable (A/P)	1,602.67
Total for Accounts Payable	$1,602.67
Credit Cards	
Mastercard	157.72
Total for Credit Cards	$157.72
Other Current Liabilities	
Arizona Dept. of Revenue Payable	–
Board of Equalization Payable	370.94
Loan Payable	4,000.00
Total for Other Current Liabilities	$4,370.94
Total for Current Liabilities	$6,131.33
Long-term Liabilities	
Notes Payable	25,000.00
Total for Long-term Liabilities	$25,000.00
Total for Liabilities	$31,131.33
Equity	
Opening Balance Equity	-9,337.50
Retained Earnings	–
Net Income	1,642.46
Total for Equity	-$7,695.04
Total for Liabilities and Equity	$23,436.29

The Dashboard and Performance Center

All versions of QuickBooks Online feature the **Dashboard** as your landing page.

If you're using **QBO Advanced**, you also have a Performance Center with additional customizations and benchmarks.

The Business Feed at the top calls your attention to overdue invoices and other trends affecting your cashflow. Use these suggestions to get paid faster.

You can see at-a-glance your biggest financial benchmarks. Everything is interactive – click on it to open the associated report.

Use the **Customize** button to rearrange and resize the tiles.

There's a great year-over year **Cash Flow Trend**. Toggle between Cash Balance and the Money In/Out column chart to compare the current period with last year (note that this Craig's Landscaping sample file doesn't have any data from the previous year).

Most charts have a drop-down arrow to change the time frames. In QBO Advanced's **Performance Center**, you can customize each chart to add and eliminate some accounts if needed.

At the bottom of the screen in accrual-based companies are lists of your open Accounts Payable and Accounts Receivable. You can click on any Customer or Vendor to jump to their open transactions.

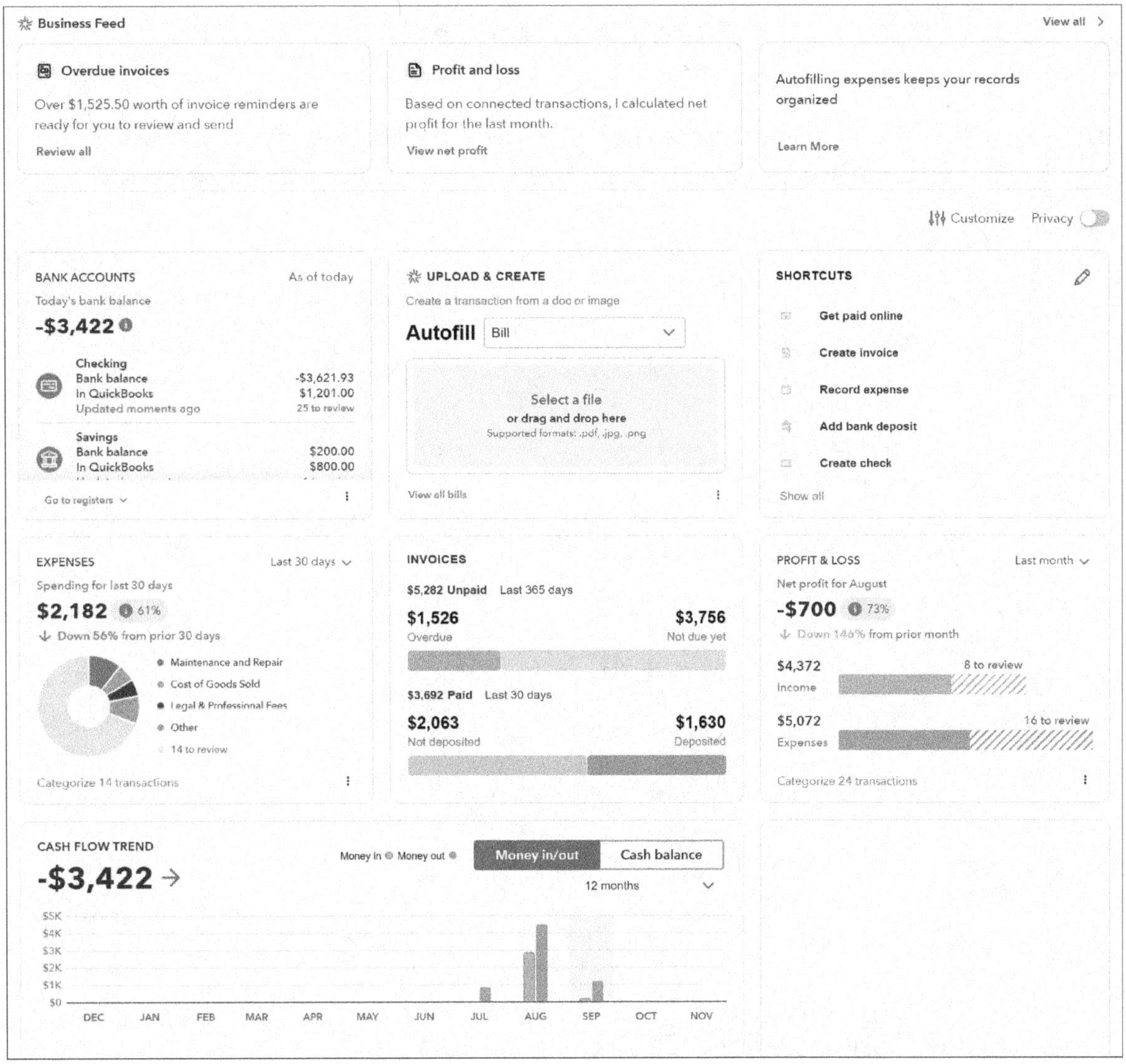
Business Feed
View all
Overdue invoices
Over $1,525.50 worth of invoice reminders are ready for you to review and send
Review all
Profit and loss
Based on connected transactions, I calculated net profit for the last month.
View net profit
Autofilling expenses keeps your records organized
Learn More
Customize
Privacy
BANK ACCOUNTS
As of today
Today's bank balance
-$3,422
Checking
Bank balance -$3,621.93
In QuickBooks $1,201.00
Updated moments ago
25 to review
Savings
Bank balance $200.00
In QuickBooks $800.00
Go to registers
UPLOAD & CREATE
Create a transaction from a doc or image
Autofill
Bill
Select a file
or drag and drop here
Supported formats: .pdf, .jpg, .png
View all bills
SHORTCUTS
Get paid online
Create invoice
Record expense
Add bank deposit
Create check
Show all
EXPENSES
Last 30 days
Spending for last 30 days
$2,182
61%
Down 56% from prior 30 days
Maintenance and Repair
Cost of Goods Sold
Legal & Professional Fees
Other
14 to review
Categorize 14 transactions
INVOICES
$5,282 Unpaid Last 365 days
$1,526
Overdue
$3,756
Not due yet
$3,692 Paid Last 30 days
$2,063
Not deposited
$1,630
Deposited
PROFIT & LOSS
Last month
Net profit for August
-$700
73%
Down 146% from prior month
$4,372
Income
8 to review
$5,072
Expenses
16 to review
Categorize 24 transactions
CASH FLOW TREND
-$3,422
Money in
Money out
Money in/out
Cash balance
12 months
$5K
$4K
$3K
$2K
$1K
$0
DEC
JAN
FEB
MAR
APR
MAY
JUN
JUL
AUG
SEP
OCT
NOV

Modern Reports

Intuit is in the process of modernizing its reports engine. Some reports, especially list and summary reports, use the new **Modern Experience**.

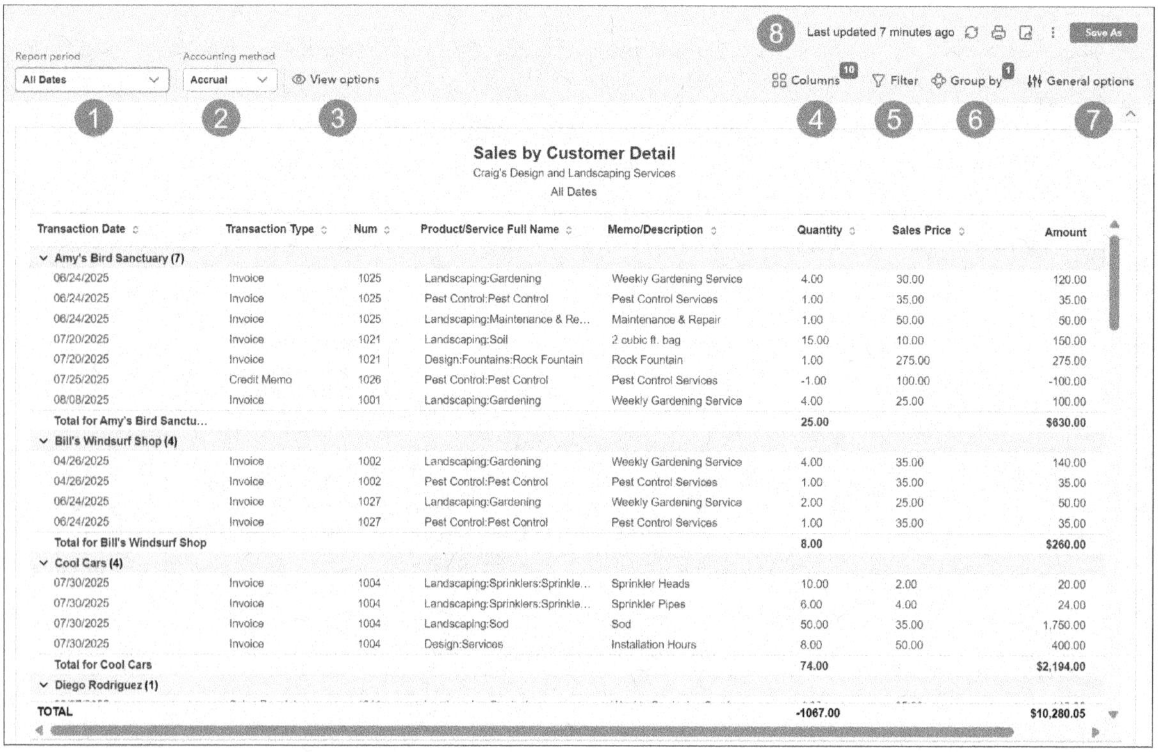

Sales by Customer Detail
Craig's Design and Landscaping Services
All Dates

Transaction Date	Transaction Type	Num	Product/Service Full Name	Memo/Description	Quantity	Sales Price	Amount
Amy's Bird Sanctuary (7)							
06/24/2025	Invoice	1025	Landscaping:Gardening	Weekly Gardening Service	4.00	30.00	120.00
06/24/2025	Invoice	1025	Pest Control:Pest Control	Pest Control Services	1.00	35.00	35.00
06/24/2025	Invoice	1025	Landscaping:Maintenance & Re...	Maintenance & Repair	1.00	50.00	50.00
07/20/2025	Invoice	1021	Landscaping:Soil	2 cubic ft. bag	15.00	10.00	150.00
07/20/2025	Invoice	1021	Design:Fountains:Rock Fountain	Rock Fountain	1.00	275.00	275.00
07/25/2025	Credit Memo	1026	Pest Control:Pest Control	Pest Control Services	-1.00	100.00	-100.00
08/08/2025	Invoice	1001	Landscaping:Gardening	Weekly Gardening Service	4.00	25.00	100.00
Total for Amy's Bird Sanctu...					25.00		$630.00
Bill's Windsurf Shop (4)							
04/26/2025	Invoice	1002	Landscaping:Gardening	Weekly Gardening Service	4.00	35.00	140.00
04/26/2025	Invoice	1002	Pest Control:Pest Control	Pest Control Services	1.00	35.00	35.00
06/24/2025	Invoice	1027	Landscaping:Gardening	Weekly Gardening Service	2.00	25.00	50.00
06/24/2025	Invoice	1027	Pest Control:Pest Control	Pest Control Services	1.00	35.00	35.00
Total for Bill's Windsurf Shop					8.00		$260.00
Cool Cars (4)							
07/30/2025	Invoice	1004	Landscaping:Sprinklers:Sprinkle...	Sprinkler Heads	10.00	2.00	20.00
07/30/2025	Invoice	1004	Landscaping:Sprinklers:Sprinkle...	Sprinkler Pipes	6.00	4.00	24.00
07/30/2025	Invoice	1004	Landscaping:Sod	Sod	50.00	35.00	1,750.00
07/30/2025	Invoice	1004	Design:Services	Installation Hours	8.00	50.00	400.00
Total for Cool Cars					74.00		$2,194.00
Diego Rodriguez (1)							
TOTAL					-1067.00		$10,280.05

1. Date range selector
2. Toggle basis between Cash and Accrual
3. Expand and collapse columns, and control spacing
4. Hide, show, and reorder columns
5. Filter data to only show what you want to see
6. Group data by the field of your choice
7. Change display options
8. Refresh, print, export, share, and Save As a custom report

Customizing Reports

Every report can be customized. You can modify them so that they have **additional columns** by Class, by Month, or by Product/Service.

Comparisons to previous years or periods are very insightful!

You can **Filter** any report so it just lists the data you want to see, like a particular Customer or Product.

You can also **Group** some reports to show you subtotals.

The possibilities are endless!

And if you're using **QBO Advanced**, you can even build your own reports including data from multiple tables, view charts, and create pivot tables.

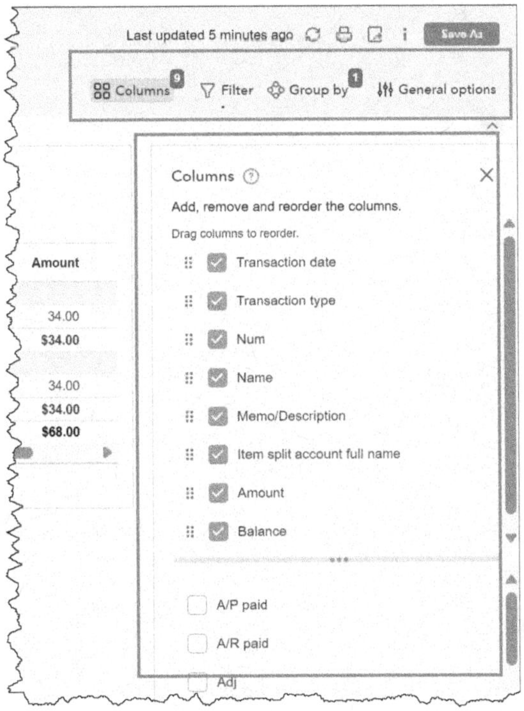

Part 3:
Making the Most of QuickBooks Online

Chapter 9: Other Transactions and Tools

Transfers

Use **Transfer** to move money between any accounts on your Balance Sheet. It's a great way to move money between checking and savings accounts.

To make a Transfer, select **+Create > Transfer.**

Enter the accounts to transfer the money to and from, the amount of the transfer, and the date of the transfer. It is helpful to put a description of the transaction in the memo field.

Transfers will automatically **Pair** in the Bank Transactions feed.

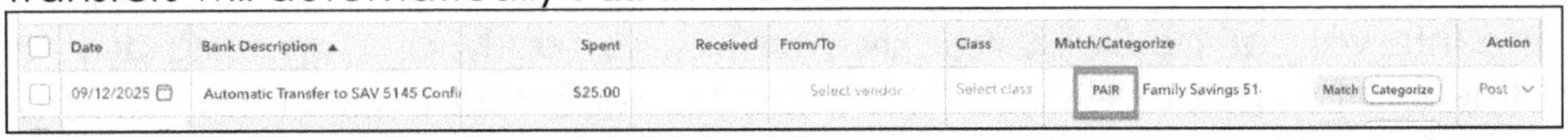

If this transfer happens on a regular basis, make it a Recurring Transaction. Click **Make Recurring** to set this up, but remember that it doesn't actually move the money for you! See page 178 for more information.

Sometimes a better option is to set up a **Rule** in the Bank Transactions feed to recognize the transfer using the last 4 digits of the account number shown in the Bank Details. Be sure only to make one checking-to-savings or savings-to-checking Rule, otherwise you may accidentally create two unconnected transactions.

Recurring Transactions

Saving **Recurring Transactions** is a feature in QBO Essentials and above, and it's well worth the upgrade for this ability alone.

If you have a transaction that repeats regularly, choose **Make recurring** in the bar at the bottom of the window. This way, you don't have to enter the transaction manually every week, month, quarter, or year.

Note that you can't use Recurring Transactions for Invoice Payments or Bill Payments, because they are "2nd-stage," meaning that QBO doesn't know what transactions to apply the payments against.

Name the Recurring Transaction with a descriptive name so you'll know what it is when you see it on the list.

- ***Scheduled*** transactions will be entered automatically, without any effort from you. These are perfect for transactions with the same dollar amount each time.
- ***Reminder*** will give you an alert when it's time to process the transaction, so that you can adjust the date or dollar amount.
- ***Unscheduled*** just puts the transaction on a list, so you can call it up and use it as needed, like a template.

The **Interval** can be Daily, Weekly, Monthly, or Yearly, on a specific day ("the 1st of the Month"), or a time period ("the 2nd Tuesday of the Month").

You can specify an **End Date** if it's only for a certain period of time.

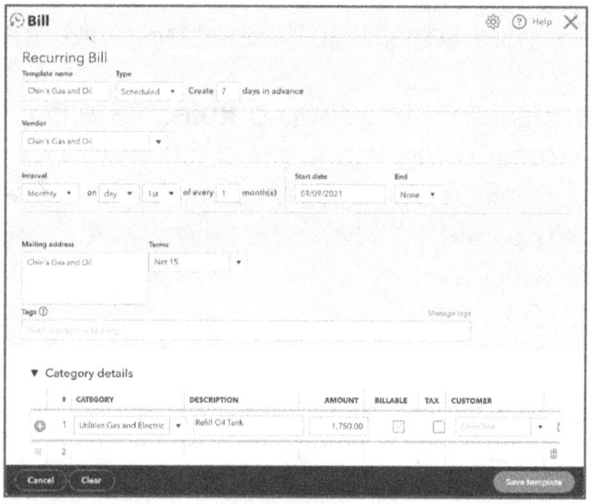

Companion Course
SCAN ME
Want to learn more?
royl.ws/bootcamp

Journal Entries

Sometimes you need to move money from one Chart of Accounts category to another in a way that's not possible through QBO's ready-made forms and features.

General Journal Entries are created on special occasions. CPAs may use **Adjusting Journal Entries** to reclassify transactions that were entered incorrectly, and for end-of-year tasks. For the most part, I recommend leaving **Journal Entries (JE)** to professionals.

If there is a proper form to achieve the transaction, please use it!
If an income or expense transaction was miscategorized, edit and fix it instead of using a Journal Entry as a band-aid! For bulk changes, use **Reclassify Transactions** at qbo.intuit.com/app/reclassify-transaction.

Most common daily transactions have a corresponding QBO tool waiting for you under the **+Create button** in the upper left corner. Every time you create any kind of transaction, QBO manages the accounting debits and credits for you behind the scenes. Business owners should only use **JEs** under rare circumstances.

For those of you who have "always used them" and prefer them, understand this: Relying on **Journal Entries** to manage your books has an important, unfortunate side effect in today's modern accounting software. While the entry made sense to you at the time, a year or two later...no one will remember why it's there, or what you hoped to achieve.

In addition, many of QBO's reports are based on transaction types, and won't recognize JEs. Even worse, the data will be wrong in many of your reports unless the date range happens to include the date of the adjustment.

And most importantly of all, QBO learns from its history. If you've been categorizing an expense incorrectly, QBO will continue to suggest the incorrect category, perpetuating the error. Patching errors with adjusting journal entries will never solve the problem.

What are Journal Entries for?

The most appropriate time to use **Journal Entries** in QBO is when you need to move funds from one category to another. Here are several examples of common use:

1. **Depreciation**. When you make a big purchase, you get to spread out the expense over time instead of taking an oversized deduction in one year. Your CPA will make annual Journal Entries to debit the Depreciation and credit the Fixed Asset, so that your vehicles and equipment hold less value on the Balance Sheet every year.

2. **Opening Balance Equity (OBE).** OBE is created automatically when setting up bank accounts in QuickBooks Online, to store the amount of money that was already in each account as of the start date of your QBO file. The company already had that money, so the dollar amount really belongs in Retained Earnings (RE). After you're done setting up QBO for the first time, use a Journal Entry to debit Opening Balance Equity and credit Retained Earnings. OBE should always equal $0 when you're done setting up your QBO file.

3. **Owner Distribution and Contribution Equity Accounts**. On January 1st of each year, these Equity categories for personal money in and out (whatever you may call them, see page 43) should be zeroed out by transferring the balances to Retained Earnings. That way, when you run a year-end Balance Sheet, you can see the total personal money contributed or distributed that year and that year only.

Let's use this last scenario as an example.

How to Create a Journal Entry

To create a Journal Entry, select **+Create** > **Journal Entry**.

Enter the **Journal Date**, and an **ID number** in the **Journal no.** box. This number will auto-increment, but many people enter a code that helps them identify the transaction. It's common for the accountant to include their initials.

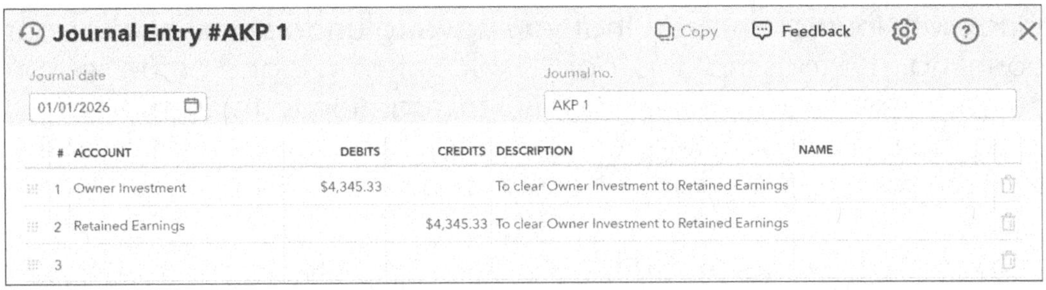

In the first row I've entered the account I used to track how much personal money I used to fund company business the previous year (*remember, don't commingle personal and business money!*).

In the **Debits** column, enter the total from last year. On the second line, enter **"Retained Earnings"** as the Account, and in the **Credits** column, copy that same number.

In the **Description** line, write careful notes about the purpose of this **Journal Entry**. It may seem obvious to you now, but a year from now it might not. If multiple people will be looking at your records, they'll need this information to understand your intention.

There is also a box to enter a **Customer Name** or **Vendor Name** if the transaction is related to an external payee.

If you're using **Classes** and **Locations** (see page 66), enter the appropriate Class for each of the lines.

Click the **Save and Close** button.

When you look at your **Balance Sheet** (see page 171) for last year, you'll still see the total Owner Investment money spent. When you look at the current year, it will start at $0 and increase throughout the year.

Follow this same procedure to zero out your Owner Draw/Shareholder Distribution account as well.

How Do the Debits and Credit Columns Work?

I joke that Debits and Credits are like your USB thumb drive. It always takes 3 tries to insert it into your computer! You try to put it in the little square slot, but it doesn't fit. So you flip it over, and it still won't go in. Then you turn it back the way you first had it...and NOW it works!

The trick with journal entries is that you have to understand a lot about accounting. The fact that this topic is so confusing is one of the reasons I encourage you to use the actual QBO transaction forms instead of JEs…and to have a bookkeeper as a trusted advisor. Even after all these years, I still have to think about it every time.

In every JE, the Debits and Credits columns must have the same total. When you spend, receive, or move money, it has to come from somewhere and go to someplace, so the amount must be the equal on both sides of the equation.

On the surface, Debits and Credits may be the opposite of what you would expect them to be when you look at a bank statement. Debiting your bank account makes it go UP. Crediting your bank account makes it go down.

Debits are not necessarily "bad" and credits are not specifically "good."

Debits increase assets and expenses.
Debits decrease revenue, liabilities and equity.
Credits decrease assets and expenses.
Credits increase revenue, liabilities and equity.

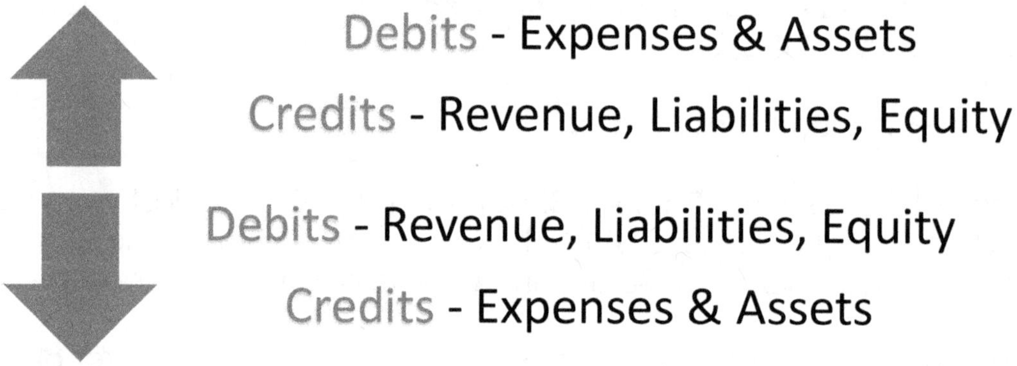

The Audit Log

QuickBooks Online keeps a running record of every change you make in the system. Under the **Settings**, click on **Audit Log**. It's a great way of seeing every single activity performed, and by whom.

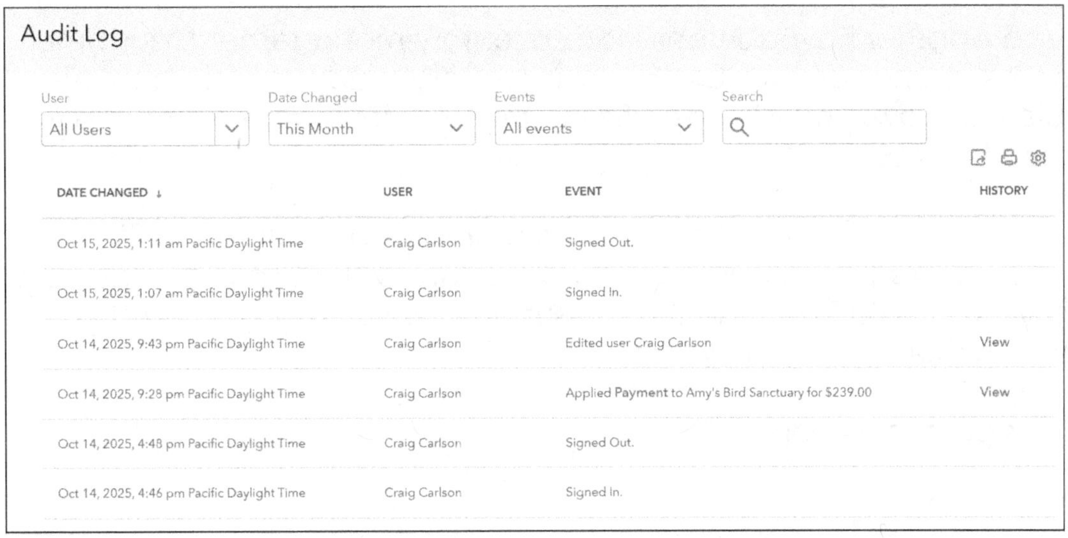

Click on the events to open them. Click **View Mode** to compare before-and-after changes.

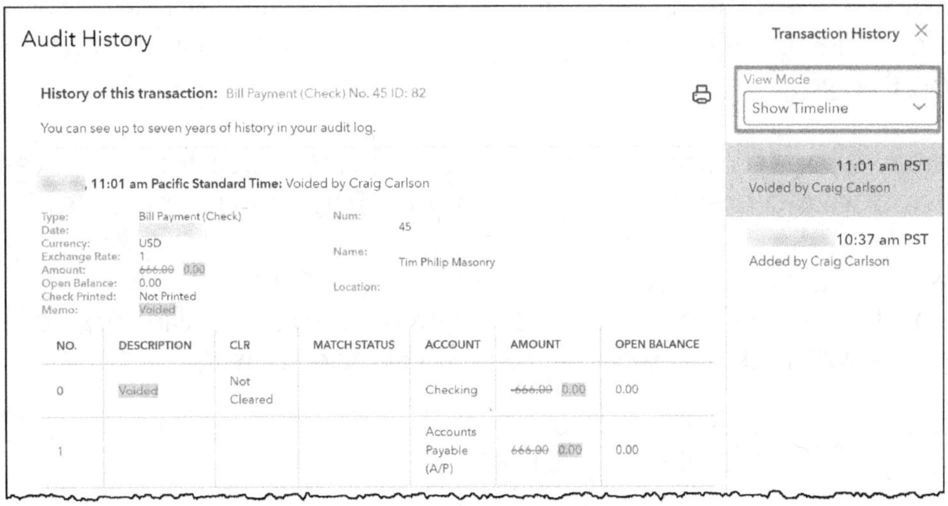

Third-Party Apps

QuickBooks Online can't do exactly everything that QuickBooks for Desktop can, but that's partially ***by design***.[1] One of the hallmarks of being web-based is that there is a rich ecosystem of plugins that extend QBO's abilities.

There are Apps for PayPal integration, inventory management, customer relationship management (CRM), storing receipts, advanced accounts payable workflows, industry-specific interfaces...you name it, and there's a solution for you.

Some people complain about the extra monthly cost, but think of it this way...if an app saves you one hour a week, and you charge $50/an hour, it will save you $200 every month. The subscription costs much less than that, which makes it worth every penny.

Visit apps.com to explore!

The QuickBooks Mobile App

QuickBooks Online also has an app for iPhone, iPad, and Android devices. The data is the same as logging into your browser, so you can get work done on the go.

It also allows you to make estimates and sales receipts for customers while onsite, and take credit card payments with Tap-to-Pay or a Bluetooth swiper.

You can also take a picture of a receipt while you're still in the store or restaurant and add the expense to QBO on the spot.

It will even track your trip mileage!

[1] The truth is that QBO does a lot of stuff that QB Desktop *doesn't* do, but you have to get past the learning curve to discover how much more efficient it is.

Backing Up

QuickBooks Online is backed up automatically on Intuit's servers, but there's no way for users to access it.

QuickBooks Online Advanced has its own system to make periodic backups, so that if you find a problem, you can roll back your file to an earlier point in time.

I personally like to save a copy after my taxes have been filed so that any future adjustments I make to the structure of my file won't impact my tax history.

I also like to make backups any time I'm about to make a big change to my QBO file, in case the update doesn't go as expected. Then I can roll back the file and try again.

One option is to select **Settings > Export Data.** Here you can export lists of your data so that you can reconstruct it in another QuickBooks file, either Online or Desktop.

My favorite backup solution is a third-party app called Rewind (http://royl.ws/rewind). Not only will Rewind create daily or weekly snapshots for rollback, but it will even allow you to Undelete a single deleted transaction, or roll back a transaction to a previous version! I install it not just on my own QBO files, but for all the clients I work with. The small monthly fee is worth your piece of mind.

To see all the QBO backup apps and choose the right option for you, visit apps.com!

Exporting to Excel

All of the lists and reports in QBO can be exported to Excel or csv for further manipulation, or for use in other software. Look to the upper right of the list for a little square with an arrow pointing out.

Once in Excel, you can manipulate and analyze your data to your heart's content.

QBO Advanced also has a tool called **Spreadsheet Sync** that integrates QuickBooks with Excel, creating a bi-directional link. You can create formatted reports that update automatically, and even use it to change your data without editing every transaction manually!

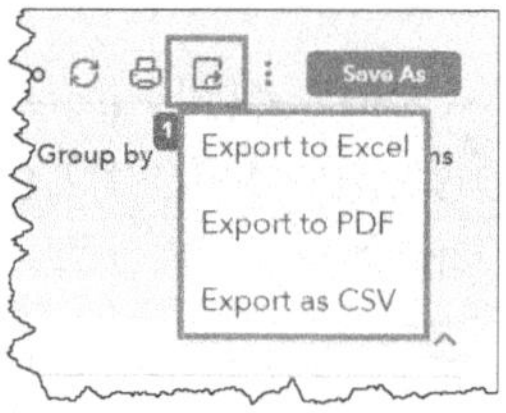

Leaving Feedback

Intuit is very responsive to our input. If something isn't working, leave **Feedback** for a bug report. Go to Settings > Feedback, and there are Feedback links in most screens that go straight to the development team responsible for that feature.

This is surprisingly important! Intuit is constantly testing out new features, and they need to know when something isn't working well.

If you have an idea for a new feature, leave that **Feedback**, too! The more people who request a feature, the more likely we are to see it in a future release. Intuit really does pay attention to every submission. The squeaky wheel gets the grease!

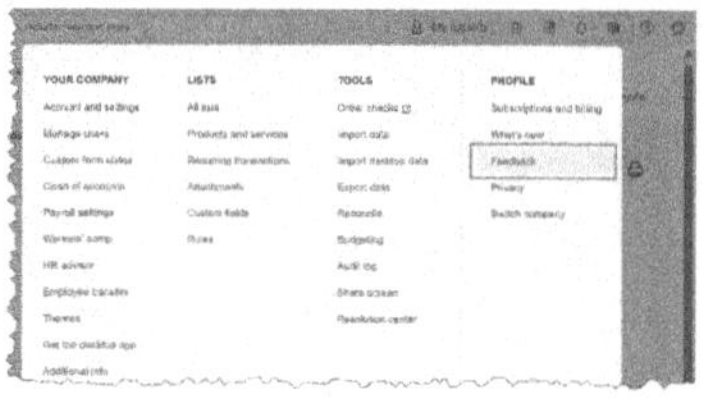

Chapter 10: Tying Up the Year for Taxes

January and February mark that time of year when business owners get anxious and accountants get busy. We're all preparing for March's tax deadlines!

If you've been keeping good records throughout the year, tying up your books for the year should just take a few hours. Then you can pass the file off to your CPA with confidence.

If you haven't been keeping good records....well, we'll talk about that in a little bit.

Here are ten steps you can take to finish off your QuickBooks bookkeeping and be prepared for the new year. Each of the steps is demonstrated at length in my video course at http://royl.ws/QBOYearEnd.

1. Confirm your A/R and A/P

It's important to start with making sure your A/R and A/P are current.

Run an **Accounts Receivable Aging Summary** report and an **Accounts Payable Aging Summary** report.

Are all the open Customer invoices actually open? Did you make deposits that should have been Invoice Payments? What are you doing to collect on the overdue invoices?

Do you need to write off any bad debt? If you're accrual-based, you will credit old uncollectible invoices to Bad Debt in the current period. If you're cash-based, you can Void them, or use a Discount to reduce the balance to zero.

For open Vendor Bills, did you pay some of them using a check instead of applying a Bill Payment? To fix this, open each check and Add the corresponding bill.

If you see any $0.00s here, it means you have an invoice and a payment, but the payment wasn't applied to the invoice. Edit the payment, check off the invoice, then save.

2. Make sure there is nothing old in Undeposited Funds / Payments to Deposit

Every time you take a customer payment, deposit it to **Undeposited Funds/Payments to Deposit**. When you see a deposit in the Bank Transactions feed, make sure it MATCHES these already-existing transactions, removing them from +Create > Bank Deposit.

If you have old transactions in **+Create > Bank Deposit**, that means you probably POSTED money in from the Bank Transactions feed, instead of MATCHING them. Your Income on your P&L is too high and you'll pay too much in taxes!

To fix this, look in your Checking account register for Deposits that say your Income account ("Sales of Product Income," "Sales," "Construction Income", etc.). Edit them. Click on the actual Payments and Sales Receipts on the list at the top so that the dollar amount is the same as the amount on the bottom. Trashcan the manual entry at the bottom. When you save the Deposit, your income will be fixed.

3. Reconcile all your bank accounts

Reconciling should happen at the end of every single month, but you can't close out the year without completing the December reconciliation. Reconcile all your accounts: checking, savings, petty cash, credit cards, PayPal/Square/Venmo, and loans.

Reconciling a bank account means comparing the transactions you have to the ones the bank has. This allows you to locate transactions that never cleared the bank and find entries the bank has that you don't.

Go to **Accounting > Reconcile**. Enter the closing date of the statement (which may not be the last day of the month), and the ending balance. Check off each matching transaction both on screen and on paper. When you're done, you should have a $0 difference.

What's important is to not just match the transactions that ARE on the statement...you also need to manage the transactions in your register that are NOT on the statement. Why are they there?

• Are they transactions that didn't clear until the following month, or checks the vendor didn't cash yet? Those are fine.
• Or, are they duplicate transactions? Those need to be deleted!
• If you have any transactions that still aren't on the statement, you need to research them and find out why they're there. Whatever they were, they didn't hit the bank!

By the time you're done, all your transactions will be present and accounted for!

Don't forget to reconcile ALL of your liability accounts, including your Sales Tax and Payroll liabilities. This is the only way to catch it if you added transactions from the banking feed as duplicates, or categorized them to these accounts instead of expenses.

My Reconciliations video at http://royl.ws/Reconciling-In-QBO includes a practical demonstration of a reconciliation, including some tips and tricks to make it easier!

4. Make sure your transactions are categorized properly

Just because your balance matches the bank, it doesn't mean all the transactions were put in the right places.

Note that bookkeepers and accountants have a **Reclassify Transactions** tool that business owners don't have, allowing us to batch edit many transactions at once instead of manually changing one at a time.

Business owners can access this same tool by going to https://qbo.intuit.com/app/reclassify-transaction.

If you have to edit manually, run a Profit and Loss report for Last Year. Click on each of the Income, Expense, and Cost of Goods amounts. Scan the list. Is each transaction supposed to be where it is? If not, click on the entry to open it, and change the category to the correct one.

Here are some traps to look out for:

- ***Personal money moved in and out of the business:*** Classify these using Equity accounts for Owner Distribution and Owner

Contribution (LLCs should use "Member" or "Partner" instead of "Owner." Corporations should use "Shareholder").

- ***Meals and Entertainment:*** Your morning Starbucks and your lunch do NOT count as Meals! The first thing to know is that there actually is no Entertainment deduction anymore. The next is that Meals is reserved for business meetings, not for keeping you from getting hypoglycemic. If you are talking business with a colleague or client, that's fine - be sure to make notes on your receipt about who you were with and what you discussed. If you're using QBO, you can take a picture of your receipt and create the transaction on the spot to save data entry time back in the office!

- ***Fuel & Auto Expenses:*** Your daily commute to work is not a business expense unless you're driving a company vehicle to job sites. Instead, fill up your gas tank and pay for your repairs with personal money, and keep a daily log of how many miles you drive every day for what purpose—QBO has a built-in tool that the Admins Users can use, and MileIQ is a fantastic app (https://www.mileiq.com, promo code APOL635A)! Then talk to your CPA about taking a standard mileage deduction. This deduction is designed to reimburse you for your gas and car maintenance.

5. Take inventory

If you sell products, you need to adjust your inventory at the end of your calendar and fiscal years. QuickBooks has inventory reports you can print out to see what you're supposed to have in stock. Take a physical count and compare the quantities.

The total price you paid for the current inventory goes into your Inventory Asset category, and the remaining difference goes to your Cost of Goods Sold.

Depending on the version of QuickBooks you're using, there may be an INVENTORY QTY ADJUSMENT tool to update your quantities.

6. Depreciate your assets

Instead of taking large purchases as an expense all in one year, you maintain them in your books as Fixed Assets. This allows you to track the value of equipment, machinery, furniture, and vehicles over time.

Every year your accountant will make adjustments to your QuickBooks file to depreciate your Fixed assets. Every year you get to take a tax deduction on that reduction in value.

Depreciation also adjusts for reductions in value - your computer is worth less now than it was five years ago. The amount of Fixed Assets shown on your Balance Sheet should be close to the resale value if you sold the items today.

7. Zero out your Owner/Shareholder Equity

After your accountant has done all their work, zero out your Owner's Contribution and Distribution accounts. Create a Journal Entry dated January 1 of the following year to transfer the 12/31 balance to Retained Earnings.

That way, your Balance Sheet for the year will only show that year's Contributions and Distributions, instead of accumulating throughout the life of the company.

8. Close the books

After your taxes have been submitted, use the **Close the Books** feature. Closing the books makes sure that your file matches what you submitted to the IRS. It prevents anyone from changing historical data without knowing what they're doing.

In QBO's **Settings > Account and Settings > Advanced**, set the date to 12/31, and put in a password. Now, when you try to change an entry before the current fiscal year, it will ask for a password first. That gives you a moment to make sure it's a good idea before you do any damage!

BUT DON'T LOSE YOUR PASSWORD!

9. Make a backup

Once your tax preparer has adjusted your books to match your taxes, run a full set of reports and save them to your computer. I also recommend printing them out! At a minimum, print your P&L and Balance Sheet, and maybe even your General Ledger transaction detail report.

Another idea is to export your data out of QBO so that you have a second set in case anything happens to your account. **Go to Settings > Export**. Export all your lists and transactions.

10. Analyze your business

QBO has somewhere between 20 and 100 reports available to you, depending on what version you're using. Plus, they're all customizable! In the beginning of this book on page 5 we discussed the Pareto Principle, the 80/20 rule, a proportion that runs through all your business.

Start by reading your Profit and Loss Statement and your Balance Sheet. These are the two fundamental reports that show your Income/Expenses, and the status of your assets and liabilities. I like to view them for All Dates, with columns by Year. That way I can look for trends over time.

Once you've perused these two reports, now go through ALL the reports available and look at your business in whole new ways. You'll be surprised at what you'll learn.

Once you know what type of customer is your best customer, find more like them next year. Once you know which of your services have the best profit margin, promote those services more. Use this analysis to make solid business decisions that will grow your company next year.

Wrapping up

This is all well and good if you've been diligent about entering your sales receipts, invoices, and payments through the year, and recording all your expenses. But what if you haven't been keeping up?

The short answer is that you have a lot to do. The good news is that most banks will allow you to download your entire list of transactions for the year, so all you have to is categorize each one.

The longer answer is that just pulling in your bank feeds, especially for your income, doesn't give you any detail for analyzing your business. You won't be able to see what you sold to whom. You won't be able to do any year-over-year reporting until the following year. If possible, at least recreate your sales history through Sales Receipts so that you have some level of detail moving forward.

If any of these 10 steps were a mystery to you, that's a sign that a bookkeeper or CPA would be a great help to you and your company. Please head over to Intuit's findaproadvisor.com website to find a QuickBooks Online certified ProAdvisor who is familiar with your industry!

ACCOUNTING

Chapter 11: The Top Dozen Mistakes People Make

Day in and day out, I work with small business owners to set up and use QuickBooks Online. Over time I have seen patterns emerge, and I find myself coaching people through the same mistakes over and over again.

Here is my list of Top 12 Errors that I see, so that you don't make them, too!

1. Not going through Account and Settings to turn on and off the features you need. Some of them aren't obvious and hinder your ability to use QBO well. See pages 23, 66, 73, and 119.

2. Adding too many accounts to the COA (page 42). Reserve your details of the items you buy and sell for the Products and Services list (page 56).

3. If you purchase Products and Services in order to sell them, be sure to "buy" them using the Item Details table instead of the Category Details table. See page 119.

4. Making new vendors for every gas station and restaurant you patronize. Use generic names like "Gas Station," "Restaurant," and "Parking" unless you have a specific reason to track one particular establishment.

5. Improperly classifying Meals. Starbucks and your lunch are not business expenses, unless it was for a business meeting. If it was, record on your paper receipt who you were with and what you talked about and include that information in the transaction memo.

6. Not recording Transfers. It's easiest to record bank transfers manually and let the Bank Transactions feed pair them. You run the risk of creating two separate debit and credit transactions that aren't linked together. See page 154.

7. When you create a Payment, always verify which Invoice it is applied to (page 91).

8. Depositing payments directly to the checking account instead of Undeposited Funds. If you group checks when taking them to the bank, use +Create > Bank Deposit to combine them to match the total amount on the Deposit slip. Record the items on your physical bank slip so you know for sure which transactions created that total! See page 94.

9. Sucking in Deposits & Income from the Bank Transactions feed. Be sure to make Sales Receipts or Invoices/Payments so that you can trace the income (page 154).

10. Uncategorized Income and Uncategorized Expenses. When you review your P&L (page 169) look for transactions here. If you see them, it means you pulled them in through the Bank Transactions feed without categorizing them!

11. Never reconciling your bank accounts...or only matching the transactions ON the bank statement and ignoring the rest. Relying on the Bank Transactions feed is not good enough! This is the only way you'll catch duplicated or missing deposits and expenses. Reconcile all your Balance Sheet accounts. See page 161.

12. Not getting help when you need it. If you're not sure how to manage a transaction, call your trusted bookkeeper or accountant, a local QuickBooks ProAdvisor at findaproadvisor.com...or me! It's much more cost effective to ask a short question and do it right into the future than it is to pay someone to go in after you and clean up incorrect entries.

Chapter 12: Where to go from here

Thank you for coming with me on this amazing journey into QuickBooks Online. Since you've made it this far and are still reading these words, this book has obviously deepened your interest in QuickBooks.

So...if that's the case...guess what? You're in luck! Your journey doesn't end here!

There's an entire world of QuickBooks resources, including a thriving ecosystem of thought-leaders, coaches, trainers, and mentors to help you navigate the waters and get set up for long-term success.

But something I discovered over the years is that the QBO ecosystem that developed was fragmented, and people were getting frustrated and lost in the shuffle.

One resource would teach you how to do X, another would teach you how to do Y, and yet another Z, but those puzzle pieces didn't fit together seamlessly to properly teach learners how to use QuickBooks Online efficiently and effectively. What's worse? All the nuance and intricacy that make this program so incredibly special...fell through the cracks!

Companion Course
SCAN ME
royl.ws/bootcamp
Want to learn more?

Then there's the whole thing of people saying, "Why pay for training? You can find everything you need on YouTube!" Well, yes, you certainly can...but getting the *actual* answer to your *actual* question is like finding a needle in a haystack.

The whole thing bothered me. The learning process shouldn't be complicated, and certainly not incomplete and confusing. It didn't have to be this way.

I knew I had to develop an umbrella solution that would take away the overwhelm that people were feeling. I knew the system had to properly educate learners so that they would love QuickBooks as much as I do!

I set out to simplify the QBO learning process, eliminate the difficulty, and enthuse the user with hidden and powerful tips and tricks, and all the while shorten the learning curve so that people like you could spend less time crunching numbers, and more time actually steering the ship.

And that's how I created the Royalwise OWLS!

The Royalwise OWLS

You've probably noticed that there are some key concepts not covered in this book, like the Sales Tax Center, running Payroll, Budgeting, and managing Loans and interest. Since it took us 200 pages just to cover the very basics, you can imagine how long this book would be if we also covered these complicated topics!

The Royalwise OWLS is my answer to this problem. Our OWLS platform is an <u>O</u>n-demand, <u>W</u>eb-based <u>L</u>earning <u>S</u>olution, crafted to be your comprehensive resource to help you learn QuickBooks Online quickly and easily without spinning your wheels hunting, searching, and piecing together the information on your own.

I've created a complete library of over 75 video courses demonstrating everything from the basics covered in this book (the QBO Bootcamp), all the way to the most advanced subjects, and everything between.

I love learning and the joy it brings people as they expand their worldview and achieve goals they never dreamed possible. I'm grateful that my teaching skills have empowered me to become the "Queen of QuickBooks" who helps real people succeed in their businesses, make more money, and earn a living doing what they love.

So, whenever you're ready, I invite you to join me at royalwise.com. It'll be a hoot!

Companion Course

SCAN ME

Want to learn more?

royl.ws/bootcamp

Learn QBO without it ever feeling like work

One more thing. You made a smart decision purchasing this book. The feedback I've received from my readers over the years on all eight of the previous editions of this book is that it's an excellent resource in of itself, especially when you need to look something up quickly.

But can I share a secret with you? When it comes to learning QBO from the ground up, books are great, but video...is even better. Yes. I said it.

You might be surprised to hear this from an author in her very own book, but it's true. According to a 2015 article by Psychology Today, our brains process video 60,000 times faster than text-based media!

And if you think about it, it makes perfect sense. As humans, we're programmed from birth to learn by watching others. Video reduces our cognitive load, which means it has the power to engage, entertain, and educate, without it even feeling like work.

Lucky for you, that is exactly what my OWLS platform is all about!

There I demonstrate everything that QBO has to offer in an easy-to-follow video format, along with words of wisdom from me and tips I gleaned from decades of experience with businesses just like yours.

The videos are divided into small, easily digestible segments for better long-term comprehension, without the information overload or overwhelm.

Take just the classes you need ala carte or subscribe to my membership program for one low monthly price.

Join me at learn.royalwise.com to get started, and I'll see you in class.

Companion Course

SCAN ME

Want to learn more?

royl.ws/bootcamp

Companion Course

SCAN ME

Want to learn more?

royl.ws/bootcamp

This is my favorite app! This browser extension adds features and shortcuts that Intuit SHOULD have put into QBO but didn't. I couldn't get my work done without it! There's a free version and a pro subscription.

Glossary

These definitions are essential for every QBO user and bookkeeper to know!

1099 Contractor
A 1099 contractor is an independent contractor or self-employed individual who provides services to a business or individual and receives a Form 1099-MISC at the end of the year to report their total income for tax purposes. 1099 contractors are responsible for their own business expenses, taxes, and social security, and have more flexibility in their work but also have less job security and stability than employees.

3rd Party App
A 3rd party app is software developed by an entity other than the manufacturer of the device or the operating system it runs on. These apps provide additional features and are often downloaded from various app stores or directly from developers. QuickBooks Online is built to support all the business solutions found at apps.com.

Account
An account provides a record of transactions that can be used to track the flow of money, manage financial resources, and make informed decisions about spending and investment.

Accountant
An accountant is a professional who specializes in the management of financial information for individuals and organizations. They use their expertise in accounting, tax laws, and financial regulations to provide advice, guidance, and financial solutions to their clients. The duties of an accountant can include: Preparing and examining financial records, Providing financial advice to clients, Preparing tax returns and other financial documents, Analyzing financial information to identify trends and make recommendations for improvement, Conducting audits to ensure that financial records are accurate and in compliance with regulatory requirements, Developing financial strategies and plans for individuals and businesses, Keeping up-to-date with changes in tax laws and financial regulations.

Accrual Basis
Accrual basis is an accounting method that records financial transactions when they are incurred, regardless of when the cash is received or paid. This method is in contrast to the cash basis method, which only records transactions when the cash is received or paid.

App
An app is a software application that runs on a computer, tablet, or mobile phone. Apps can be used for a wide range of purposes, such as productivity, entertainment, social networking, and more.

Integration Transactions
The Integration Transactions tab in the Bank Transactions Center provides a centralized location for managing your transactions imported from Amazon for Business, Square POS, and other 3rd party platforms.

Asset
An asset is a resource owned or controlled by an entity, expected to provide future economic benefits. Assets can be tangible, like buildings and machinery, or intangible, such as patents and trademarks.

Audit
An audit is a systematic and independent examination of financial records and statements to assess the accuracy, validity, and reliability of financial reports. The purpose of an audit is to provide assurance that an organization's financial reports are in compliance with accounting standards and that they present a fair and accurate view of the organization's financial position and performance.

Balance Sheet Report
A balance sheet is a financial statement that provides a snapshot of a company's financial position at a specific point in time. It shows the company's assets, liabilities, and equity, and helps to give a picture of the company's financial health. The balance sheet must always balance, meaning that assets equal liabilities + equity. The balance sheet is an important tool for understanding a company's financial position, as it provides information on the company's ability to pay debts, its liquidity, and its solvency.

Bank Deposit
Making a Bank Deposit in QBO combines several individual customer payments into one batch so that your bank register matches the deposit in your bank.

Bank Transactions Feed
QuickBooks Online's banking feed is a feature that allows you to connect your bank and credit card accounts to your QuickBooks Online account. Once you have connected your accounts, QuickBooks Online automatically imports your bank and credit card transactions into your account, making it easy to reconcile your accounts and keep your financial records up to date.

Banking
Banking refers to the financial activities and services provided by banks and other financial institutions. Banks play a critical role in the economy by accepting deposits, providing loans, and facilitating the movement of money through the economy.

Bill
A bill is a document that represents a demand for payment for goods or services provided. In most cases, bills are issued by a vendor or supplier to a customer and include information such as the date of the transaction, a description of the goods or services provided, the quantity and cost of each item, any applicable taxes or fees, and the total amount due.

Bookkeeper
A bookkeeper is a professional who is responsible for recording and managing a business's financial transactions. They maintain accurate financial records, including accounts payable and receivable, bank transactions, and payroll, and ensure that the financial information is organized and up-to-date. The duties of a bookkeeper can include: Recording and categorizing financial transactions, Reconciling bank statements, Maintaining accounts payable and receivable, Processing payroll and tracking employee time off, Preparing and sending invoices to customers, Keeping track of fixed assets, Providing financial reports to management and stakeholders.

Cash Basis
Cash basis is an accounting method that records financial transactions only when cash is received or paid. This method is in contrast to the accrual basis method, which records transactions when they are incurred, regardless of when the cash is received or paid.

Cash Flow
Cash flow refers to the movement of money into and out of a business, investment, or financial account. It is crucial for evaluating the liquidity and overall financial health of an enterprise.

Chart of Accounts
The chart of accounts is a systematic list of a company's financial accounts, used to categorize and track its financial transactions. It is an essential tool in accounting and financial management, as it provides a framework for organizing and recording financial information. The chart of accounts typically includes categories such as assets, liabilities, equity, revenue, expenses, and cost of goods sold.

Check
A check is a written order to a financial institution to pay a specific amount of money to a specified recipient, from an account held in the account holder's name. Checks are typically used for personal and business transactions, and serve as a form of payment that is more secure than cash and more convenient than making a transfer directly from a bank account.

Class
In the context of accounting and finance, a "class" refers to a category or grouping of similar financial transactions. A class is a way to categorize and track financial information in a meaningful way, making it easier to understand the financial performance of a business.

Clearing Account
A Clearing Account is a temporary account used to gather and hold amounts to be transferred between two or more accounts at a later time. It's like a holding area where transactions can be recorded and separated before being finalized. These accounts are often used for managing complex or multi-step transactions and can simplify reconciliation processes. Once the transactions are completed, the clearing account's balance should be zero. It ensures that the books are kept clean and organized, and transactions can be traced easily.

Contractor
A contractor, also called a Subcontractor or Independent Contractor, is an individual or entity hired to perform specific tasks or services for another party based on the terms outlined in a contract. Unlike an employee, a contractor typically operates independently, provides their own tools and resources, and is not subject to the hiring party's direct control or supervision in terms of how the work is executed.

Control Account
A control account in accounting is a general ledger account that summarizes the transactions of subsidiary accounts or individual transactions related to a particular asset, liability, revenue, or expense category. The purpose of a control account is to provide a summary of the transactions in the subsidiary accounts that make up the balance of the control account

Cost of Goods (COGS)
The cost of goods (COGS) is a term used in accounting and finance to refer to the direct costs associated with producing a product or providing a service. COGS includes all of the costs

that are directly related to the production of a product or the delivery of a service, such as raw materials, labor, and manufacturing overhead.

Credit
A credit is a bookkeeping entry that records a sum of money being added to an account. In double-entry accounting, a credit entry is made to record a transaction that increases the balance of an liability or a revenue account, or decreases the balance of an asset or an expense account.

Credit Card
A credit card is a payment card that allows the cardholder to borrow money up to a certain limit in order to purchase goods and services. The card issuer extends a line of credit to the cardholder and the cardholder repays the borrowed amount, along with any interest or fees, to the issuer. Credit cards are a common and convenient form of payment, but it is important for users to be mindful of the interest rates and fees associated with credit card usage and to pay their balances in full and on time to avoid paying unnecessary interest charges.

Credit Memo
A Credit Memo, also known as a credit note or Credit Memorandum, is a document used in accounting and finance to indicate a reduction in the amount owed by a customer. A Credit Memo is issued by a company or vendor to a customer in response to a return of goods, a cancellation of an order, or a correction of an invoice.

Customer
A customer is a person or organization that purchases goods or services from a business. They may also be called Clients, Members, Donors, Tenants, and Patients.

Daily Sales Receipt
Also called a Z-Tape, this daily summary, typically entered with a $0 Sales Receipt or Journal Entry, records the total amount of sales that occur within a single business day. It adds income by department, and subtracts the totals by payment method.

Debit
A debit is a bookkeeping entry that records a sum of money being taken out of an account. In double-entry accounting, a debit entry is made to record a transaction that increases the balance of a asset or an expense account, or decreases the balance of a liability or a revenue account.

Debits & Credits
Debits and credits are terms used in accounting to describe the movement of money into and out of an account. They are used to record transactions in double-entry accounting, which is a system of bookkeeping that uses two entries for every transaction in order to maintain the accuracy and integrity of financial records.

Deposit
A deposit is a financial transaction in which money is placed into an account with a bank or financial institution. Deposits can be made into savings accounts, checking accounts, or other types of accounts, and can be made using cash, check, or electronic methods such as online or mobile banking.

Depreciation
Depreciation is an accounting method used to allocate the cost of a tangible or physical asset over its useful life. It reflects the decrease in value of an asset as it ages, is used, or wears out. This process allows businesses to spread the expense of an asset over the years it is in use, thereby matching the cost of the asset with the revenue it generates.

Direct Connect
Direct Connect establishes a secure connection between your QuickBooks Online account and your bank or financial institution to automatically download your transactions on a regular basis, typically daily.

Economic Nexus
Economic nexus refers to a tax presence established in a particular jurisdiction based solely on a business's economic activity there, without requiring a physical presence. This concept has become increasingly relevant in the context of sales tax for online sellers, where a certain volume or value of sales into a state can trigger tax collection obligations, even if the seller has no physical operations or presence in that state.

Employee
An employee is a person who is hired by an organization to perform a specific job or set of tasks.

Envelopes
QuickBooks Checking's Envelopes feature allows you to allocate and separate funds within your checking account for specific purposes, much like a digital version of the envelope budgeting system or Profit First. You can create multiple envelopes for various expenses such as payroll, sales tax, and owner pay.

Equity
Equity is a financial term that refers to the ownership interest in an asset, such as a business or a property.

Estimate
Estimates are provisional or approximate calculations of the expected cost, quantity, or duration of a future event or project. They can be used to predict the outcome of a proposed project, plan for future expenditures, or determine a budget for a project or event.

Expenses
Expenses are costs that a business or individual incurs in order to produce goods or services, or to maintain their operations. Expenses can include both direct costs, such as the cost of raw materials or labor, and indirect costs, such as overhead expenses like rent or utilities.

Find Match
Find Match is a Bank Transactions feed tool that allows you to quickly match transactions in your account to their corresponding bank or credit card transactions, if for some reason the match doesn't happen automatically.

Fixed Asset
A fixed asset is a long-term tangible piece of property or equipment that a company owns and uses in its operations to generate income. Fixed assets are not intended for sale but are to be used and depreciated over their useful life.

Funds
"Funds" can refer to a pool of money that is managed and invested by a financial institution, the money available in a bank account, or money set aside for specific purposes by a government. The specific meaning of the term depends on the context in which it is used.

Income
The money a person or business receives in exchange for goods or services provided, or from other sources such as investments. This can include wages and salaries, commissions, rent, dividends, and interest earned on savings and investments.

Integration
Integrations enable different software applications to communicate and work together. This can streamline workflows, automate tasks, and create a more cohesive user experience by sharing data and functionalities between apps.

Intuit
Intuit Inc. is an American software company that develops financial and tax preparation software and related services for individuals, accountants, and small businesses. The company's flagship products include QuickBooks, TurboTax, Mailchimp, and Credit Karma. Their mission is "Powering prosperity around the world."

Inventory
Inventory refers to the goods and materials that a company holds for sale or for use in the production of other goods. Inventory management is the process of tracking, controlling, and maintaining an accurate record of a company's inventory levels, with the goal of ensuring that the company has the right amount of inventory at the right time, in the right place, and at the right cost.

Invoice
An invoice is a document that is issued by a seller to a buyer, indicating the goods or services provided and the amount due for payment. An invoice serves as a request for payment and is an important record of the transaction between the buyer and seller.

Job Costing
Job costing is a method of accounting that tracks the costs associated with a specific job or project, including direct costs such as materials, labor, and equipment, and indirect costs such as overhead expenses. The goal of job costing is to determine the total cost of the job and determine the profit or loss for the project.

Journal Entries
A journal entry is a financial accounting transaction that is recorded in a company's general ledger. It includes information about the date, accounts affected, debit and credit amounts, and a narrative description of the transaction, and is used to keep a record of financial transactions and to ensure the accuracy and completeness of the company's financial records.

Liability
A liability is an obligation that an entity owes to another party, which arises from past events or transactions and is expected to result in an outflow of economic resources from the entity in the future. Liabilities can be current or long-term. Current liabilities are obligations that are expected to be settled within one year, while long-term liabilities are obligations that are expected to be settled more than one year from the reporting date.

Line of Credit
A line of credit is a type of financial arrangement in which a lender agrees to provide a borrower with a predetermined amount of money, which the borrower can draw upon and repay as needed. Lines of credit are often used by businesses to cover short-term cash flow needs, such as inventory purchases or payroll expenses.

Loan
A loan is a financial arrangement between two parties, in which one party (the lender) provides money, assets, or property to another party (the borrower), who agrees to repay the loan with interest over a specified period of time. Loans are typically used to finance large purchases or investments that would otherwise be difficult or impossible to afford upfront.

Merchant Services
Merchant services refer to the suite of financial products and services that enable businesses to accept electronic payments from customers.

Operating Account
A company's main checking account, used as the source of funds for everyday expenses.

Overhead
Overhead refers to the ongoing business expenses not directly tied to creating a product or service. These are necessary costs for running a business but do not directly contribute to the production or delivery of goods and services. When using Classes, Overhead is commonly assigned to indicate that the operational expense isn't tied to a specific revenue stream.

Owner Draw
An owner's draw, also known as an owner's distribution, is an amount of money taken out of a business's profits by the owner for personal use.

Partial Payment
A partial payment is a payment that only covers a portion of the total amount owed for a transaction or an invoice.

Payee
A payee is a person or entity to whom a payment is made. In the context of banking and finance, a payee is typically the recipient of a check or electronic payment.

Payment
Payment refers to the exchange of funds between two parties in exchange for goods, services, or debt repayment.

Pay Down Credit Card
This QBO feature applies your payment to the correct credit card from the correct bank account, eliminating duplicate transaction errors that occur if other workflows are used.

Payment Processor
A payment processor is a third-party service provider that enables merchants to accept electronic payments, such as credit card or debit card transactions, through a variety of channels, including online, in-store, and mobile. Payment processors act as intermediaries between the merchant and the financial institutions that issue the payment methods used by customers.

Payroll
Payroll refers to the total amount of wages, salaries, and other employee compensations that a business pays out during a specific period. It also encompasses the process of calculating, distributing, and reporting these payments to employees and relevant authorities.

Payroll Contributions
Payroll contributions refer to amounts that employees elect or are required to have withheld from their paychecks to fund certain benefits or accounts. Examples include contributions to retirement plans, health savings accounts, or insurance premiums.

Payroll Deductions
Payroll deductions are amounts taken out of an employee's paycheck by the employer for various purposes. These can include federal and state taxes, Social Security, health insurance premiums, retirement contributions, and other benefits or mandatory charges.

Payroll Garnishments
Payroll garnishments are legally mandated deductions taken directly from an employee's paycheck by the employer. They are used to settle debts like unpaid taxes, child support, or court judgments, ensuring creditors receive the amounts owed by the employee.

Prepaid Expenses
Prepaid expenses are payments made for services or goods that will be received or used in the future. Initially categorized as assets, they're later adjusted and recognized as expenses on the income statement as the benefit is realized. This is frequently done in Accrual-based accounting for annual service contracts so that the expense can be recognized monthly, or when an expense (like a conference or airfare) is paid for several months ahead of time.

Product
A product is a tangible or intangible item that is produced or created to meet the needs or wants of customers. Products can be physical items such as a book, a computer, or a car, or they can be intangible items such as software, music, or a movie.

Products & Services
In general, businesses offer both products and services to their customers to meet their needs and provide value. The mix of products and services that a business offers can vary depending on the industry, target market, and overall business strategy.

Profit & Loss
A Profit and Loss (P&L) statement is a financial report that shows a company's revenue and expenses over a specific period of time, typically a month or a year. The purpose of the P&L statement is to show the company's profitability and to help management make informed decisions about how to allocate resources and improve operations.

Progress Invoicing
Progress invoicing, also known as incremental billing, is a billing method used to bill a customer for the completion of specific stages or milestones within a project. The customer is billed periodically as the work progresses, rather than at the end of the project, which helps to mitigate the risk of non-payment and ensures that both parties are on the same page regarding the progress of the project.

Purchase Order
A purchase order (PO) is a document that a buyer uses to request goods or services from a supplier. It is used to formally communicate the specifics of the purchase and provides a

legal contract between the buyer and the supplier. Purchase orders are used to ensure that both the buyer and the supplier have a clear understanding of the terms of the transaction, and to track the costs of goods and services in accounting.

QuickBooks Advanced Suite
QuickBooks Advanced is a version of QuickBooks Online, a cloud-based accounting software produced by Intuit Inc. It is designed for medium-sized businesses that need more advanced features including advanced custom reporting, batch importing, and accrual accounting automations.

QuickBooks Checking
A checking account built into QuickBooks Online, powered by Green Dot Bank. It is integrated with QB Payments, Payroll, and Sales Tax, helping you manage liabilities. You can create up to five savings envelopes that earn interest.

QuickBooks Desktop Enterprise
QuickBooks Desktop is financial management software that is designed for businesses to manage their accounting and financial operations. It is a desktop-based software, as opposed to its cloud-based counterpart, QuickBooks Online.

QuickBooks Essentials Suite
QuickBooks Essentials is a version of QuickBooks Online, produced by Intuit Inc. It is designed for small businesses that need basic accounting and bookkeeping features, but with more functionality than the standard QuickBooks Solopreneur product.

QuickBooks Online (QBO)
QuickBooks Online is a cloud-based accounting software designed to help small and medium-sized businesses manage their finances. It offers a wide range of features, including invoicing, bill payment, expense tracking, and financial reporting, and is known for its ease of use and accessibility from anywhere with an internet connection.

QuickBooks Payments
QB Payments is Intuit's Merchant Services, fully integrated in QuickBooks. This service allows you to accept credit card payments and ACH bank transfers within QBO, send invoices for electronic payment, and create recurring payments. The rates are competitive with other payment processing solutions, but because it's built in to QBO, it takes less time and effort to manage.

QuickBooks Plus
QuickBooks Plus is a version of QuickBooks Online, a cloud-based accounting software produced by Intuit Inc. It is designed for small and medium-sized businesses that need more advanced features and additional capabilities such as class and location tracking, advanced reporting, increased limits, and automated billing.

Receipts
A receipt is a document that confirms a transaction between a buyer and a seller. It provides evidence of the purchase of goods or services and serves as a record of the transaction for both the buyer and the seller.

Receipt Capture
With Receipt Capture, you can take a photo of a receipt using your smartphone or forward an email to a dedicated email address, and the image will be automatically uploaded to your QuickBooks Online account. Once the receipt is captured, QuickBooks Online will extract the

relevant data, such as the vendor, date, and amount, and create a transaction in your account. You can then review and categorize the transaction, and attach the receipt image for future reference.

Reconciling
Reconciling is the process of comparing the transactions in your accounting system with those on your bank or credit card statement to ensure that they match. This helps ensure that your financial records are accurate and up-to-date. To reconcile your accounts, you'll need to compare each transaction with the corresponding transaction on your statement. If there are discrepancies, you'll need to investigate the issue and resolve it before finishing.

Refund
A refund is the return of money to a customer in exchange for goods or services that were not provided, were defective, or did not meet the customer's expectations. Refunds can be processed in a variety of ways, depending on the original payment method and the policies of the business or organization.

Reports
A financial report is a formal document that provides an overview of an entity's financial performance and position over a specific period. It includes key financial statements such as the income statement, balance sheet, and statement of cash flows. Financial reports serve as crucial tools for decision-making, performance evaluation, and assessing the financial health and stability of an organization.

Revenue
Revenue is the income generated from a business's sales or other activities over a given period of time. It represents the total amount of money a business earns before deducting expenses, taxes, and other costs.

Rules
QuickBooks Online's Rules feature is a tool that allows you to automate the categorization of transactions in your account. With Rules, you can set up conditions that determine how transactions in your Bank Transactions feed should be categorized, and QuickBooks Online will automatically apply those rules to future transactions that meet those conditions.

Sale(s)
A sale refers to the exchange of goods or services for money or other consideration. It is a transaction in which a business or individual sells something to a customer. The process of making a sale typically includes the negotiation of terms, the delivery of the goods or services, and the receipt of payment. The amount received from the sale is typically recorded as revenue, which is an important financial metric used to measure a business's performance over time.

Sales Receipt
A sales receipt is a document that serves as proof of a transaction between a buyer and a seller. It typically includes the date of the sale, the items or services purchased, the price of each item, and the total amount paid. Sales receipts can be printed or electronic and are often provided to the customer at the time of purchase. They can be used for record-keeping purposes, for tax purposes, and as evidence of payment in the case of a dispute. In the context of accounting, sales receipts are typically recorded as cash sales in the company's financial records.

Sales Tax
Sales tax is a consumption tax imposed by the government on the sale of goods and services. Typically, the tax is collected by the retailer from the consumer at the point of sale and then remitted to the relevant government authority.

Service
A service is an intangible offering that provides value to customers without a physical product being involved. Services are often experiences or results that a customer receives from a business. Examples of services include consulting, education, healthcare, and entertainment.

Sole Proprietor
A sole proprietor is a type of business structure in which an individual operates a business as a single entity without creating a separate legal entity. This means that the business and the owner are considered to be one and the same for tax purposes, and the owner is personally liable for the business's debts and obligations.

Startup
A startup is a new company that is in the initial stages of operations and is focused on developing a unique product or service with the aim of scaling up and eventually becoming a profitable business. Startups are typically characterized by innovation, high growth potential, and a willingness to take risks in order to achieve their goals.

Statement
A statement is a document that summarizes financial transactions, account activity, or other information over a specified period of time. Statements are often used in finance, accounting, and banking, and can be used to provide information to individuals, organizations, or businesses.

Statement of Cash Flows
A Statement of Cash Flows is a financial statement that provides a summary of a company's cash inflows and outflows during a specific accounting period, categorized into operating, investing, and financing activities. It helps stakeholders understand how a company generates and uses cash, highlighting its liquidity position and ability to meet financial obligations. This statement complements the income statement and balance sheet, offering a comprehensive view of a company's financial health. It answers the age-old question, "If my P&L says I made a profit, why isn't there that much money in my bank account?"

Subcontracting
Subcontracting is the practice of hiring another company or individual to perform part of a larger project that has been contracted to your own business. In subcontracting, the subcontractor is responsible for completing a specific part of the project, while the main contractor is responsible for the overall management of the project.

Tagging
Tagging is a feature that allows you to add custom labels, or "tags," to transactions in your account. Tags are customizable labels that you can assign to transactions to help you categorize and organize them in a way that makes sense for your business.

Taxes
Taxes are mandatory financial charges imposed by a government on individuals, businesses, or transactions to generate revenue for public expenditures. They can take various forms,

such as income, property, sales, or payroll, and are enforced by law with non-compliance subject to penalties.

Third-Party App
A third-party app is an application that is created and maintained by a company or individual other than the manufacturer of the platform it runs on. In the context of financial software, such as QuickBooks, third-party apps refer to add-ons or integrations that provide additional functionality or enhance the capabilities of the main software. These apps are designed to work seamlessly with the main software and can help users streamline their work processes, automate certain tasks, and get more value out of their financial management system.

Transaction
A transaction is an exchange of goods, services, or financial instruments between two parties. Transactions can take many forms and can involve the exchange of physical goods, such as when a customer buys a product from a store, or the exchange of financial instruments, such as when a stock is bought or sold on a stock exchange.

Transfer
A transfer is a financial transaction in which money is moved from one account to another, either within the same bank or financial institution or between different banks or financial institutions.

Undeposited Funds
Undeposited funds is a term used in accounting to describe funds that have been received but have not yet been deposited into a bank account. Undeposited funds are considered a liability and it is important for businesses to monitor and manage them to ensure that they are deposited in a timely manner and that the funds are properly accounted for.

Value Pricing
Pricing your services based on the benefits to clients instead of based on the number of hours worked. This allows you to scale your operations because you are not limited by time.

Vendor
A vendor is a person or organization that supplies goods or services to another person or organization. In business, a vendor is typically a supplier of raw materials, components, or finished products that are used by a company in its operations or sold to its customers.

Voiding
Voiding a transaction means canceling or nullifying its effect in a financial or accounting system. While the record of the transaction remains in the system for audit purposes, its financial impact is negated, making it appear as though it never occurred monetarily.

Workflow
Workflow is the set of tasks, processes, and decisions that are involved in completing a specific business or organizational activity. It refers to the way work is organized and managed, from start to finish, in order to achieve specific goals or objectives.

Zero-dollar checks
Zero-dollar checks are entries in accounting systems used to record non-cash transactions or to adjust certain accounts without affecting the cash balance. While they appear as checks in the system, they have a net value of zero, ensuring no actual money is moved or issued.

Index

QuickBooks Online
BOOTCAMP
QuickBooks Online
BOOTCAMP

www.ingramcontent.com/pod-product-compliance
Lightning Source LLC
LaVergne TN
LVHW060448061126
851857LV00016B/1766

* 9 7 8 0 9 8 9 3 9 9 2 6 5 *